JAMES MARTIN ESTES

Christian Magistrate and State Church: The reforming career of Johannes Brenz

UNIVERSITY OF TORONTO PRESS

Toronto Buffalo London

JON BALSERAK
07888-736-644
23 AUG 2005

© University of Toronto Press 1982
Toronto Buffalo London
Printed in Canada

ISBN 0-8020-5589-3

Canadian Cataloguing in Publication Data

Estes, James Martin, 1934–
    Christian magistrate and state church

    Bibliography: p,
    Includes index.
    ISBN 0-8020-5589-3

    1. Brenz, Johann, 1499–1570. 2. Lutheran Church –
    Germany (West) – Württemberg – History – 16th century.
    3. Church and state – Lutheran Church – History – 16th
    century. I. Title.

    BR350.B73E87   284.1'4347   C82-094518-8

For my mother
In memory of my father

Contents

Preface

In early modern times, two native sons of the little imperial city of Weil der Stadt left town to become figures of major historical importance. One of them was Johannes Kepler (1571–1630), who became a renowned mathematician and astronomer. The other was Johannes Brenz (1499–1570), the Lutheran reformer of Schwäbisch Hall and Württemberg, who became one of the principal founders of state-church Protestantism in Germany. If Kepler's name is far better known to educated people today than Brenz's, it is not simply because mathematics and astronomy are still in style while state churches are not. Another reason is that while historians of science have given Kepler his due, historians of the German Reformation, in their obsessive preoccupation with Luther, have tended to ignore Brenz and a great many other so-called lesser reformers. Only in the last two decades or so has this tendency been decisively reversed. Although the flood of Luther literature continues, the presses are also turning out a substantial number of much-needed works on men like Andreas Osiander, Lazarus Spengler, Wolfgang Capito, Brenz, and many others whose careers shaped the Reformation.

For convenience' sake, Brenz's career can be said to fall into two categories, theology and church organization, though the distinction is highly artificial and will not be rigorously adhered to in the chapters which follow. In his own day Brenz was most widely known as a theologian because that was the aspect of his career most evident in his prodigious output of published works. In numerous pamphlets and treatises he presented his views on matters as various as the Peasants' Revolt, the sacramentarian controversy, and the treatment of Anabaptists, to name just a few. His catechisms were second only to Luther's in popularity and influence. The same is true of his voluminous biblical commentaries, upon which Luther himself heaped extravagant praise. While Brenz seldom left his Southwest-German homeland, and then only briefly, his Latin works, and Latin versions of his German works, carried his ideas throughout Europe. His writings were much admired by English divines and received official sanction in the reign of Edward VI. Even in Spain, where his views were not generally admired, the authorities had to take the trouble to place on the Index a prayer book which included as an introduction Brenz's catechism of 1527.

Far more interesting for the secular historian than Brenz the theologian is Brenz the church organizer, a role in which he was superior not only to Luther but to all the other Lutheran reformers as well. He was the chief architect of the Lutheran territorial state church in the Duchy of Württemberg, a church whose polity became the model for Protestant Germany and thus profoundly affected the history of that country until recent times. If this aspect of Brenz's career has been less widely known and appreciated, both in his own day and since, the main reason is that the work was done in the relatively anonymous role of princely adviser. Much of his writing on the subject of church order consisted of memoranda and correspondence which ended up in the archives rather than in the bookstalls. Those of his ecclesiastical ordinances which were published (quite a few were not) appeared not in his name but in that of the prince or city council under whose authority they were issued. And Brenz was not the sort of person to try to steal the spotlight by advertising his own role. So the historian has to reconstruct and to evaluate what few contemporaries were in a position to see clearly or to appreciate fully. That is the purpose of this book.

In whatever city or principality he was responsible for at the moment, Brenz's efforts as a church organizer were directed chiefly at the establishment and maintenance of three things: orthodoxy and uniformity of doctrine, a set order of common ceremonies, and a decent standard of public morals. The particular doctrines, ceremonies, and moral standards involved will not be a major topic of concern here. The aim rather will be to investigate why Brenz assigned the regulation of such matters to the secular authorities, and what arguments he advanced to justify doing so; what means he devised for enforcing the desired doctrinal, ceremonial, and moral standards, and how effective those means were; and what measures he recommended for dealing with the external and internal enemies of the order thus established. The result of this effort will be, I hope, a fairly clear picture of Brenz's contribution to the institutionalization of the Reformation.

Chapter one of this book is devoted to a brief chronicle of Brenz's career as a church organizer. Its purpose is to provide the necessary background for the ensuing chapters, which take up the subject matter in thematical rather than chronological units. Chapter six deals with topics which I have never addressed in print before. Chapters two through five, on the other hand, have grown out of preliminary studies published in the period 1968–73:

'Church Order and the Christian Magistrate According to Johannes Brenz,' *Archiv für Reformationsgeschichte* 59 (1968):5–23 [chapters two and three]
'The Two Kingdoms and the State Church According to Johannes Brenz and an Anonymous Colleague,' ibid., 61 (1970):35–49 [chapter three]
'Johannes Brenz and the Problem of Ecclesiastical Discipline,' *Church History* 41 (1972): 464–79 [chapter five]
'Johannes Brenz and the Institutionalization of the Reformation in Württemberg,' *Central European History* 6 (1973):44–59 [chapter four]

Subsequent research has produced changes in the treatment of the material. In all cases, the current version is longer, more detailed, and based on a substantially larger body of primary sources and secondary literature. I have, of course, taken the opportunity to correct numerous small errors of fact and judgment, but more significant changes have been made as well. Especially in chapters two and three, there is so much new material, the arguments have been so extensively recast, and the conclusions have been so much altered, that the earlier articles have been rendered obsolete.

Unless otherwise noted, all translations in the text are my own. In translating biblical passages I have followed the Authorized Version, making such changes as were necessary to render accurately the Latin or German version in question.

It is a pleasure to acknowledge the debt I owe to those who helped me produce this book. Two grants from the Social Sciences and Humanities Research Council of Canada, in 1974 and 1978, made possible the necessary research in Germany. That research was greatly facilitated by the generous cooperation of the officials and personnel of the following institutions: the Hauptstaatsarchiv Stuttgart; the Württembergische Landesbibliothek, Stuttgart; the Stadtarchiv Schwäbisch Hall; the Bayerisches Staatsarchiv Nürnberg; and the Evangelisches Stift, Tübingen. Hans-Martin Maurer and Kuno Ulshöfer, head archivists in Stuttgart and Schwäbisch Hall respectively, went out of their way to provide me with needed information. At home in Toronto I have benefited from the friendly assistance of the staffs of the library of the Pontifical Institute of Medieval Studies and the libraries of Victoria University (in the University of Toronto), particularly the library of the Centre for Reformation and Renaissance Studies.
  That this book has a documentary basis significantly broader than that of the articles which preceded it is in large measure the result of help graciously given by the doyen of Brenz scholars, Martin Brecht, formerly Ephorus of the Tübinger Stift and now Professor of Church History at the University of Münster/Westf.

During my visit to Germany in 1974 he drew my attention to the *Ratswahlpredigte* which play so crucial a role in chapter three, and provided me with typed transcripts of the documents from the Staatsarchiv Nürnberg used in chapter five. He also made it possible for me to use the page proofs of volume two of Brenz's *Frühschriften* well in advance of its publication.

My Toronto colleague, Norman Zacour, rendered invaluable aid with the deciphering of Latin manuscripts. Another Toronto associate, Hartwig Mayer, guided me through some murky passages of sixteenth-century bureaucratic German. The following colleagues read all or part of the manuscript at one stage or another in its development and made suggestions which led to substantial improvements in the quality of the final version: James M. Kittelson of the Ohio State University; James K. McConica, CSB, of the Pontifical Institute of Medieval Studies; Willard Piepenburg of York University; and, last but most important, Martin Brecht. Jean Houston and Judy Williams of the University of Toronto Press provided painstaking, skilful, and considerate editorial assistance.

Naturally, none of the persons named above is in any way responsible for the errors and misjudgments which remain: they are uniquely my own.

Finally, it is a pleasant duty indeed to acknowledge that this book has been published with the help of grants from the Canadian Federation for the Humanities, using funds provided by the Social Sciences and Humanities Research Council of Canada, and from the Publications Fund of the University of Toronto Press.

CHRISTIAN MAGISTRATE AND STATE CHURCH

1

Brenz's Career in Brief

The extant sources tell us very little about Brenz's life before the onset of his public career in Schwäbisch Hall. We do not know, for example, what the Catholic Brenz really thought nor can we trace the inner process which made him into a Lutheran. We might know more if Brenz had not so consistently abstained from personal reflections in his writings or if someone had recorded his dinnertime reminiscences. The following is a summary of the little that is known.[1]

Brenz's family belonged to the governing elite of Weil der Stadt. His father served repeatedly as *Schultheiss* (mayor), an office which his grandfather had also held. Destined by his family for theological studies, Brenz attended schools in Weil der Stadt, Heidelberg, and Vaihingen. Then, beginning in 1513, he attended the University of Heidelberg, where he took his MA in 1518.

During the years in Heidelberg, Brenz belonged to a group of humanistically minded teachers and students, several of whom later became important leaders of the Reformation in southwestern Germany. His most influential teacher was Johannes Oecolampadius, the future reformer of Basel. From Oecolampadius Brenz learned his Greek, which he later taught to Martin Bucer. It was also under the guidance of Oecolampadius, whom he served for a time as a sort of graduate assistant, that Brenz absorbed the thought and aims of Christian humanism. The influence of this tradition would still be evident in Brenz's writings long after other influences had come to predominate.

Once he had completed his MA, Brenz began the formal study of theology. The traditional scholastic theology, which he must have heard in the lectures of the theology professors, evidently made little impression on him. At any rate, there is little reference to it in his later writings. The decisive influence on the formation of Brenz's theological outlook was the confrontation with Luther, which began when the Saxon reformer defended his new theology at the Heidelberg Disputation of April 1518. Brenz and a number of his fellow students, including Bucer, attended. Profoundly impressed by what they saw and heard in the disputation, they afterward obtained a private audience with Luther, from which they emerged enthusiastic supporters of his cause. Brenz was the one who would in due course most completely absorb Luther's teaching and become the most influential spokesman for Lutheran orthodoxy in southwestern Germany.

In 1519 Brenz became rector of the *Bursa Suevorum*[2] and at about the same time went through the formalities of becoming a Bachelor of Theology. As Master of Arts, Brenz had to teach subjects such as grammar and logic to students in the arts faculty. But what really attracted attention to him were the lectures on the New Testament which be began to give at this time. Such large crowds came that the lectures had to be moved from the *bursa* to a larger lecture hall in the university. Since a mere unordained Bachelor of Theology was not entitled to offer lectures, the university banned them. In 1520, by virtue of his authority as vicar and canon (though still not ordained) of the Church of the Holy Spirit in Heidelberg, Brenz began once more to lecture on the Bible. The unmistakably Lutheran content of these lectures finally caused the Palatine Elector, Ludwig V, to ban them (August 1522) and to institute a formal investigation of Brenz. A few weeks later the call to serve as town preacher in Schwäbisch Hall provided a welcome exit from the difficult situation in Heidelberg.

THE REFORMATION IN SCHWÄBISCH HALL

Situated between the Duchy of Württemberg and the Margraviate of Brandenburg-Ansbach, Schwäbisch Hall was a free imperial city of about five thousand souls whose modest but solid prosperity was based on the production and sale of salt.[3] Following the example of many other cities, Hall in 1502 established a town preachership (*Prädikatur*) at St Michael's Church, the principal church of the city. The incumbent of the preachership was to be a learned man who would provide intellectual leadership to the city's clergy. Johann Eisenmenger (a.k.a. Isenmann), a native of Hall and a member of Brenz's circle in Heidelberg, recommended Brenz for the post when it fell vacant in 1522. It is likely that the partisans of Brenz's appointment inside the city council were a small group led by the salt refiner Hans Wetzel, whose son had received his MA in Heidelberg at the same time that Brenz received his, and who had connections by marriage with the Eisenmenger family. On 8 September 1522 Brenz delivered a trial sermon, after which the council unanimously approved his appointment. It certainly took some courage to appoint a man who was already in trouble for his Lutheran teachings. On the other hand, confessional lines were not yet clearly drawn in 1522, and it is not likely that any besides Wetzel and his allies realized the full significance of the appointment.[4]

There had been no Lutheran preaching in Hall before Brenz's appointment, and the populace was still attached to the old ceremonies and usages. So he decided, much to the satisfaction of the cautious city fathers, to proceed slowly and to observe the ancient forms as much as possible, at least for the time being. Accordingly, in the spring of 1523 he took holy orders and went home to Weil der Stadt to celebrate his first mass. In Hall he celebrated mass in the traditional manner, save only for the omission of all reference to it as a sacrifice. At the same time, however, he began to employ his exceptional skills as a preacher and exegete to prepare public opinion for more far-reaching changes. The first foray against the old religion was a sermon (5 July 1523) attacking the cult of the saints.[5] Another, preached the same year, expounded the Lutheran view of the true church.[6]

The following year, 1524, proved to be the year of the real onset of the Reformation in Hall.[7] Brenz defeated his most vigorous opponents, the local Franciscans, in a disputation arranged by the city council.[8] Soon thereafter the monks voluntarily surrendered their monastery to the city council, which turned it into a school.[9] Major changes also began to be made in the old papal ceremonies. With great difficulty, Brenz and Eisenmenger, who had returned to Hall to become pastor at St Michael's, persuaded their Hall congregation to abolish the feast of Corpus Christi, which had been a great favourite of the populace but which was inconsistent with the Lutheran doctrine of the sacrament.[10] Most important of all, perhaps, the city council began to legislate in accordance with the principles of the Reformation. Many of the traditional privileges which set the clergy apart from ordinary citizens were abolished. Clergymen were henceforth required to pay taxes and to bear the normal civic burdens if they acquired property. Moreover, they were granted permission to marry and, like all other residents, forbidden to keep concubines.[11] The council also began to take punitive action against some of Brenz's more indiscreet opponents. A certain priest who spoke ill of Brenz, denounced his teaching, and then started a brawl in the churchyard, was banished from the city.[12]

It took until the end of 1526 for this first phase of the Reformation in Hall to reach its conclusion. Perhaps the fears and anxieties that accompanied the Peasants' Revolt slowed things down a bit. At any rate, in 1526, probably on Christmas Day, Brenz officiated at the first fully reformed celebration of the Lord's Supper at St Michael's. By this time the doctrine, the ceremonies, and the personnel of the city's principal churches were completely Lutheran in character. But in St John's Church, which was not under the patronage of the council, and in St Mary's Chapel, mass continued to be celebrated.[13] Moreover, the parishes in

Hall's subject rural territory still had not been reformed, and much had to be done if the reformed order in the city itself were to acquire stability and durability.

Brenz set down his proposals for dealing with these problems in a long memorandum entitled 'Reformation of the Church in the Hall Territory,' which he submitted to the city council in the first weeks of 1527.[14] He demanded that the city council ban the celebration of mass in its territory and institute in all the churches ceremonies modelled on those already adopted at St Michael's. He also demanded that qualified clergymen be appointed to the rural parishes; that an ecclesiastical court be established to enforce moral discipline; that a poor chest be set up; and that certain changes in marriage law be made. In a section on schools, Brenz, adopting ideas first articulated by Luther, called on the city council to establish free public schools which would provide elementary instruction in German to boys destined for manual trades, and more advanced instruction in Latin to those destined for university study and professional careers. He also took over from Luther the novel idea that little girls be taught reading and writing by a qualified woman. 'For Scripture belongs not to men alone but to women as well.'[15]

This was a broadly conceived, well-thought-out scheme of reformation.[16] One could call it a comprehensive scheme were it not for the lack of two things. One was detailed recommendations for an organ (or organs) of church government. These would come a few years later. The other missing ingredient was a plan for meeting the church's financial needs. Two years earlier Brenz had enunciated the idea of a central church treasury, administered by the government, and it appears that some such arrangement had already been established in Hall.[17]

In the 'Reformation' Brenz had in fact demanded a good deal more than he was able to get. The proposal for a morals court proved extremely controversial and had to be dropped.[18] Mass continued to be celebrated at St John's and St Mary's until 1534, when the council finally put an end to it.[19] And the reform of the rural parishes had to be postponed even longer than that. All but one of them were under the patronage of other governments, such as the Counts of Hohenlohe, that were hostile to the Reformation.[20] In the 'Reformation' Brenz had urged the city council to buy up all the patronage rights. He had also urged that, regardless of the outcome of the attempts at purchase, the council order all the village pastors to preach nothing but the 'holy, pure, clear gospel' and to reject all contrary doctrine. As authority for such an order Brenz had cited a resolution adopted by the free cities at their recent diet in Speyer (July 1524).[21] The council, however, appears to have taken no action in response to either recommendation. Purchase of the patronage rights would doubtless have cost more than the council was willing to spend,[22] even if the patrons had been willing to sell. Nor did the council feel strong enough, politically or militarily, to enforce its will on the rural pastors over the opposition of the Catholic patrons and their ally, the emperor. Brenz, the son and grandson of city magistrates in Weil der Stadt and intimate friend of leading council members in Schwäbisch Hall, understood such political factors and sympathized with the magistrates' difficulties in dealing with them. Thus, even though he chafed at the delays, and was quick to urge the exploitation of any opportunity to push the reformation of the rural parishes, he had the patience and good sense not to alienate the council with unrealistic demands for action.

In the period before 1540 there is only one recorded instance in which the city fathers acted to provide a rural congregation with an evangelical preacher. Sometime in the mid-1520s the peasants in the village of Rieden petitioned the city council in Hall to send them a preacher. Since the church in question was under the patronage of the abbot of Murrhardt (Württemberg), the council asked Brenz for his advice. Because of his scrupulous regard for the legal rights of the patrons and the priests appointed by them, Brenz recommended that the priest be left unmolested in his living but that the council bear the expense of a special pastor from whom the peasant congregation could request the sacrament should the regular priest refuse to administer it to them in the evangelical manner.[23] In this case the council acted in accordance with Brenz's recommendation. Whether or not anything similar was done in any of the other rural parishes is not known. Of the rural pastors only one, the chronicler Johann Herolt, is known to have been sympathetic to the Reformation in this early period.[24]

In 1529 the city council tried unsuccessfully to force the rural clergy into conformity with the Hall church order by exerting pressure on the rural chapter. In that year the Bishop of Würzburg instructed the chapter dean, who at the time was the chronicler Herolt, to call a chapter meeting and proceed to the election of a new dean. Since the chapter had always met at St Michael's Church, Herolt sought permission from the city council for the meeting. Presumably at Brenz's urging, the council, to which the pope in 1487 had granted the *advocatio ecclesiae* over the chapter, declared that it would not permit the chapter to meet unless the pastors agreed to adopt the Hall church order and recognize the city pastor and preacher as superintendents. When one group of pastors refused, the council stuck to its refusal to let the chapter meet. The result was another decade of ecclesiastical disorder in the rural parishes. In Herolt's words: 'Since then we have had neither dean nor chapter, the rural churches are in complete disorder, everyone teaches whatever doctrine and observes whatever ceremonies suit his fancy.'[25]

Not until 1540, two years after Hall's belated entrance into the Schmalkaldic League, did the council forbid the celebration of mass in any church in its territory and order all pastors to conform to the ceremonies used in the city churches.[26] The sources record the protest of only one patron, the dean of the Comburg, a monastery not far from the city, whose advocate was the lord of the Limburg, a fortress located above the city. The *Reichskammergericht* rejected the dean's complaint on the ground that Hall had in 1540 purchased the Limburg and received an imperial bill of enfeoffment.[27] In February of the following year, when the parish of Münckheim fell vacant, the patron, the Count of Hohenlohe, failed to appoint a new pastor despite the requests of the parishioners that he do so. So in the fall of that year the Hall city council collected the grain tithes and in 1542 appointed a new pastor. The count protested this invasion of his rights and the case was submitted for arbitration to Elector John Frederick of Saxony, Prince Philip of Hessen (the co-leaders of the Schmalkaldic League), and Elector Ludwig V of the Palatinate. The cities of Nuremberg, Augsburg, 'and several others' strongly supported Hall's case. The resulting agreement (January 1543) stipulated that the count would retain the right of appointment but that the pastor would have to be examined and approved by the 'superintendents and visitors' in Hall and conform to the Hall church order.[28] Meanwhile, in 1541 the old rural chapter was transformed into a central organ of church government (it sent out the superintendents and visitors mentioned above)[29] and in 1543 a new church order for the city and territory was published.[30] These measures brought to long-postponed fruition Brenz's efforts to give the Hall territory a uniform ecclesiastical constitution.

FIRST VENTURES OUTSIDE HALL

In the meantime, Brenz had already begun to address himself to problems whose scope far exceeded the narrow confines of Schwäbisch Hall and to respond to the requests of other governments for advice and assistance.

In the spring and summer of 1525 the problem was the Peasants' Revolt, which Brenz opposed as firmly as did Luther but without succumbing to the bitterness and rancour that disfigured the Saxon reformer's hard book against the peasants.[31] In his commentary on the Twelve Articles, written at the request of Elector Ludwig of the Palatinate, Brenz displayed a sympathetic understanding of many of the peasants' demands even while condemning as unchristian their attempt to secure those demands by means of rebellion against legitimate authority.[32] After the peasants had been defeated, Brenz urged the victorious governments to deal leniently with them.[33]

In the fall of the same year the problem was the great intramural Protestant dispute over the Lord's Supper. In September, Johannes Oecolampadius, now a professor in Basel, addressed to the pastors 'in Swabia,' many of whom had been his students in Heidelberg, a treatise aimed at winning them over to the Zwinglian view of the sacrament. Brenz, who was unequivocally on Luther's side in this dispute, now took up the cudgels against his revered mentor. His reply to Oecolampadius, the so-called *Syngramma Suevicum*, was signed by thirteen other pastors from the Swabian/Franconian region at a conference held in Hall in October 1525. Widely circulated in Latin and in several German translations, hailed by Luther and deplored by Zwingli, the *Syngramma* was the opening salvo of Brenz's campaign to keep southwest German Protestantism safely in the Lutheran camp.[34]

Although essentially a wrangle among theologians, the sacramentarian controversy was a problem for politicians as well, for it threatened to frustrate plans for a common Protestant front against the powerful Catholic opposition. In the summer of 1529, when Philip of Hessen was planning the Marburg Colloquy (October 1529) as an attempt to reconcile the two Protestant factions, Margrave George of Brandenburg-Ansbach recommended that he include Brenz, the author of the *Syngramma* and an 'admirable, learned, good-tempered man,' among the Lutheran theologians invited. Brenz did indeed attend the colloquy, but made no significant contribution to the debate. However, the incident is noteworthy because it is evidence of the role which Brenz had come to play in the pious margrave's ecclesiastical politics. Just who had first brought Brenz to George's attention is not clear. Probably it was Brenz's friend Adam Weiss, pastor in Crailsheim. At any rate, by the time George recommended him to Landgrave Philip, Brenz was already the margrave's favourite adviser on major questions of theology and church order. In the period 1529–33 Brenz provided advice on such issues as resistance to the emperor and the treatment of Anabaptists. In 1530 he accompanied Margrave George to the Diet of Augsburg, where he played an important part in the behind-the-scenes negotiations with the Catholics.[35] Then, in 1531–2, he helped with the preparation of the Brandenburg-Nuremberg Church Order of 1533.

In 1530 the margrave and the city council of Nuremberg decided to cooperate in the preparation of a common church order for their adjoining territories. It took two years of complicated negotiations to produce agreement on a final draft. On the Nuremberg side, the principal architect of the order was Andreas Osiander, and the core of the finished document derived from his original draft. On the Ansbach side, Brenz, who was already well known and highly regarded in Nuremberg, was the leading figure. Three times in 1531 he journeyed to Ansbach to lead the deliberations of the margrave's theologians on the preparation of the order. After the contents had been agreed upon, Brenz and Osiander spent six weeks in September and October 1532 preparing the final draft. Brenz was then asked to write a preface and a conclusion for the order, which was printed in December and promulgated in the new year.[36] Since the governments in Ansbach and Nuremberg had agreed only to observe uniformity of doctrine and ceremonies, not to establish common administrative institutions, the Church Order of 1533[37] makes no provision for the latter. However, some of the memoranda which Brenz wrote during the deliberations on the order contain his earliest discussion of the need for administrative machinery to enforce ecclesiastical legislation.[38]

THE BEGINNINGS OF THE REFORMATION IN WÜRTTEMBERG

Not long after Brenz had completed his work on the Brandenburg-Nuremberg Church Order, Duke Ulrich of Württemberg summoned him to assist in the preparation of a church order for his duchy. A series of interesting and important developments forms the background of that summons.[39]

In 1498 Duke Ulrich, still a child, succeeded to the Württemberg throne. Although intelligent and gifted, he developed into a headstrong, unstable, and violent young man who heedlessly and repeatedly abused his subjects and offended his neighbours. In 1515 he even went so far as to murder a courtier whose wife he coveted. When in 1519 he forcibly annexed the free imperial city of Reutlingen to his domains, he had finally gone too far. The Swabian League, an alliance of South German princes and cities, invaded Württemberg and forced Ulrich into exile.

Württemberg was a rich prize. Its approximately 8000 square kilometres (about one quarter the area of the present-day state of Baden-Württemberg), its 250,000 inhabitants, and its flourishing agriculture and wine production made it the most important territory in southwestern Germany. The Habsburgs, always alert to any opportunity to advance the fortunes of their house, immediately launched a determined effort to acquire Württemberg, thus closing the gap between their possessions in Hither and Anterior Austria and establishing their hegemony in Southwest Germany. In 1520 the Swabian League ceded Württemberg to Charles V, who in 1522 incorporated it into the possessions of his brother, Archduke Ferdinand.

While all this was a tribute to the brilliance of Habsburg diplomacy, it was also illegal. Neither the Swabian League nor the Habsburgs had the right to dispose of a principality which in imperial law still belonged to its hereditary ruler. Thus the Austrian regime in Württemberg always bore the taint of usurpation, and its harsh treatment of those who sympathized with the exiled duke added to its unpopularity. So did its ruthless enforcement of the imperial edicts against the Protestant heresy, which had begun to win adherents in all levels of Württemberg society.

Meanwhile Ulrich, who had himself adopted the Protestant faith (1523–4), and who had twice failed to reconquer his duchy (1519, 1525), found an effective champion of his rights in Philip of Hessen, at whose court he resided from 1526. By restoring Ulrich to Württemberg, Philip hoped to strike a blow for the rights of the territorial princes, to weaken the overmighty Habsburgs, and to advance the cause of Protestantism in South Germany. After years of careful planning and preparation, Philip, whose army was paid mostly with French money, defeated the troops of the Austrian regent (May 1534) and occupied the duchy.

By the Treaty of Kaaden (June 1534) Ulrich, now a far more self-controlled person than he had been in his youth, got back Württemberg, albeit as a fief of Austria. His intention to introduce the Reformation into the duchy was clear, and both the Zwinglians and the Lutherans sought to gain the upper hand in that process. On the Lutheran side, for example, Ulrich's former court preacher, Johann Geyling, one of the signers of the *Syngramma*, urged the duke to entrust the implementation of the Reformation to Johannes Brenz, whom Ulrich had met at the Marburg Colloquy. Such a clear-cut decision in favour of Lutheranism would have been in accord with the Treaty of Kaaden, which permitted Ulrich to adhere to the Augsburg Confession (i.e. Lutheranism) but forbade the toleration of 'Sacramentarians' (i.e., Zwinglians). On the other hand, Ulrich's personal religious development had been influenced by both sides and his ties to the Swiss reformers were old and strong. Moreover, his patron and protector, Landgrave Philip, had attempted to reconcile the confessions at the Marburg Colloquy and continued to tolerate men of various theological tendencies in his lands. So Ulrich decided to make Württemberg the scene of his own unique experiment in confessional coexistence. This made it inadvisable to employ anyone who, like Brenz, was a prominent and uncompromising representative of either party. Instead, the reformation of the duchy was entrusted to two theologians who were not yet known as polemecists on either side: the Zwinglian Ambrosius Blarer from Konstanz, and the Lutheran Erhard Schnepf, a native of Heilbronn who was called from his chair of theology at Marburg. While they were formally obligated to cooperate with one another and to decide basic issues in common, they were given separate geographical areas to work in: the southern portion of the duchy, with headquarters at Tübingen, went to Blarer, while the northern portion, with headquarters at Stuttgart, went to Schnepf.

After patching together a compromise formula on the most contentious theological issue, the question of the real presence in the sacrament (July 1534), the two set to work. The break with the Catholic past was sudden and sharp. In May 1534 Württemberg had been a Catholic land. Within a year it was a Protestant land, at least externally: Protestant preaching services and the Protestant Lord's Supper had everywhere replaced the mass. In contrast to the general pattern in Germany, this was a classic case of reformation from above. The main losers were those clergymen, perhaps a majority of them, who refused to conform and lost their livings to Protestant newcomers. The majority of the population, however, either approved of the changes or were passive toward them. A few tears were shed at the last celebration of mass in Stuttgart, but there was no open resistance anywhere.

Still, there were problems to be dealt with. It soon became apparent that it was necessary to provide the new territorial church with uniform ceremonies and institutions. Apparently the execution of this task produced serious disagreements between Blarer and Schnepf. So Duke Ulrich now decided that he could not do without the assistance of Brenz, whose reputation as an expert in matters of ecclesiastical organization was already well established. At Ulrich's request, Brenz spent several weeks in Stuttgart in the summer of 1535 for this purpose.[40] After examining Schnepf's draft of a church order (i.e., order of worship), Brenz recommended the inclusion of a number of specific provisions, such as the extensive use of Latin in church services, retention of the traditional priestly vestments, and the adoption of the Augsburg Confession as the official confession of the Württemberg Church.[41] Blarer, who had complained of Schnepf's complete subservience to Brenz,[42] managed to prevent the inclusion of these Lutheran excesses.[43] However, Brenz's catechism was appended to the published order (1536),[44] thus putting doctrinal instruction in the Württemberg Church on a thoroughly Lutheran basis. At Brenz's suggestion, the church order was inaugurated by means of a visitation (1536), and subsequent visitations were undertaken to enforce it.[45] Brenz's other suggestion, that superintendents be appointed to supervise the pastors in their work,[46] was not adopted until sixteen years later (below).

Soon after the Church Order of 1536 had been issued, Duke Ulrich once again summoned Brenz to Württemberg, this time to assist in the reform of the University of Tübingen.[47] The resistance of the solidly Catholic faculty to interference in their corporate rights had made the reformation of the university difficult. The eventual departure of the hard-line Catholics made possible the appointment of a number of distinguished scholars in several faculties, but none such had been found for the faculty of theology. Blarer, who was responsible for the reorganization of the university, was clearly not equal to the task. Furthermore, the partisans of Lutheranism were determined to have a voice in the reform of an institution so vital to the training of future pastors. Melanchthon, who was asked to do the job but was not free, recommended Brenz. So from April 1537 to April 1538 Brenz served as ducal commissioner and professor of theology at Tübingen. As commissioner he succeeded in bringing order to the academic and financial affairs of the university, and as professor of theology he quietly but effectively instilled the views of conservative Lutheranism.

By this time Duke Ulrich's unique experiment in confessional harmony was breaking down. The differences in opinion had been repeatedly papered over but never resolved. And Duke Ulrich, unlike Landgrave Philip, was unable to provide the sort of leadership that would impose cooperation on men of disparate views. Just why he decided to drop Blarer is a matter of guesswork. Schnepf, who lived in

Stuttgart, had the advantage of closer contact with the duke, whose secular counsellors also apparently influenced him in the same direction. One of them, the chancellor Nikolaus Mayer, was a friend of Brenz's from Heidelberg days. Brenz's quietly persuasive advocacy of Lutheranism probably counted for something as well. At any rate, Blarer was released from the duke's service in 1538, and Württemberg became an unequivocally Lutheran territory.[48]

EXPULSION FROM HALL AND SUCCESS IN WÜRTTEMBERG

In the midst of all his efforts on behalf of the Reformation outside Schwäbisch Hall, Brenz had not neglected the needs of his congregation there. Indeed, his loyalty to that congregation was such that in 1543 he turned down flattering calls from the universities of Leipzig and Tübingen.[49] That same year the city council made him town preacher for life with a generous salary and a free residence.[50] Just a few years later, however, Brenz's career in the Franconian city came to an end as a result of Charles V's victories in his war (1546–7) with the Schmalkaldic League, which Hall had joined in 1538. In December 1546 Hall surrendered to the emperor's Spanish troops. To avoid arrest, Brenz had to flee by night and remain in hiding outside the city. Spanish soldiers occupied his house and destroyed most of his books and papers. Early in January 1547, after the emperor's forces had departed to score further triumphs, Brenz was able to return to the city and to his pulpit.[51] The final defeat of the League came in April 1547. In the fall and winter of 1547–8, Brenz again received attractive offers from elsewhere: the University of Leipzig renewed its call; the Margrave of Brandenburg-Ansbach offered him a canonry in Feuchtwangen; and Bucer tried to persuade him to come to Strassburg to succeed the deceased Matthäus Zell. But once again Brenz declined all offers in order to stay with his beleaguered flock in Hall.[52] He was not, however, permitted to stay for long. In May 1548 the Imperial Diet at Augsburg approved the emperor's plan for the reimposition of Catholicism in all Protestant regions, the so-called Interim. The Hall city council had no choice but to accept the Interim and to endure its enforcement by the emperor's Spanish troops. But Brenz formally refused to abide by the provisions of the Interim, as a consequence of which the imperial government ordered his arrest. Thus on 24 June 1548, his forty-ninth birthday, Brenz, given only a few minutes' warning, had to flee Schwäbisch Hall, never to return.[53]

Now an outlaw with a price on his head, Brenz fled to Württemberg, where Duke Ulrich, who had also been on the losing side in the Schmalkaldic War, was himself on the verge of having to impose the Interim and admit Spanish troops. On top of that, he was in danger of being deprived of Württemberg all over again on the ground that he had been an unfaithful vassal of Austria. Nevertheless, he had the courage to offer refuge to Brenz, whom he wanted to retain in his service on a permanent basis as soon as circumstances permitted. For the time being, Brenz had to be kept out of sight in order to escape detection by the agents the emperor had sent to find him. Part of the time he was hidden in ducal fortresses, but in September 1548 he had to flee via Strassburg to Basel, where he remained till July 1549. In the late summer of 1550 he was finally brought out of isolation and allowed to live more freely in the vicinity of Urach, a favourite residence of the duke, though it was still not possible to give him public office. During this whole period, Brenz played the role of princely counsellor as actively as his straitened circumstances permitted, doing so not only for Duke Ulrich but also for Ulrich's son and heir, Duke Christopher, in whose reign (1550–68) Brenz's career would reach its fulfilment.[54]

Christopher was born in the spring of 1515.[55] Not quite six months later, his mother, one of the principal targets of the young Duke Ulrich's ungovernable temper, fled to her native Bavaria, leaving her children behind. After his father was expelled from Württemberg, the five-year-old Christopher came under the guardianship of Emperor Charles, who sent him off to be raised at the court of Archduke Ferdinand. Only after he had joined the emperor's court at the age of fifteen did Christopher gradually learn of his father's fate and come to realize that his Habsburg guardians had no intention of letting him succeed to his legitimate inheritance. So in 1532 he fled the imperial court, found refuge with his Bavarian relatives, and publicly asserted the legitimacy of the claim of his house to Württemberg.

Christopher's association with the Bavarian dukes, who had played a major role in Ulrich's defeat in 1519, and who openly advocated giving Württemberg to Christopher rather than Ulrich, caused the naturally suspicious Ulrich to distrust his son. Ulrich was probably also jealous of Christopher's superior gifts and more appealing personality. So when Ulrich was restored to Württemberg in 1534, he refused to let Christopher join him there, sending him off instead to reside at a safe distance at the court of Francis I of France.

Not until eight years later, in 1542, after having settled his quarrel with Bavaria, was Ulrich ready for reconciliation with his son, whom he made regent in the county of Mömpelgard (Montbéliard), an Alsatian possession of the House of Württemberg. Christopher, who had spent all his life in the strict Catholic environment of the Austrian, Bavarian, and French courts, was now the heir to a Lutheran duchy and the regent in a county whose leading theologian (Pierre Toussaint) was a Zwinglian. Determined to make up his own mind about the conflicting claims of the various confessions, Christopher studied the works of representatives of all of them. Just exactly what he read or how long the process took is not known, but the result is clear: Christopher emerged a convinced

Lutheran with an unusually thorough and independent grasp of theological issues and a deep sense of his responsibility to foster the true faith among his subjects. He was, in brief, the very perfect model of a modern Christian prince as Brenz understood that term.

In the period following his expulsion from Schwäbisch Hall (1548-51), Brenz was offered high ecclesiastical office in Magdeburg, Prussia (the bishopric of Samland), Denmark, and England (the deceased Bucer's professorship at Cambridge). But, out of loyalty and gratitude toward Dukes Ulrich and Christopher, and in the growing belief that the Interim was only a temporary setback, Brenz chose to remain in the service of the House of Württemberg.[56]

There were good reasons for thinking that the situation under the Interim was not entirely hopeless.[57] Catholic doctrine and ceremonies had indeed been reintroduced and the central administrative institutions of the territorial church had been put out of business. On the other hand, the overwhelming majority of the Württemberg clergy refused to accept the Interim. An estimated three to four hundred of them were dismissed from office as a result. But it was impossible to find anywhere near that many priests to replace them. Those that were found were often poorly qualified and had to endure the open hostility of the populace, which for the most part remained stubbornly loyal to Protestantism. Furthermore, the duke and his officials, with encouragement and counsel from Brenz, proved adroit at exploiting every opportunity to defeat the spirit of the Interim while obeying its letter. For example, the dismissed pastors were soon reemployed as preachers or catechists, which allowed them to minister to their flocks without interfering with the priests who said mass as the Interim required. In a long memorandum, Brenz showed the preachers how to exploit the contradictory provisions of the Interim in order to defend the true faith 'out of the Interim against the Interim.'[58] All in all, it was a confused, unstable, and unhappy situation but not a hopeless one. Any serious weakening of the authority that had imposed the Interim would produce the better times that Brenz hoped for.

In the midst of all this, Duke Ulrich died (November 1550). Duke Christopher, who was impatient to start the work of Protestant restoration, immediately summoned Brenz to his side. At first, since the Interim was still in force, and since Christopher was having difficulty winning imperial recognition of his succession (King Ferdinand still hoped to regain Württemberg for himself), Brenz had to go on serving without public office and it was necessary to proceed cautiously in ecclesiastical matters.[59] Maurice of Saxony's successful campaign against Charles V in the spring of 1552 finally made it possible to abolish the Interim in Württemberg (30 June), to secure King Ferdinand's formal recognition of Christopher's succession (August), and to proceed openly with the work of ecclesiastical reorganization.[60] In January 1553 Christopher formally named Brenz his chief councillor in ecclesiastical matters for life and appointed him to the provostship (*Probstei*) of the Collegiate Church (*Stiftskirche*) in Stuttgart, the most prestigious ecclesiastical post in the duchy.[61]

By this time the work of ecclesiastical reorganization, begun quietly in 1551, was already far advanced. It was completed in 1559 with the publication of the so-called Great Church Order.[62] Put together under Brenz's supervision,[63] the Church Order of 1559 incorporated all the major ecclesiastical legislation of the previous decade. Section one is Brenz's *Confessio Virtembergica*,[64] written in 1551 for presentation at the Council of Trent[65] and subsequently adopted as an official confession of the Württemberg church. Section two is the 'little' Church Order (i.e., order of worship) of 1553.[66] Section four is the Marriage Court Ordinance of 1553,[67] and section eight is the Welfare Ordinance of 1552.[68]

Section five contains the ordinances for the Württemberg school system.[69] These were written in 1559 by a committee of three which included Brenz.[70] The most authentically Brenzian of the ordinances was that for the so-called cloister schools, junior seminaries established in fourteen of the duchy's fifteen monasteries, where deserving but needy teen-age boys were prepared at public expense for theological studies at the University of Tübingen.[71] First established in Brenz's Cloister Ordinance of 1556,[72] these schools were the long-postponed realization of an idea first articulated in 1529 in a memorandum written for Margrave George of Brandenburg-Ansbach.[73] Of the remaining school ordinances, the most important are those for Latin and German schools.[74] Many schools in both categories had been established since the introduction of the Reformation in 1534. In 1559 they were, for the first time, given a common order and subjected to effective central control.[75] Moreover, the church order called for a significant increase in the number of German schools,[76] the aim being to make elementary education (reading, writing, Bible, catechism, and hymn-singing) for boys and girls generally available in both town and countryside. This goal was not achieved quickly, but Württemberg, under Brenz's leadership, was the first sizeable principality to set out toward it.

The remaining sections of the Great Church Order are, from the point of view of this study, the most important of all. They are devoted to the system of church government which Brenz had devised to enforce the provisions of the ordinances and enactments noted above.[77] The central governing body, the consistory, had been established in 1553. Superintendents responsible for the intermediate and local levels of administration had been appointed in the period 1551–3. A centralized church treasury had been created by 1552, and an order of moral discipline had been put into operation by 1554. All the basic features of this system had their origin in various proposals Brenz had made in the 1520s and 1530s but had only partially achieved in practice. The elaboration of these ideas into a coherent, effective, and durable ecclesiastical polity, soon to be imitated all over Protestant Germany, was Brenz's greatest accomplishment as a reformer.[78]

Brenz died on 10 September 1570, by which time his system of church government had already been adopted by half a dozen other German territories. At his own request, he was buried beneath the pulpit of the Collegiate Church in Stuttgart, where a simple flagstone still marks his resting place.

2

The Background of the
State Church

Whatever the spiritual forces and popular enthusiasms that sustained its begin-nings, the Protestant Reformation in Germany ultimately survived only where it won the support and protection of the secular magistrates. There was no other way to deal with the multiple dangers of armed Catholicism on the right, radical sectarianism on the left, and a good deal of confusion and disorder in the Protestant middle. However, the secular magistrates in question did much more than provide the Protestant movement with physical protection and material support: they assumed full control of ecclesiastical affairs and established that *landesherrliche Kirchenregiment* which was to endure until 1918/19. It is now generally recognized that this is not what Luther really wanted, that it ran counter to his understanding of the appropriate distinction between secular and spiritual authority. He dreamed, albeit in rather vague terms, of a church able to govern itself, and approved of governmental intervention in the internal affairs of the church only as a temporary measure to deal with an emergency. On a few occasions he referred to the magistrates in this connection as *Notbischöfe*, 'emergency bishops,'[1] meaning that they were to step into the breach created by the disappear-ance of the old hierarchy and the absence of new institutions of church govern-ment to replace it.

Brenz, although deeply influenced by Luther in this matter as in all others, took the quite different view that the state church was not a temporary expedient but the ideal church polity. He described the Christian magistrate not as *Notbischof* but as *gubernator et ordinator rerum ecclesiasticarum.*[2] Since the great majority of reformers agreed with Brenz rather than with Luther, an examination of the genesis and content of Brenz's view should throw some light on the historical process that imposed magisterial control upon German Protestantism. Two things form the historical background of Brenz's view of the office of Christian magistrate: 1/Luther's thought on the role of the magistrate in ecclesiastical matters; and 2 / pre-Reformation developments in the theory and practice of *landesherrliche Kirchenregiment.*

LUTHER AND THE STATE CHURCH

The question of Luther's intentions concerning the external organization of the church is a difficult one that has been answered in a number of ways without ever being definitively settled. The main reason for the difficulty is that Luther, whose talents lay outside the field of organization, and who had to come to terms with difficult and diverse circumstances, did not always express his intentions precisely or consistently. This is not the place to go through all the evidence and resolve all the difficulties. The attempt, rather, will be simply to say as much about Luther as is necessary to reveal the nature of his influence on Brenz.[3]

For this purpose, the following three points need to be made. First, Luther repeatedly called upon the secular authorities for help in reforming the church, and in so doing he contributed to the process which turned the German territorial rulers into the heads of territorial state churches. However (and this is the second point), the state was never Luther's first recourse and he was never comfortable with the development of state control of the church. For while his view of the church and of secular government made it possible for him to assign a limited, helping role to the secular authorities, that same view made it impossible for him to assign to them routine authority over the internal affairs of the church. Third, in his early reformatory writings Luther laid down some basic principles and definitions which, as it turned out, could be used for their own purposes by reformers who, in contrast to Luther, did assign routine authority over the internal affairs of the church to the secular authorities.

Luther spoke of the church in two ways, as the visible church and the invisible church.[4] The invisible church is the fellowship of all those whom the word has awakened to true faith in Christ, who rules over them. The members of this fellowship are widely dispersed in time and space and are unknown to one another, for only God can read the hearts of men and know for sure who the true believers are. Thus the existence of this church and of Christ's rule over it is invisible save to the eye of faith. The visible church, on the other hand, is the earthly institution in whose congregations the word is preached and the sacraments administered. Its members are known and include not only true believers but also those who hear the word without responding in true faith. Though imperfect and fallible like any earthly institution, the visible church is an essential part of God's plan of salvation, for it is through its ministry of the word, instituted by Christ himself, that men are called to membership in the invisible church.

Luther thought that the structure, ceremonies, and usages of the visible church should be in harmony with the nature of the invisible church. This meant, first of all, that the church had to be organized in accordance with God's word. Anything which could not be justified by the Bible's witness to Christ could not be regarded as Christian *de jure divino*. On this basis Luther eventually rejected the Catholic mass, canon law, monasticism, clerical celibacy, and much else besides, as human additions to the gospel. On the other hand, he insisted that any external order which was not contrary to God's word was acceptable. The essence of Christianity, he said, is faith in God's promises , not the performance of prescribed works. And God has commanded the church only to preach the gospel, not to observe any particular external forms. Hence no particular ceremonies or practices, not even those of the ancient church, are binding on conscience. Christians are free to observe whatever forms seem most likely to assure the preaching of the word and the administration of the sacraments in a decent and orderly fashion.[5]

Moreover, the obedience which Christians render to Christ, and the fellowship they share, are voluntary. For faith is something freely given in response to the word; it cannot be coerced. Hence the rule of force is completely out of place in spiritual matters. It is both unchristian and futile to burn heretics or to attempt in any other way to enforce faith with the sword.[6]

Finally, all Christians are equal, since all have the same faith and are in like measure sons and heirs of God. This means that scriptural injunctions concerning the ministry of the word apply equally to all Christians. Thus every Christian is empowered to preach the word, administer the sacraments, judge doctrine, proclaim the forgiveness of sins to those who repent, and excommunicate those who do not. In other words, all Christians are priests. But precisely because this priesthood is the common possession of all believers, no individual should presume to exercise the priestly office in a Christian community without the express command and call of that community. Clergymen, then, are simply those whom the community designates to exercise, on behalf of all, rights and duties common to all. They minister to the community, they do not rule it. If they preach false doctrine, introduce ungodly ceremonies, lead evil lives, or are just incompetent, the community that placed them in office can remove them, appoint someone else and institute necessary reforms.[7]

Judged by these standards, the papal church was, in Luther's view, the kingdom of Antichrist indeed. Its hierarchy, far more interested in the defence of rank and privilege than in the performance of its pastoral duties, claimed to be a separate estate, superior in authority to mere laymen; to have divine authority to impose ceremonies and doctrines contrary to God's word; to have the right, in cooperation with the secular arm, to punish the disobedient with fire and sword; and to be exempt from judgment by the whole church (i.e., a council) on the basis of Scripture. So Luther called on Christians in general to exercise their priestly responsibilities by taking the reformation of the church into their own hands.

What specifically was to be done and who precisely was to do it? As we shall see, Luther's answer to that question varied according to the circumstances of the moment, which changed significantly over the years. But from the beginning he assigned an important role to the secular rulers, which was not a simple thing for him to do, given his view of the nature of secular authority.

It is an oft-repeated theme in Luther's writings that the authority of the secular rulers extends only to 'life and property and external affairs on earth' and that they may not encroach upon God's authority over souls.[8] In other words, church government is not part of their office. This is true even of Christian magistrates. The *person* may be Christian (and thus share in the priesthood of all believers), but the *office* is not.[9] It is purely secular, 'serves no purpose' in God's kingdom,[10] and gives the ruler no right to lord it over his fellow Christians in the church the way he does his subjects in the state.

On the other hand, secular authority is of divine origin and its proper exercise is of benefit to the church. If all men were true believers, secular government would be completely unnecessary, for men ruled by the Holy Spirit love everyone, harm no one, and cheerfully suffer injustice at the hands of anyone. What need of laws, courts, judges, princes, and swords in such circumstances? In reality, however, 'there are few true believers, and still fewer who live a Christian life.' They are a minority of sheep among a majority of wolves and lions. Unless restrained, the many that are wicked would devour the few that are good, and 'no one could support wife and child, feed himself, or serve God.' To prevent this, God has established secular government to maintain external peace and prevent evil deeds. Thus there are two governments ordained by God: spiritual and secular. While the two must be carefully distinguished, both must be allowed to remain, for 'neither one is sufficient in the world without the other.' Secular government cannot make anyone righteous in the eyes of God, and spiritual government cannot keep that external peace and order in the world which is the essential prerequisite of its own proper functioning.[11]

So Luther did in fact see secular and spiritual authority as coordinate elements in a divine scheme for the government of the world. This made it possible for him, in certain extraordinary circumstances, to ask the secular authorities to intervene in spiritual affairs.

The first such request was the *Address to the Christian Nobility* (1520),[12] in which Luther called upon the emperor and estates of Germany to summon a church council. Only because the existing ecclesiastical authorities, 'to whom the task more properly belongs,' were so indifferent to reform did Luther regard the intervention of the secular authorities as essential.[13] But he by no means simply turned the task of reforming the church over to them. In his reform proposals[14] he distinguished between those things which fall under the jurisdiction of secular government and those which do not.[15] In the first category he placed abuses that were secular in nature even though committed by members of the 'spiritual estate' (i.e., the clergy). The Roman curia, for example, was by virtue of its collection of annates guilty of the secular crime of robbery. Hence, even though rulers who forbade the collection of annates were in fact serving the true interests of the church, they were by no means interfering in spiritual matters. They were merely doing their routine, God-given duty to protect the property and honour of their subjects. In the category of those things beyond the routine jurisdiction of secular authority Luther placed such things as changes in ceremonies, monastic reform, the abolition of clerical celibacy, and the reform of the papal court. These were spiritual matters which came under the jurisdiction of spiritual authority, in this case the council which Luther wanted. But there were serious obstacles in the way of a council.

According to the 'Romanists,' only the pope had the right to summon a council and give effect to its decrees. But the pope, who was himself 'an offence to Christendom,' could scarcely be expected to summon a truly free council or confirm its decisions. In such a situation, said Luther, every Christian, every participant in the priesthood of all believers, is duty-bound to do whatever he can to bring about such a council. But 'no one can do this so well as the secular authorities.' Not only are they fellow Christians and fellow priests, they are also the incumbents of an 'office and work which they have received from God over everyone,' and which they should exercise 'whenever it is necessary and profitable' to do so.[16]

In other words: of all the lay members of the church, only the secular rulers occupy, by the grace of God, an office which gives them influence and authority over every member of society. Thus, when the church is in the throes of a crisis which its responsible leaders cannot or will not deal with, the secular authorities are in the best position to intervene effectively. Consequently, it is their duty as Christians to do so. The aim of their intervention is not to usurp the authority of their fellow Christians, but to make it possible for them to exercise it once more. As Luther put it, the job of the Christian rulers was 'to rouse the Christian people and call them together [in a council].'[17] He assumed that if the secular authorities took the initiative, ordinary Christians (*der hauff*), and perhaps even some bishops and theologians, would find the courage to defy papal anathemas, attend the council, and carry out the work of ecclesiastical reformation.[18] Thus the effect of this limited intervention by secular authority in spiritual matters would be to put spiritual authority back into working order, thereby restoring the normal balance between the two divinely ordained governments and eliminating the reason for the intervention.

The pattern established here is the one Luther tried to adhere to throughout his career: a limitation to emergencies of any direct governmental role in the process of ecclesiastical reform; a distinction between those things the magistrates undertake by virtue of their secular authority and those they undertake by virtue of their membership in the church; and an insistence that governmental intervention be limited to what is necessary to restore the healthy functioning of spiritual authority.

The Edict of Worms (1521), in which the emperor and the diet condemned Luther and his supporters, dashed Luther's hopes for a large-scale reform by means of a council. But the Reformation continued nevertheless, centred for the next few years primarily in the towns, where emerging evangelical congregations sought to replace traditional doctrine and ceremonies with preaching and worship in harmony with Luther's teachings. In the *Address to the Christian Nobility* Luther had briefly stated the view that each individual congregation possessed all the gifts and rights that flow from the gospel and was therefore competent to reform itself whether pope and bishop liked it or not.[19] So in the years immediately following the publication of the Edict, Luther, who was most immediately concerned with developments in Saxony, supported and encouraged the reform efforts of his followers by developing the 'congregationalist' implications of his thought.

The first task facing the new congregations was to find suitable pastors, which bishops, abbots, and other prelates refused to provide. Luther argued that every congregation had the right to judge the doctrine preached to it, to dismiss a pastor who preached contrary to Scripture, and to appoint a suitable pastor in his place.[20] His purpose was not by any means to establish a democratic right of congregations to determine the truth by majority vote, but rather to insist that 'a Christian congregation in possession of the gospel' had not only the right but also the duty 'to avoid, to flee, to depose, and to withdraw from the authority' of a corrupt hierarchy that taught and ruled 'contrary to God and his word.'[21] Luther thought that if there had been good bishops who wanted to serve the gospel by appointing good pastors, it would have been possible to allow them to do so. But even good bishops, he insisted, should not appoint good pastors 'without the will, the election, and the call of the congregation.' For the time being, however, there were no such good bishops, so congregational self-help was necessary.[22]

Once a congregation had a suitable pastor, the next step was to replace the mass and other Catholic ceremonies with forms of worship in harmony with the new doctrine. In this respect also Luther upheld the independence of the local congregation.[23]

In actual practice, however, this independence of the local congregation could only be exercised with the cooperation and assistance of the local secular authorities. For one thing, the reform parties in the towns operated on the well-nigh universal assumption, which Luther shared, that the boundaries and membership of the ecclesiastical congregation (*kirchliche Gemeinde*) and the civic community (*bürgerliche Gemeinde*) ought to coincide. This decision to operate within the framework of the political community made it necessary at the very least to institute reforms with the consent of the secular authorities in order to avoid any appearance of disorder or tumult.[24]

Moreover, the continuing crisis in the church was something which individual congregations, for all their theoretical autonomy, could not deal with on their own. The help of the secular rulers was still necessary. Once again, as in 1520, Luther distinguished between those things which he expected from the magistrates as magistrates, and those which he expected from them as fellow Christians.

From secular authority as such he demanded a ban on the Roman mass, which continued to be celebrated in monastic and collegiate churches. The popish mass, he said, is nothing more than public blasphemy, a secular crime, the toleration of which will bring God's wrath upon land and people.[25] (A few years later Luther would add the argument, borrowed from the Nuremberg reformers, that the coexistence in one jurisdiction of contrary forms of doctrine and worship is a source of 'mobs and rebellion.')[26] In other words, the celebration of mass, like the collection of annates, is something which poses a threat to the temporal well-being of the populace, for which the secular government is directly responsible. Moreover, banning the mass constitutes no interference in the spiritual realm, for individuals are left free to believe what they want. The government simply represses external abominations; it does not force anyone to faith or the gospel.[27]

From the magistrates 'as Christian brothers' Luther expected help with the appointment of evangelical preachers, just as he had earlier asked for their help in summoning a council.[28] There were all kinds of practical problems – the shortage of qualified preachers, magisterial control of ecclesiastical endowments, disputed claims to benefices, and so forth – that forced the fledgling congregations to turn to their magistrates for help.[29]

As in 1520, Luther again set definite limits to the intervention of the secular authorities in the internal affairs of the church. City hall could ban the mass and appoint a pastor, but it was the pastor who had the right and duty to determine what form of worship would replace the old Catholic ceremonies.[30]

For a time Luther was content to allow the Reformation in Saxony to proceed on the basis of the efforts of the individual congregations and the local authorities, and he rarely sought the help of the elector in ecclesiastical matters. But by the mid-1520s circumstances had driven him to the conclusion that Saxony must have a uniform church order and that the intervention of the elector was necessary in order to achieve it.

For one thing, church finances were in a state of disorder. Much of the wealth of the abandoned monasteries was being appropriated by the nobles and others for their own use rather than being used for the religious, educational, and charitable purposes intended by the founders.[31] Moreover, many of the congregations that had been happy to call evangelical pastors were unwilling to pay them a decent salary. As a result, material want threatened to undermine the effective performance of the church's ministry.[32]

For another thing, public worship was also in a state of confusion and disorder. The unrestricted exercise of congregational freedom in externals had produced a bewildering variety of ceremonies which 'confused and offended' the people. Not only did each community have its own order of worship but also, in the larger towns, every parish had its own peculiar ceremonies. To make things even more complicated, mass continued to be celebrated in the monastic and collegiate churches.[33] The confusion of Protestant ceremonies interfered with the orderly, effective instruction of the people, while the juxtaposition of Catholic and Protestant worship contained the seeds of endless strife.

The first problem, church finances, was, in Luther's view, something within the jurisdiction of secular authority as such. According to him, all the abandoned monasteries and foundations fell into the hands of the elector, who thus had the duty of seeing to it that they were inspected, set in order, and that the income be used to support those churches and schools not already adequately endowed. Moreover, he attributed to the elector, as 'supreme guardian of the younger generation,' the power to compel communities who had the wherewithal to do so 'to support schools, preacherships, and parishes' just as one would compel them 'to contribute to ... the building of bridges and roads, or any other of the country's needs.' Otherwise, he said, 'the land will be filled with wild, loose-living people.'[34]

The second problem, that of achieving uniformity of ceremonies, was more complicated. Luther continued to regard the suppression of mass as something which the authorities, in this case the elector, could undertake by virtue of their secular office.[35] But he also continued to believe the things he had said about the rights of congregations and the power of the church to establish its own ceremonies. So when in the summer of 1525 he began to urge that a common order of worship be observed in each principality, he argued that that common order should be the result of the voluntary cooperation, the brotherly understanding, of the pastors, who would consider 'the edification of the lay folk' more important than their own freedom to alter ceremonies as often as they wished.[36] And he continued to defend the general validity of this voluntaristic approach even after he had decided that conditions in Saxony were such that the intervention of the elector was necessary to secure uniformity of ceremonies.[37]

It was the impressions gathered during his travels through the countryside during the Peasants' Revolt that convinced Luther of the necessity of princely action to bring order and stability into the affairs of the Saxon church. Beginning in the autumn of 1525, he urged upon the elector the necessity of undertaking a visitation of all the parishes and schools in his domains.[38] When the visitation commission was finally appointed, it consisted, as Luther had recommended, of two experts on property and finance, and two on doctrine and personnel.[39] Early in 1527 the long, difficult process of visitation began.

In 1528 Melanchthon's *Unterricht der Visitatoren*, a summary of the doctrinal and ceremonial regulations to be imposed by the visitation, was published with a preface by Luther[40] in which he undertook to justify the whole enterprise with arguments that were simply an adaptation of those he had used in 1520 in the *Address*. For a long time, he said, the bishops have failed to perform their original and primary function of visiting pastors and congregations. As a result, the church has become 'grievously confused, scattered, and torn.' In this emergency the reformers wished to have 'the true episcopal office and practice of visitation reestablished.' However, none of them 'felt a call [from God]' or had 'a definite command [from the Saxon congregations] to do this.' So they have appealed to the elector 'that out of Christian love (since he is not obligated to do so as a temporal sovereign) ... and for the welfare of the wretched Christians of his territory,' he 'call and ordain to this office several competent persons.'[41] The elector's job, in other words, was to appoint the visitors, not take over the government of the church. Once in office, the visitors were to function as officials of the church, not of the elector. Similarly, the *Unterricht* was, in Luther's view, not an electoral decree but a 'witness and confession'[42] of the faith of the reformers.[43]

In these circumstances, Luther continued, the visitors have no authority to 'issue any strict commands' as if they were 'publishing a new form of papal decrees.' But good, devout pastors will 'willingly, without any compulsion' accept what the visitors impose (i.e., the contents of the *Unterricht*) 'until God the Holy Spirit brings to pass something that is better, through them or through us.' If some obstinately and perversely refuse to accept the common order, the elector will be asked to take action against them. For while the elector 'is not obligated to teach and rule in spiritual affairs, he is obligated as temporal sovereign to so order things that strife, rioting, and rebellion do not arise among his subjects.'[44]

Luther's view of the role of the magistrate in the church remained essentially one man's opinion. There was in it a tension, which he could not satisfactorily resolve, between the need for secular force on the one hand and the desire for Christian freedom on the other. There were two possible solutions: 1 / sectarian withdrawal and the renunciation of secular force; or 2 / acceptance of the state church and the curtailment of Christian freedom. Luther resolutely refused to adopt either solution, which made it necessary for him to elaborate a complicated and cumbersome system in which the church was materially dependent upon the prince yet spiritually independent of him, while the prince was supposed to act now as secular ruler, now as Christian brother, without getting the two roles confused. Those who did the actual work of institutional reform – princes, city councillors, jurists, and Luther's fellow reformers – preferred the simpler view, which had a long history behind it,[45] that the prince as prince was responsible for both the temporal and spiritual welfare of his subjects, and that the visible church was subject to him as its administrative head. It was in this spirit that the elector responded to Luther's appeal to aid the church. Whether or not the princely view had already prevailed over Luther's in the elector's own *Instruktion* to the visitors (1527),[46] as Karl Holl argued,[47] is a question that has recently been the subject of dispute.[48] But if the issue was still unclear in 1527/8, the emergence of the state church was unmistakable in the ordinances of the following years.[49]

This development, to which Luther, driven by necessity, had contributed, put him in a dilemma. On the one hand, he was dismayed and frightened by the confusion of spiritual and secular authority which the state church seemed to him to involve.[50] On the other hand, he had nothing to gain by mounting a vigorous protest. At best he would have become involved in a dispute with his fellow reformers, including his beloved Melanchthon, who disagreed with him on this issue.[51] At worst he would have sabotaged what was, for all its defects in his eyes, the only available means for bringing the true word and the true sacraments to the 'wretched Christians' of Germany. So he acquiesced in silence. He did not abandon his own point of view, but he did not press it either.[52]

The irony in all this is that some of the things Luther said about the nature and extent of secular authority could, in other hands, be made to support the state church. For example (to summarize some points already discussed): Luther argued that the secular magistrate as magistrate has the right and duty to repress any religious activities (e.g., the public celebration of mass, factious preaching) which threaten temporal peace and order. He also argued that this constitutes no interference in spiritual affairs because no one is thereby forced to believe anything. But, having argued that the magistrate has the duty to curb or forbid something bad (false preaching and worship), he resisted the logical conclusion that this implies the corresponding duty to impose something good (true preaching and worship). Such action would, in Luther's view, have constituted unwarranted interference in spiritual affairs.

An advocate of the state church might reasonably have commented on all this as follows. 'If false preaching and worship threaten secular welfare, then surely true preaching and worship promote it. If this be so, then the magistrate as magistrate has just as legitimate an interest in establishing and enforcing true preaching and worship as he does in banning false preaching and worship. Moreover, if the repression of false preaching and worship constitutes no interference in spiritual affairs, then surely enforcing true preaching and worship does not do so either. After all, Luther teaches that ceremonies as such are not sacred or binding on consciences but are simply convenient external means for preaching the word and administering the sacraments. And he also says that secular authority extends over all external matters on earth. It would seem to follow from this that a magistrate who establishes and maintains true preaching and worship, and who leaves individuals free to believe as they wish in private, is not interfering in spiritual matters at all but simply doing his duty to maintain peace and good order in his territory. Finally, if the magistrate, by virtue of his secular office, has this much authority in ecclesiastical affairs, then there is no antithesis between the magistrate's role as magistrate and his role as Christian brother, and the limitation to emergencies of magisterial intervention in matters of internal church order disappears. In other words, it is the duty of the Christian magistrate, not only as Christian brother but also as secular magistrate, to serve God and his fellow Christians by establishing and maintaining true preaching and worship in his domains.'

The advocates of the state church did not in fact confront Luther in this fashion with the unforeseen implications of his own ideas, and their own arguments were, as we shall see, much more than just wilful reinterpretations of his. Thus the preceding paragraph is not a fair indication of the way they argued their case. But that paragraph does make clear, if it was not clear already, that Luther's doctrine of church and state was, for all the consistent fidelity to certain basic principles that lay at its core, a rather ramshackle affair whose component parts were not held together by airtight logic. Thus it was perfectly natural for Luther's followers, Brenz among them, to take from his thought on church and state whatever could legitimately be used for their own, quite different purposes. The following chapter will provide a number of examples of Brenz and others doing just that.

The immediate question, though, is why Brenz wanted to put Luther's ideas to such use. The answer is that Brenz read his Luther and his Bible in the light of an *a priori* commitment to magisterial control of ecclesiastical affairs. It used to be thought that it was the crisis of the Peasants' Revolt which first produced this commitment.[53] Modern research, however, has proved that it was part of Brenz's thinking from the very beginning of his activity as a reformer and that it was, in fact, the product of the political and intellectual climate from which he emerged and in which he worked.[54]

PRE-REFORMATION ANTECEDENTS OF THE STATE CHURCH

In the one hundred years or so before the Reformation, the German territorial rulers, both princes and city councils, acquired such extensive control over ecclesiastical affairs in their territories that in a great many cases one can, with only modest exaggeration, speak of them as the virtual heads of 'territorial churches'

(*Landeskirchen*). This was in large measure the inevitable result of the development of the early modern state in the German territories. The details of the story and the degree of control established were different in each case. Still, the process was essentially the same everywhere and can, with considerable oversimplification, be summarized as follows.[55]

Like the Italian *signori* and the kings of France before them, many German princes of the fifteenth and early sixteenth centuries strove not only to enlarge and consolidate their territorial possessions but also to make themselves truly sovereign by concentrating all governmental authority in their own hands. To achieve this second aim they had to destroy or at least severely restrict the traditional autonomy of individuals, communities, or corporations, and replace the old notion of specific personal obligations to one's lord or other local interest with the notion of everyone's general obligation to the 'common good' or 'common weal' (*der gemein nutz, das gemein wohl*). While success in this endeavour had its definite limits, it was impressive nevertheless. By the end of the fifteenth century, give or take a decade or two, the German princes ruled more territory and more subjects with fewer restrictions than ever before. An analogous development had taken place on a much smaller scale in those cities which had managed to retain their independence and acquire subject territories. In fact, in the areas of political theory and practical administration, the cities were usually several jumps ahead of the princes and provided them with models to imitate.

Among the institutions which the rulers had to bring into line was the church, whose activities affected the well-being of the lay community in many ways. Education and charity, for example, were largely in the hands of the clergy. Certain aspects of lay life (e.g., all matters related to marriage and wills) fell under the jurisdiction of the ecclesiastical courts. Furthermore, the church had over the centuries acquired an immense endowment in land. The estates of the monasteries, in particular, were a vital element in the economy of most territories.

Naturally, the territorial rulers wished to regulate such matters in the interest of the common weal, but there were serious obstacles in the way. The clergy claimed exemption from those taxes which fell on the lay community and from the jurisdiction of the secular courts, even in matters that were essentially secular in nature. Furthermore, the clergy as a whole, as well as the church courts, owed obedience to, and paid taxes and fees to, a hierarchy that was, from the point of view of the territorial state, foreign. In the case of most German territories, even the local bishop was an outsider, since he resided outside the territory and was usually a prince of the empire in his own right. This meant that the ruler usually could not make the church serve the common weal by securing control over the episcopacy; instead, he had to substitute his own authority for that of the foreign bishop.

One way to do this was to usurp the jurisdiction of the episcopal courts. Every effort was made to bring all cases not purely doctrinal in nature under the jurisdiction of the secular courts. Of these non-doctrinal cases, ones deemed purely secular in nature were assigned to the regular courts, while cases ecclesiastical in nature were assigned to special courts or commissions staffed largely or entirely by clerics who based their decisions on canon law. This process won the support of many clerical litigants, who found the sound and speedy justice of the prince's courts preferable to the ineffective and dilatory procedures of the church courts.

Another way to undercut the authority of the bishop was to exploit certain well-established rights in ecclesiastical affairs in order to secure control over the clergy and gain access to their wealth. To begin with, the territorial rulers possessed in varying degrees the right of patronage or advowson over the secular clergy in their territories. Patronage was the right accorded to any person or corporation that endowed a parish, chapel, or other ecclesiastical foundation, to 'present' the clerics who would officiate in the foundation. In theory the church authorities could reject a candidate, but in practice the patron had the right to appoint and dismiss the priests in the churches under his patronage pretty much as he pleased. Any individual or corporation could be a patron, but the secular rulers, eager to increase their influence over the clergy and to secure for themselves a portion of the income from church benefices, eagerly sought, through purchase or by other means, to concentrate in their hands the patronage of as many as possible of the ecclesiastical posts in their territories.

Further, each territorial ruler enjoyed certain rights as 'church advocate' (*advocatus ecclesiae, Kirchenvogt, Schutz- und Schirmvogt*, etc.). A church advocate was a lay person entrusted with the external protection of an ecclesiastical foundation. The emperor and all the imperial estates were acknowledged in a general way to be protectors of the church, and from time to time acted in concert to defend the general interests of the churches in the Empire. But this left open the question of who was the specific protector of each individual ecclesiastical foundation. Naturally, each territorial ruler sought to have the ecclesiastical foundations of his territory acknowledge him, rather than some neighbouring rival, as their protector. In fact, rulers were inclined to impose their protection whether it had been formally acknowledged or not. While protection could be afforded to any ecclesiastical institution, and sometimes served as the pretext for intervention in the affairs of a church which was not under the ruler's patronage, it was especially useful for the purpose of controlling the affairs of the monasteries in the interest of the common weal. In return for protection in times of war and feud, the monasteries paid annual protection money, supplied carts and horses for military transport, lent money and supplies in wartime, and rendered such other services as may have been agreed upon. Thus, at least in times of emergency, the material resources of the monasteries were at the disposal of the ruler. The importance of these resources was sufficient to justify, in the eyes of many rulers, 'protection' in the form of intervention in the management of monastic property and in the election of abbots.

In this campaign to expand their authority at the expense of that of the bishops, the German rulers were not content simply to eliminate the jurisdiction of the ecclesiastical courts in temporal matters, to secure the political loyalty of the clergy, or to gain access to the material resources of the church: they intervened in religious matters as well, claiming the right to regulate the clergy in the exercise of their spiritual office and the populace in the observance of their religious duties.

This too was done in the name of the common weal. To men of that time it was obvious that disorders in a community's religious life produced grave consequences in its temporal affairs as well. The excessive number and the riotous celebration of church holidays, for example, tended to reduce the productivity of labour and to produce disorder. But this inseparability of the spiritual and temporal welfare of the community could also be seen at a much more sophisticated level. Wars, rebellions, epidemics, floods – any natural disasters or man-made catastrophes – tended to be interpreted as God's punishment upon the community for its sins. Thus it was in the interest of the common weal that steps be taken to avert or assuage the wrath of God by improving public morals and by maintaining orthodoxy of doctrine and worship. Not only because they were guardians of the common weal but also because they were commonly thought to have been given their authority by God, to whom they were responsible for its exercise, it seemed only proper that the secular rulers should take the initiative in such matters, particularly if the clergy were lax in doing so.

The secular authorities exercised their responsibility for the spiritual welfare of their subjects in a number of ways. First of all, they enjoined the undertaking of certain pilgrimages or processions, the sale of some indulgences, and the observance of some religious holidays, while forbidding others, according to their understanding of the temporal and spiritual needs of the community. Second, in the great burst of law-making by which they strove to promote the common weal, they increasingly assumed direct responsibility for enforcing acceptable standards of Christian morality in the lay community. The last three decades of the fifteenth century saw the first widespread appearance of territorial police ordinances (*Polizeiordnungen, Landesordnungen*), which contained not only regulations for such things as weights and measures, coinage, dress, and care of the poor, but also sections banning such things as cursing, swearing, overdrinking, fornication, adultery, gambling, indecent dances, and so forth.

Third, as patrons and as church advocates the territorial rulers assumed the right to regulate the clergy in the performance of their duties and, whenever necessary, to initiate reforms. Thus the priests under the patronage of the ruler would be required to do such things as reside in their benefices, avoid pluralism, preach at certain times and places and in an edifying manner, and so forth. Rulers also found it expedient to send out visitation commissions to 'protect' the monasteries by requiring them to adhere to their old rule or even to adopt a new, stricter rule. The obvious and generally recognized need for such reforms in this period, and the equally obvious inadequacy of the hierarchy's own reform efforts, encouraged this sort of intervention in ecclesiastical affairs. The community was not to be denied the spiritual treasures that the church could bestow simply because of the negligence or corruption of a group of outsiders (i.e., the bishop and his officials). The more genuinely pious the ruler, the more far-reaching and systematic this aspect of his ecclesiastical policy was likely to be. As time passed, what was officially defined as helpful intervention in emergencies came to seem more and more like the exercise of routine jurisdiction.

It is hardly surprising that reform-minded clerics, many of whom served the secular princes as advisers and judges, should have aided and abetted all this poaching on the jurisdiction of the bishops. Nor should it be surprising that the popes did the same thing. The period of the greatest strides in the development of territorial sovereignty in Germany roughly coincided with the period in which the popes were struggling to recover that primacy in the church which had been challenged by the conciliar movement. The German bishops had been among the strongest supporters of conciliar supremacy. In the decades following the dissolution of the Council of Basel (1449), that is, following the defeat of the conciliar movement, the papacy, in return for support of its claims to supremacy in the church, formally conceded to many territorial rulers those rights in ecclesiastical affairs which they had wrested or were trying to wrest from the jurisdiction of the bishops. Moreover, the popes provided the necessary charters for a number of new *Landesuniversitäten* (territorial universities) – e.g., Tübingen in Württemberg (1477) and Wittenberg in Saxony (1502) – thus enabling the territorial rulers to assume direct responsibility for the training of qualified clergymen.

By the end of the fifteenth century the trend toward the development of *Landeskirchen* had gone so far that it had become common for German princes, such as the Duke of Württemberg in 1495, to boast that they were pope in their own territories. The boast would have been less vainglorious if they had said 'bishop' instead of 'pope,' for it was the bishops, not the pope, whose authority had been curtailed. Bishops were still important personages: among other things, they were still indispensable at ordinations and confirmations, and their authority in doctrinal matters (including the sacrament of marriage) was not questioned. But the territorial rulers could, if they wished, intervene in just about every other aspect of episcopal jurisdiction over the affairs of the clergy and the lives of the laity. Small wonder that the ruler's subjects, clerical and lay, were becoming accustomed to thinking of him rather than the bishop as their protector and guide in ecclesiastical matters.

On the eve of the Reformation, the Christian humanists were the principal advocates of the authority of the secular magistrates in religious matters. There were two reasons for this. First, although the humanists hoped for a spiritual regeneration of society, they had pretty much lost hope that the initiative would come from the ecclesiastical hierarchy, and the very idea of appealing to the passions of the mob was anathema to them. On the other hand, many of them were either natives or adopted sons of Upper-German imperial cities, where the idea of magisterial control of religious affairs for the sake of the common weal had been earliest and most thoroughly worked out. Since the 'common weal' (*publica utilitas*) was a high-minded idea of impeccably classical pedigree, it was logical for the humanists to take it up, adorn it with scriptural learning, and elaborate the notion of the 'Christian magistrate' who seeks the common weal, not merely by securing the external well-being of his subjects but also by providing for their religious and moral instruction as well. The best-known expression of this view is Erasmus's *Education of a Christian Prince* (1516).[56] Erasmus, typically, elaborated no concrete programme of institutional reform on the basis of this view of the Christian magistracy. But during the Reformation many young Erasmians (or former Erasmians) did.

So it is no accident that the best-known advocates of the state church among the German reformers were, in contrast to Luther, men of Upper-German urban background who came to the Reformation via Erasmian humanism. Their tendency to look to the secular magistrates for religious reform was a product of the political and intellectual traditions in which they had been nurtured before the Reformation and which continued to shape their thought and actions after they had become Protestant reformers. Thus Brenz, the son and grandson of city councillors and *Schultheisse* in Weil der Stadt, and member of a humanist circle in Heidelberg, came to the Reformation predisposed to demand from the secular authorities the orderly institution of the desired reforms and to justify those demands on the grounds of the Christian magistrate's duty to the common good.[57] Moreover, his experience as a reformer reinforced this predisposition at every turn.

For example, it was the exercise of the secular authorities' prerogatives as patrons and church advocates which provided the legal basis for initiating the Reformation. In Schwäbisch Hall it was the city council's patronage of St Michael's Church which enabled it to appoint known reformers, Brenz and Eisenmenger, as preacher and pastor and to shield them from interference by the Bishop of Würzburg.[58] In Württemberg the duke's prerogatives as patron played just as important a role. As of 1534, the year the Reformation was introduced there, the duke was patron of thirty-four per cent of the parishes in the duchy, an unusually high figure. Most of the rest were in the hands of monasteries and other ecclesiastical institutions firmly under the duke's control as church advocate.[59] Thus Duke Ulrich was able to launch the reformation of his duchy by dismissing from the churches under his patronage all those pastors who would not submit to the reform, appointing suitable Protestants in their places, and ordering the same thing to be done in all those churches whose patrons were his subjects.[60] Ulrich also devoted considerable attention to monastic reform, justifying his actions in part on the basis of his protectorate over the monasteries.[61]

If magisterial control of ecclesiastical appointments was crucial to the inauguration of the Reformation, so too was the old notion of the magistrate's obligation to use his God-given authority to secure the common weal. Indeed, that notion was an essential ingredient in the arguments that Brenz used to persuade the cautious, conservative magistrates in Schwäbisch Hall and elsewhere to undertake the fundamental reforms of the early years of the Reformation. This is a matter which will be discussed fully in the following chapter, so it need not detain us for the present.

While it is thus legitimate to emphasize the continuity between the *Landeskirchentum* of the pre-Reformation period and the *landesherrliche Kirchenregiment* of the Protestant Reformation, it is important to remember that there was a significant element of discontinuity as well. Before the Reformation, magistrates may have abridged episcopal jurisdiction and extended their own authority over ecclesiastical and religious affairs, but they had always considered it their obligation to uphold the cardinal doctrines and sacred rites of the Catholic faith as defined by popes and councils. In the Reformation, by contrast, magistrates eliminated episcopal jurisdiction and used their authority to replace Catholic doctrines and ceremonies with new ones. They did not lay claim to the dogmatic authority of the bishops (or of popes and councils); that fell to Scripture itself (as interpreted by the learned theologians of the state church). But they did bring the entire institutional structure of the church and the entire public exercise of religion under their sole authority.

Brenz was fully aware that the magistrates had thus acquired a far greater role in the life of the church than the one they had played before the Reformation. Moreover, he had not advocated such a development lightly. Writing in the 1530s, he observed that it should really have been the bishops who abolished the godless mass and dismissed the priests who obstinately adhered to it. Instead, the bishops had persecuted the gospel. So the Holy Spirit had called the secular authorities to the task of reformation. If they had not responded, God would have called someone else.[62] Brenz might also have observed in this connection that the secular authorities had not been particularly eager to take on the assigned task and that one of his major accomplishments had been to persuade them to do so.

3

The Justification of the
State Church

The extant writings in which Brenz discussed the responsibility of the secular magistrate for the establishment and maintenance of true religion fall into three periods. In the 1520s the traditional arguments summarized in the preceding chapter (with some ideas from Luther blended in) served Brenz well. Then, beginning in 1530, changing circumstances forced Brenz to reassess and, in some measure, to revise his thinking on the subject. Finally, the result of that rethinking, Brenz's mature thought on the office of Christian magistrate, was set forth in works of the 1540s and 1550s.

THE EARLY WRITINGS, 1524-9

The 1520s were the time of the reformers' earliest efforts to bring about an orderly transformation of ecclesiastical institutions in conformity with the new doctrine. Brenz's early writings on the office of Christian magistrate consist primarily of appeals to the secular authorities in Schwäbisch Hall, Brandenburg-Ansbach, and elsewhere to take positive action to bring about that transformation. The problem was not to persuade the magistrates that they had authority in ecclesiastical matters – they already believed that – but to persuade them to use that authority in behalf of the Reformation despite the apparent risks involved. For the 1520s were also the time of events, like the Knights' Rebellion and the Peasants' Revolt, which aroused fears that the spread of Protestant doctrine constituted a threat to the established social and political order. These fears, fanned by the enemies of the Reformation, were enough to cause even the convinced Lutherans among the German rulers to be anxious and hesitant about carrying through major changes in church order.[1] Brenz's strategy for overcoming these scruples was to turn the argument around by insisting that magisterial support of the Reformation was not only a moral duty but the best way to keep peace and order as well. In other words, he placed great emphasis on the political and social benefits of supporting the Reformation.

Brenz wanted the authorities to do essentially two things. The first was to 'promote' the true preaching of the word. The earliest of the early writings concentrate on this theme.[2] Then, after Protestant preaching had been established, the emphasis shifted to a demand for the establishment of true worship in conformity with that word, that is, for the substitution of Protestant worship for the Roman mass.[3] The arguments in support of these demands were identical and are thus lumped together here.

Brenz first of all reminded the magistrates of the nature of the authority they exercised. The authority of a ruler over his subjects is the same as that of a father over his children. Indeed, in the days of Adam, Noah, Abraham, Isaac, and Jacob, there was no earthly authority higher than that of a father. Every father was 'pope, bishop, king, and emperor over his household.' But when the children became unruly and disobedient, secular authority took the place of paternal authority. Thus the attitude of a ruler toward his subjects should be paternal, which is to say that he should seek their material and spiritual welfare above all else.[4]

Secular authority, moreover, comes from God and is exercised over a people who belong to God. Knowledge of this fact and the acceptance of its consequences are what distinguish a Christian magistrate from a heathen one. A heathen ruler thinks that his territory is nothing more than a fief received from the wordly emperor and that he has only to enforce secular laws without regard to God's word. A Christian ruler, by contrast, knows from the word of God that his territory is not merely a fief of the Empire but, much more, a trust from God (Dan. 4:17; John 19:11; Rom. 13:1), and that he must therefore rule it not only in accordance with secular law but, much more, in accordance with the 'word, law, and command' of God (Deut. 17:18–19). Since God has commanded that his word be preached to every creature (Mk. 16:15) and that false worship give way to true worship (Matt. 15:1–9), a Christian ruler must use all appropriate means for carrying these divine commands into effect.[5] Furthermore, God established the secular sword for the purpose of keeping the peace and order in society. That is why Paul commands that Christians pray for all in authority, 'in order that we might lead a quiet and peaceable life in all godliness and honesty' (1 Tim. 2:2). But this purpose can only be satisfactorily fulfilled if the ruler provides for true preaching and worship. For there is no more reliable source of peace and order than true preaching and worship, while there is no greater source of conflict and disorder than false preaching and worship (Lev. 26:14ff.; Deut. 28:15ff.).[6]

Brenz supported this contention with an array of examples drawn from recent experience and from Old-Testament history. The Peasants' Revolt, during which Schwäbisch Hall narrowly escaped being occupied by a peasant army, provided

Brenz with his major example of the dangers of false preaching. His view of the revolt, as expressed in his commentary on the Twelve Articles (1525), was that the rebellious peasants, inspired by false preachers, had misused Luther's purely religious concept of Christian freedom to justify rebellion against legitimate authority for the achievement of purely secular ends such as the abolition of serfdom. Had the peasants understood the gospel correctly, they would have known that it affirms absolutely the right of government to regulate such secular matters and forbids subjects to rebel against their rulers, no matter how foolish or tyrannical they may be.[7] The moral: true preaching is a source of peace, order, and obedience; consequently, a government which wishes to fulfil its obligation to maintain peace will establish true preaching in all the churches attended by its subjects.[8]

Two years later, Brenz once more evoked the memory of the peasant uprising in the 'Hall Reformation,' where he urged the city council to cause the 'pure word of God' to be preached in all the churches in its territory. There is, he said, no greater cause of peaceful and honourable conduct, whereas there is no greater cause of violence and insurrection than the misinterpretation and false preaching of God's word, 'as events in our times unfortunately have shown.'[9] In the concluding section of the same document Brenz took the council to task for not doing anything effective to provide the rural parishes with suitable pastors, admonishing the city fathers not to be like those governments which value their subjects' welfare so little that they entrust their spiritual care to men whom they would scarcely trust to herd swine. It is for this reason, he said, that God sometimes uses the peasants as his instruments for punishing secular rulers. The city council should avoid deserving such punishment by providing for the spiritual needs of its subjects.[10]

Brenz also argued that governmental provision for uniform preaching would prevent the strife which factious preaching causes, first among clergymen and then in the congregations. As the histories of the ancient church testify, 'factious teaching produces sects, sects produce strife, and strife leads to violence.'[11]

With respect to the effects of true and false worship, numerous examples from the Old-Testament histories supplemented those drawn from the recent history of Germany. Thus, when the children of Israel forsook God to worship Baal and Ashtaroth, God angrily delivered them into the hands of their enemies (Judg. 2:11–23). On the other hand, God set the descendants of King Jehu on the throne of Israel for four generations because Jehu, who was otherwise a pretty worthless fellow, destroyed the house of Baal and slew the worshippers of Baal as well as the family of King Ahab, who had established the idolatrous cult (2 Kings 10:18–31). Similarly, because King Hezekiah of Judah destroyed pagan idols and kept God's commandments, God prospered him and gave him victory over the Syrian invaders (2 Kings 18:1–8, and chap. 19). The stories of Kings Josiah (2 Kings 22 and 23) and Jehoshaphat (2 Chron. 17 and 19) of Judah teach the same lesson. Brenz cautioned against dismissing these as mere Old-Testament tales no longer relevant in the Christian era. For, he said, the Holy Spirit caused them to be written down in order that every God-fearing ruler might know from the example of the chosen people what good fortune will befall him and his people if he establishes true divine worship, and what judgment and punishment will come upon him and his subjects if he promotes or tolerates worship contrary to God's word.[12]

The false worship which Brenz wanted the Jehus and Josiahs of his day to abolish was, of course, the Catholic mass, which continued to be celebrated in Hall's rural parishes long after its disappearance from the city churches. Abuse of the Lord's Supper or mass, said Brenz in the 'Hall Reformation,' is surely one of the greatest sins on earth. Members of the Corinthian congregation were punished with sickness and death for a relatively minor abuse of it (1 Cor. 1:29–30). But the Roman mass is a far more evil misuse. It is a blasphemous, 'completely idolatrous' perversion of the sacrament into a supposed sacrifice for the sins of the living and the dead. This blasphemy so arouses God to anger that he inflicts upon the land whose government tolerates it famine, pestilence, and dangerous wars, as in the case of the Peasants' Revolt. (A few years later, the imminent Turkish invasion of the Empire served as Brenz's main example.) Thus the celebration of mass is not only an affront to the glory of God but also a threat to public peace. 'Therefore ... a faithful, Christian government must ... turn aside God's wrath by abolishing the blasphemous abuse of the mass, in order that the mercy bestowed upon the government, city, and territory of Hall in the recent peasants' war not be lost, and in order that a new, greater wrath of God, with factions and destruction of land and people, not be brought on by negligence in promoting God's glory and by toleration of publicly recognized blasphemy.'[13]

In addition to keeping the peace, the secular magistrates are, said Brenz, responsible for maintaining a respectable standard of public morality (*weltlich erberkeit und frumkeit*) among their subjects.[14] Once again he argued that the establishment of true preaching and worship is a necessary means toward this end. In particular, he saw preaching as a means for dealing with what he thought was the generally wild, lawless, and immoral behaviour of the peasants in Hall's rural territory. In an undated memorandum from this period, Brenz lamented that whereas in the cities many hundreds of burghers could live close together with relatively little public strife and lewdness, the rural areas were hotbeds of vice and violence. In the villages young people behaved shamelessly at dances while nearly every public occasion – church holiday, wedding, or whatever – soon degenerated into a drunken brawl with someone ending up maimed or killed. Brenz blamed this on the long-standing neglect of the spiritual needs of the peasants. More specifically, the peasants had not had discipline and the fear of God instilled in them from childhood onward by means of public preaching. So Brenz appealed to the city council which, like all secular governments, had been established 'for the sake of the common weal,' to establish in the rural parishes that true preaching by means of which an 'honourable, peaceful, and godly life among the subjects' would be produced. Even though the people themselves, who were 'like sheep gone astray,' might not demand or desire such action, the secular magistrates, 'as the enlightened parties,' must nevertheless take the initiative in providing their subjects with the word of God.[15]

As for the effects of worship upon public morality, Brenz was content to cite St Paul's catalogue of the iniquities of those who 'worship the creature more than the creator' (Rom. 1:21–32) as evidence that false worship is a major cause of shameful and immoral behaviour. He went on to recommend that a Christian ruler who wished to live up to his obligation to maintain secular decency could do no better than to replace ungodly worship with true divine worship, so that the true, divine peace and honour begun in church would overflow into everyday life.[16]

In addition to these arguments based on the received notions of the office of Christian magistrate, Brenz also used arguments derived from Luther's doctrine of the priesthood of all believers. Brenz's conclusions, however, were quite different from Luther's. For Luther, as we have seen, the priesthood of all believers served to place severe limits on the role the magistrate as magistrate could play in ecclesiastical affairs.[17] In Brenz's case, the reverse was true. Given his *a priori* commitment to the view that church government is part of the office of Christian magistrate, he could only appeal to the magistrate's personal obligations as a participant in the priesthood of all believers in order to reinforce the magistrate's public obligations as the bearer of secular authority. And, in fact, he did so repeatedly.

For example, like Luther, Brenz used the priesthood of all believers to take ecclesiastical authority away from the Catholic hierarchy and give it to the Christian congregation or community. But for Brenz the exercise of this authority automatically fell to the magistrate as the responsible agent for the community:

[I]t is not cowls, tonsures, or annointing by a bishop that empower one to perform the priestly offices in the community, but rather the command and election of that Christian community or whoever is, as secular government, authorized to act for the community ...[18]

Similarly, Brenz wrote in his commentary on the Twelve Articles that Christ's command to the apostles to go forth and preach the gospel to every creature (Mk. 16:15) obligates the Christian magistrate as a Christian to promote the preaching of the gospel.[19] By itself this argument only proves that the magistrate has the same authority in the church as any other Christian – precisely Luther's point. But Brenz did not use the argument by itself; he used it in conjunction with other arguments, summarized above, based on the magistrate's duty as magistrate to provide for true preaching and worship. Used in this way, the priesthood of all believers became just one more reason for magisterial control of church government, not the principal theoretical obstacle to it. The Christian magistrate is not just another member of the church: because he is the magistrate, he is, to use the term coined later by Melanchthon, the 'foremost member' (*praecipuum membrum*), with the same commanding role in ecclesiastical matters that he has in secular matters.

This characteristic emphasis on the magistrate's dual role as secular ruler and Christian brother occurs again in the opening paragraph of the 'Hall Reformation' of 1527:

Since God our saviour has graciously permitted Christians to secure secular power over their own territories, cities, and villages, the secular rulers, as members of Christ and children of God, both for the salvation of their souls and by virtue of their office, are responsible for regulating and ordering all those things which Christ commanded to be observed in a Christian community [i.e., the preaching of the gospel and the administration of the sacraments], for the benefit of their subjects (according to secular power) and their brothers (according to Christ, for they are also co-heirs with them).[20]

Thus Brenz's prior commitment to the authority of the magistrate in the church left no room in his thought for that independence of the church from state control which Luther had deduced from the priesthood of all believers. Not even as an ideal to be achieved in some future, happier time did the idea of such independence enter Brenz's mind.

Given a situation in which, as at the time of the ancient church, Christians were a minority and the magistrates were not Christian, Brenz's solution to the problem of church order might well have been the kind of congregational autonomy which Luther had championed in the early 1520s. But Brenz was conscious of living at a time when God had 'graciously permitted Christians to secure secular power over their own territories, cities, and villages.' Under these happy circumstances, the secular magistrate had to play the commanding role that God had assigned to him, that of 'governor in things ecclesiastical.'[21] It was not that ordinary Christians, in Brenz's view, were without responsibility in ecclesiastical matters, but that they had a different office. As he wrote in 1535, Christ has commanded everyone to serve the building of his church: the magistrates by the supervision of church order, the pastors by preaching and administering the sacraments, and the common people by saying their prayers.[22] In other words, ecclesiastical affairs, like secular affairs, were to be subjected to the fatherly tutelage of the increasingly absolutist secular rulers, and the ordinary Christian was to be a passive, obedient subject in ecclesiastical and secular affairs alike.

At this point one may ask if the assignment of so much authority in the church to the magistrate did not contradict the doctrine of the two kingdoms as the reformers understood it. In other words, did not the state church involve unwarranted interference by secular authority in purely spiritual matters? In the period before 1530 Brenz had less to say about this important question than one might expect. Not that he ignored the doctrine of the two kingdoms; his views on that subject, which derived from those of Luther,[23] were fully set forth in the early writings on the Christian magistracy, principally in the commentary on the Twelve Articles.

According to Brenz, the spiritual realm is, in St Paul's words, 'righteousness, peace, and joy in the Holy Ghost' (Rom. 14:17). Adam was born into this kingdom, but his sin made him and his descendants exiles from it until God became man in Jesus Christ, reconquered the kingdom, and restored to it all those who believe in him. Appropriately, Christ himself became king in this realm (Ps. 8:6; John 13:13; Eph. 1:20-3). But he does not rule in the manner of worldly kings (Matt. 20:25-8), for he calls all the faithful his brothers (Heb. 2:11) and makes of them 'lords, kings, and emperors' (1 Pet. 2:9; Rev. 1:5-6). His kingdom, in other words, is not of this world (John 18:36); his dominion is not over land and people, fields and meadows, but rather over sin, temptation, death, and hell (Eph. 6:12), and that person is greatest in his kingdom who, through him, has most thoroughly fought and overcome sin, temptation, death, and hell.[24]

Because the citizens of the spiritual kingdom are ruled by the word of God alone, they have no need of swords, judges, lawyers, hangmen, magistrates, or princes. For they keep perfect peace and suffer all injustice and evil without seeking revenge; they lend without interest; if someone takes away their coat, they let him have their cloak also; they lay charges against no one in court but leave vengeance to God, etc. However, such exemplary creatures are extremely rare, and are scattered here and there throughout the world. They are a few just men in Sodom and Gomorrah, a minority of sheep among a majority of wolves. This means that the world cannot possibly be governed by the word of God alone. If that were attempted, the evil majority would devour the few real Christians as wolves devour scattered sheep. To prevent this, God has established secular government and given it coercive power ('the sword') with which to govern the secular realm (Rom. 13:4).[25]

The secular realm, the kingdom of this world, is distinct from the spiritual realm and different from it. In the invisible world of the spirit there is no such thing as time, place, or other external circumstance, and the faithful possess all its goods equally. In the external world, by contrast, there are infinite distinctions of time, place, size, shape, and composition, as well as of rank, station, wealth, and personal attributes. Moreover, the affairs of this world – business, commerce, manufactures, and the like, as well as swords, racks, and gallows to punish the wicked – have nothing to do with the spiritual kingdom.[26]

Secular government is, to be sure, a divine ordinance, and the regulations it makes to secure the peace, order, and common good of the secular realm are to be deemed judgments of God (Prov. 16:10–15). However, such regulations are of no use to the Christian realm. They make no one pious or just in the eyes of God, but serve only to keep peace and order in the secular realm. Civic virtue and godly piety are two entirely different things. The statutes, ordinances, regulations, and punishments of secular government can guide and force men to civic virtue, but no prince or emperor, no creature in heaven or earth, can force anyone to true piety. Only the word of God can make a man pious.[27]

Now, how could Brenz begin his commentary on the Twelve Articles by claiming that the ordinances of secular government are of no use to the spiritual kingdom, and then proceed, in the same work, to claim that the magistrates must provide their subjects with true preaching and worship and shield them from the false?[28] The juxtaposition of the two claims in the same work indicates that there was no contradiction in Brenz's mind. It did not occur to him to forestall possible misunderstanding by demonstrating the consistency of the two claims because no one had raised the issue. Not until 1530 would Brenz be confronted with the charge that the state church constituted a violation of the biblical distinction between secular and spiritual authority.[29] Meanwhile, when he took up the subject of the two kingdoms, it was to deal with issues that had nothing to do with the church/state problem. In the commentary on the Twelve Articles, for example, the emphasis on the God-given authority of secular government to regulate secular affairs, and on the irrelevance of those regulations to salvation, served simply to demonstrate the illegitimacy of a rebellion over secular grievances in the name of the gospel.[30]

Supposing that Brenz had addressed himself to the task of harmonizing his doctrine of the Christian magistracy with his doctrine of the two kingdoms, what would he have said? There are in his early writings some comments on the church and its ceremonies which make possible at least a partial answer to that question.

He pointed out, for example, that the word 'church' may be used in two different ways. In one sense it is the equivalent of 'spiritual realm' and thus refers to the invisible fellowship of all the elect in Christ, the community of God's people, ruled by Christ. This church is not bound to any time or place, but exists at all times and in all places where true faith in Christ is found. In the other sense, 'church' refers to an external gathering of people, both good and evil, in which the word of God is preached and the sacraments are administered.[31] Moreover, this visible church has certain external ceremonies which, though useful and necessary, are not in themselves essential to salvation. That is, they are not part of the spiritual realm. For this reason, Brenz was most anxious that ordinary Christians not make the mistake of regarding the performance of ceremonies prescribed and enforced by the magistrates as a sacred obligation meriting grace.[32] So in his first reformed order of worship, the *Frühmessordnung* of 1526, he appended an afterword solemnly warning against this neo-popish error. Ecclesiastical ceremonies, he said, are simply a matter of external order and discipline, and a person who observes them is only well disciplined (*zuchtig*), not pious (*frumb*), 'for piety pertains to higher things than ceremonies.' As long as the word is preached and the sacraments administered in an orderly fashion and nothing is done contrary to his word, God does not care what ceremonies are observed in the church. Thus the city council may freely alter or replace them as the need and benefit of the church require.[33]

The implications of all this seem clear. If the church order for which the magistrate is responsible is simply a matter of external discipline and not of inner piety, it follows that the magistrate's authority extends only to externals, not to faith itself. In other words, the control of church order is something within the legitimate sphere of secular authority and involves no violation of the spiritual realm. Starting in 1530 Brenz would have to explain his views on this matter more explicitly and in far greater detail.

1530: A TURNING POINT

The last of the works in which Brenz defended the state church with the arguments summarized in the preceding section bears the date 1 June 1529.[34] There is a gap of eleven years between it and the first of the series of later works dealing with the same issue. The argument he used in these later works is quite different from that in the earlier works. In the earlier writings Brenz had argued, first, that because the magistrate's power is a trust from God he must use it in accordance with God's will by establishing true preaching and worship; and second, that in so doing the magistrate best accomplishes the goal of his office, namely to keep secular peace and order. The emphasis was, as we have seen, on the second part of the argument. In the later works, by contrast, the second part of the argument is virtually eliminated, and the case for the state church is based entirely on a much expanded version of the first part.

The earliest version, or at least the earliest extant version, of Brenz's revised doctrine of the Christian magistrate is found in four *Ratswahlpredigten*, sermons on the theme *De officio magistratus*, preached on the occasion of city-council elections in Schwäbisch Hall in 1541, 1543, 1545, and 1546.[35] The ideas worked out in these Election Day Sermons of the 1540s are repeated in the 1550s in the prefaces to several of Duke Christopher's published ecclesiastical ordinances, and are echoed in certain other writings of the 1540s and 1550s as well.

Because of the gap in the sources, the process of thought which led from the stand taken in the earlier writings to that taken in the later writings cannot be reconstructed in detail. It is possible, however, both to establish when and why Brenz decided to revise his argument for the state church and to identify at least some of the factors that influenced the process of revision.

In the spring of 1530, in the midst of controversy, Brenz suddenly discovered that his argument in support of magisterial authority in ecclesiastical matters had some major loopholes. The controversy, which concerned the treatment of Anabaptists, took place not in Schwäbisch Hall, where Anabaptism was not a problem, but in Nuremberg. Three times in the period 1528–30 Brenz's Nuremberg colleagues sought his opinion in the matter, and each time Brenz responded with a written memorandum.[36] For present purposes, the most important of these memoranda is the last one, written in May 1530, but the one immediately preceding it (March 1530) merits brief attention as well.[37]

The title of the March memorandum states the question that Brenz had been asked to deal with: 'Whether a Government Violates Conscience when it Forcibly Banishes False Teachers.'[38] Brenz's answer was a rather clumsy affair. Citing Jean Gerson, he argued first that true conscience (*Gewissen*) exists only where there is true knowledge (*Wissen*) of truth as revealed by the Holy Spirit.[39] Thus the adherents of false doctrine actually have no consciences to be violated but only vain delusions to be banished. Furthermore, the government does not force them to faith contrary to their so-called consciences but only forbids them to spread harmful doctrine. Indeed, even if a tyrant were to banish true Christians from his land, their consciences would not thereby be violated, for physical punishment of the body does not affect the conscience. If this is so in the case of true believers, it is even more so in the case of the teachers of false doctrine. On the other hand, although God alone can know and rule hearts and consciences, over which no man has power, nevertheless every man, but especially the magistrate, should do his best to serve and help consciences in his office or calling. After all, if the government is obligated to serve God, who is a spirit and thus far more deeply hidden from us than is any human heart, why should the government not also be able to serve consciences by comforting the weak, praising the strong, and also by preventing or punishing the teaching of false doctrine? In so doing it neither burdens the conscience nor forces anyone to act contrary to his conscience but simply serves God by promoting the truth.

Brenz himself was evidently not happy with the notion of conscience derived from Gerson, for he never used it again. In his very next statement on the subject, the memorandum about to be discussed, he acknowledged the existence of erring consciences with rights that must be respected. On the other hand, the idea of the magistrate serving the conscience without ruling it (or serving God's kingdom without violating it) was one that he did not have to abandon.

Brenz wrote the May memorandum in an attempt to rebut the arguments of an anonymous Nuremberger who, although he was a convinced Lutheran and a member of the governing elite of Nuremberg, thought that secular authorities had no right to use their sword in matters of faith but must tolerate Anabaptists, Jews, and other religious dissidents.[40] His reasoning was, essentially, that the New Testament distinguishes between two realms on earth: the secular realm, governed by the magistrate, who wields the sword in order to keep external peace and order; and the spiritual realm, governed by Christ through his word, whereby men are called to faith and eternal life. The New Testament also teaches that these two realms are to be kept strictly separate and that neither authority is to interfere in the sphere of the other. Furthermore, only the word of God is able to awaken true faith or to destroy false faith; the secular sword is powerless against it. Therefore, the magistrate should stick to his job, the preservation of external peace and order, and refrain from any interference in matters of faith, whether true or false.

In his reply,[41] Brenz undertook the difficult task of maintaining the distinction between secular and spiritual authority while at the same time justifying governmental action against Anabaptists or other teachers of false doctrine. He readily admitted that the New Testament distinguishes between the spiritual and secular realms, each with its own distinct purpose and ruling authority. He also conceded that 'it is not appropriate for secular authority to defend the true faith with force or to drive out or punish false faith by force.'[42] But he then drew an extremely fine distinction between personal faith on the one hand and external works or deeds done in pursuit of that faith on the other. Personal faith, whether true or false, is no concern of the government as long as it remains the private conviction of an individual. But the proclamation of that faith, or worship in accordance with it, whether in public or in secret, is a proper concern of the magistrate as guardian of public peace and order. If the new preaching and worship are useful and peaceful, the magistrate must promote them, but if they are demonstrably scandalous and factious, the magistrate must abolish them.[43] Brenz then went on to argue, for the last time, that false preaching and worship are a source of civic disorder, and to evoke, also for the last time, the spectre of the Peasants' Revolt.[44] The point he wanted to make was that a government which abolishes such false preaching and worship, and punishes the obstinate teachers of false doctrine, is only acting in restraint of external offences; private faith is unmolested and consciences are left free.[45] Brenz was consistent and fair-minded enough to argue that the same was true in the case of action by a heretical government against adherents of the true faith. Magisterial control over externals is complete, even if they exercise that control unjustly by persecuting the true faith.[46]

Unfortunately for Brenz, the anonymous Nuremberger had already heard the argument about false preaching as a source of tumult or rebellion (*aufruhr*) and in his memorandum had raised objections for which Brenz had no really satisfactory answer. The first argument was that tumult is not the product of true or false faith or the teaching of it, but is something caused by evil men who may happen to be the adherents of one faith or the other. Hence neither tumult nor the fear of it is any justification for invading Christ's kingdom by banning the preaching or worship of any sect. Indeed, Christ, his apostles, and the prophets before them were all the cause of tumult and were denounced as rebels. Should one on that account ban the preaching of the true faith?[47] Brenz's answer was that the prophets and apostles had been called by God and could prove their calling by performing miracles. Thus their offence against the established order was justified. The leaders of a new sect must prove their calling in the same way if they wish to justify their breach of the established order. On the other hand, pastors who have been regularly called and appointed by the government, and who thus are no threat to the peace of the community, do not need to justify their calling in this way.[48]

Even more damaging to Brenz's case was the purely empirical argument that it is perfectly possible for a government to keep peace and order while tolerating false doctrine and worship. 'For over a hundred years in the Kingdom of Bohemia there have been Jews as well as three [Christian] faiths, and their kings have nevertheless maintained external peace and prevented all tumult for reasons of faith.'[49] In reply, Brenz admitted that there are cases where a people divided in religion accepts a ruler only on condition that every sect retain the right to observe its religion, as the Jews accepted the Romans and the Bohemians accepted King Ferdinand.[50] A government may also have good reason for permitting the establishment of a new sect, as was perhaps the case with the admission of the Jews into Frankfurt and Worms. But Brenz denied that rulers in whose territory religious unity has been established are obligated to permit the establishment of a new sect.[51] If they were, some God-fearing bishop would certainly have denounced those Christian emperors who issued decrees against various heresies. But the ancient histories record no incidence of such a denunciation.[52]

All this amounted to an admission that there is no necessary connection between false preaching or worship and civic disorder. Indeed, Brenz had already said as much two years earlier in his first statement on the treatment of Anabaptists.[53] But if there is no necessary connection between false preaching or worship and civic disorder, then neither is there any necessary connection between true preaching or worship and civic peace. Thus, although Brenz was only arguing the issue of the treatment of Anabaptists, it was really the magistrate's control of ecclesiastical affairs in general that was at stake, and one of Brenz's main arguments in support of that control had been fatally damaged. Why should the magistrate shoulder the burden of enforcing doctrinal and liturgical uniformity if he can keep peace and order just as well without all that trouble and expense? Why not, as the anonymous Nuremberger recommended, follow Gamaliel's advice to 'refrain from these men, and let them alone: for if this counsel or this work be of men it will come to nought: but if it be of God, ye cannot overthrow it' (Acts 5:38–9)?[54] The argument that the magistrate is not compelled to tolerate a new sect was no answer. What was needed was a good, solid reason for intolerance. For the moment all that Brenz could think to do was to fall back on the argument that 'secular government must prevent not only those things which by their nature cause tumult but also those things which cause indecency or public scandal,' such as bigamy and cursing. Now, even if the preaching or worship of a false sect produces no tumult, it does cause disorder, confusion, and faction among Christians. 'Why then should it not behoove the government to take action?'[55] The real question, of course, was *why*, not *why not*.

Thus in the spring of 1530 Brenz found himself in something of a quandary. Faced for the first time with serious, biblically grounded objections to the state church, advanced by an adherent of the Reformation and rendering his favourite argument in support of the state church useless, the best he had been able to do was defend the rather weak proposition that a Christian magistrate is *not obligated* to tolerate a new sect but *may* with good conscience take action to abolish it.[56] What Brenz needed, as he perhaps already realized, was a new argument as compelling as the old one but not so easily undermined by empirical considerations. It seems that his Nuremberg colleagues were the first, though by no means the last or the most important, to assist him in the process of rethinking his position.

INFLUENCES ON BRENZ'S LATER THOUGHT

At least two of the Nuremberg reformers also wrote replies to the arguments of their anonymous fellow citizen. While the originals of these counter-memoranda have disappeared, copies evidently made for Brenz's personal use have survived in the Brentiana collection of the Schwäbisch Hall archives. Since the author is not named in either case, and since the available evidence is so sparse and confusing, the problem of attribution has as yet found no definitive solution. The most persuasive of the learned guesses so far[57] ascribes the longer and more ambitious of the two counter-memoranda to Osiander,[58] the other to Wenzeslaus Linck.[59] The important thing here is not who wrote the documents but the fact that their contents seem to have influenced the general direction if not the precise formulation of Brenz's later thought on the subject of the Christian magistracy.

Like Brenz, the Nurembergers readily conceded that the spiritual and the secular realms are distinct and that secular authority may not interfere in the spiritual realm.[60] At the same time, however, they took the view that the two realms are not opposed to one another like God and Mammon or good and evil, but are partners like law and gospel or body and soul, working hand in hand in the service of a common goal, neither one able to do its job properly without the other.[61] From this standpoint they defended the following proposition:

Although things which pertain directly and of necessity to the spiritual realm should be dealt with in a spiritual manner and entrusted to the clergy, who have the ministry of the word: nevertheless, to the extent that such things are external or temporal and can be separated from the spiritual realm, a Christian magistrate may and should deal with them in the defence of truth.[62]

This meant, first of all, that the external aspects of church order, precisely because they are external, not essential to salvation, not binding on conscience, are not part of the spiritual realm but rather part of the temporal realm.[63] The Nurembergers thought it 'indisputable' that church property, income, vestments, and so forth are 'earthly, temporal things' and thus under the authority of the magistrate.[64] The question of preaching and the administration of the sacraments was, they admitted, more difficult. Nevertheless, the same principle applied. While preaching and the sacraments are indeed essential components of the spiritual realm,[65] the accompanying procedures and ceremonies are not. They are temporal matters[66] which the magistrate should regulate in such a way as to promote the welfare of God's kingdom. For God established secular authority primarily for the purpose of serving his kingdom in this fashion. That is why St Paul refers to the secular magistrate as God's servant for the benefit of the good and the punishment of the wicked (Rom. 13:3–4).[67] Thus a magistrate who promotes true preaching and worship by establishing wholesome and useful ceremonies, or who by appropriate means prevents false preaching and worship, is in no way guilty of usurping God's authority over faith and conscience. He is simply doing his duty to God and his fellow Christians within his proper sphere of authority.[68] Indeed, the wrath of God awaits him if he does not use his authority in this way (Ps. 2:10–12; Wisd. 6:1–6).[69]

The only caution which the Nurembergers voiced was that the magistrate be absolutely sure, on the basis of God's word, that any measures undertaken actually promote God's kingdom and in no way hinder it. Thus, for example, before taking punitive action against an unauthorized preacher, the magistrate must make absolutely sure that it is false preaching rather than true preaching he is banning. He must not make Pilate's mistake of condemning Jesus and freeing Barabbas.[70]

Naturally, only a Christian magistrate can be expected to understand all this or be trusted to act in the appropriate spirit, that is, to serve God's kingdom out of love rather than to tyrannize over it.[71]

Now, if the primary purpose of secular authority is to serve God's kingdom, then the question of the temporal side effects of true or false preaching or worship becomes secondary at best, and the anonymous memorandist's example of a state which is peaceful even though divided in religion becomes irrelevant. For 'tumult or temporal harm is not the chief reason why false sects or erring rabble should not be tolerated but, much more, God's honour and the salvation of souls.'[72] On this basis the Nurembergers could readily concede that false preaching does not necessarily produce tumult yet still insist that it is the secular magistrate's duty to oppose it.[73] Indeed, even if false preaching were to produce 'great temporal profit, security, and fortune,' a Christian government would have to oppose it 'for the sake of the glory of God.'[74]

While this brief summary hardly does justice to all the complexities, not to mention the difficulties, of the Nurembergers' defence of magisterial authority in ecclesiastical affairs, it does suffice to reveal the way in which they seem to have influenced Brenz. Most of their arguments had fairly exact counterparts in Brenz's writings up to 1530. For example, the argument that the externals of church order are part of the secular realm and thus under the control of the Christian magistrate was essentially the position that Brenz took in his reply to the anonymous memorandum.[75] Again, the idea of the magistrate serving God's kingdom without tyrannizing over it was analogous to Brenz's idea, enunciated in the memorandum of March 1530, that the magistrate may serve consciences but not rule them.[76] On one important issue, however, the correspondence was not so close. The Nurembergers' argument that secular authority was established to serve God's kingdom was indeed akin to Brenz's idea, much used in the 1520s, that because the magistrate has his authority from God he must use it in accordance with the will of God.[77] But while the Nurembergers had been able to make good use of their version of the argument in their reply to the anonymous memorandum, Brenz had not been able to make similar use of his. The reason was that while the Nurembergers had formulated a conception of the purpose of secular authority which rendered irrelevant the question of the temporal effects of true or false preaching, Brenz had not. In his thought, the idea of the magistrate's obligation to rule in accordance with the will of God had always been inextricably bound up with his assertion of the secular benefits of true preaching and worship. His reasoning had been: the magistrate must use his authority in accordance with God's will; God's will is that the magistrate maintain peace and order; since true preaching and worship are bulwarks of peace and order ... and so forth. He had never had to defend the state church in any other way, and it had apparently never occurred to him that the magistrate *as magistrate* had a divine mission loftier than that of keeping peace and order. Thus, when suddenly confronted with a critique of the state church which did such mortal damage to his principal argument in support of it, he was, in contrast to the more experienced Nurembergers, in no position to argue that God requires the magistrate to establish true preaching and worship and root out the false regardless of the temporal consequences. But in the years after 1530, he would advance that argument over and over again. It is therefore reasonable to assume that it was Brenz's Nuremberg colleagues who first showed him how it could be done.

In addition to the arguments of the anonymous Nuremberger, there were, or soon would be, more general considerations leading Brenz away from his initial reliance on the assertion of a direct connection between true preaching and civic order. In the 1520s the Reformation had been a new movement struggling to establish itself in the face of fears that Lutheranism and social unrest went hand in hand. In such circumstances the emphasis on true preaching and worship as sources of secular peace and order had been ideally suited to the task of winning and keeping the support of princes and town councilmen. By the 1530s, however, the peasants had been defeated and Lutheranism was a well-established, expanding movement whose compatibility with order and good government hardly needed further demonstration. Furthermore, once the initial step of abolishing mass and instituting Protestant preaching and worship had been taken, attention shifted from the campaign against 'idolatry and blasphemy' to other problems. Chief among these was the discipline of morals. By the early 1530s, as we shall see, Brenz had come to the conclusion that the secular authorities would have to become more deeply involved in the censure of morals than they really wished.[78] But it was not possible to persuade them that offences like adultery, fornication, and indecent dances were a threat to the public peace in the way that murder and robbery or idolatry and blasphemy were. So to inspire the authorities to action on such problems, Brenz had to find some argument that did not hinge on the preservation of public tranquillity.

Thus, whether it was to justify magisterial authority over ecclesiastical affairs or to convince the magistrates to use that authority in the desired way, Brenz had good reason to discuss the magistrate's duties along the lines laid out in the memoranda attributed to Osiander and Linck. In two respects, however, the position Brenz took in his later works differed from that taken by his Nuremberg colleagues. First, he shifted emphasis away from the question of the boundary between secular and spiritual authority. And second, he incorporated into his thought some new ideas borrowed from his friend, Philip Melanchthon.

The shift of emphasis was already evident in the mid-1530s. It was in the 1530s that the governments of Ansbach/Nuremberg and Württemberg began in earnest to prescribe uniform ceremonies. Critics of this policy – mostly pastors who wanted to follow their own lights in such matters – protested that consciences were being burdened with 'doctrines of men' (Matt. 15:9), which was another way of saying that the authorities were committing the popish error of invading the spiritual realm by imposing human inventions upon Christian consciences.

The Brandenburg-Nuremberg Church Order of 1533, in a section entitled 'Concerning the Doctrines of Men,'[79] written by Osiander, took note of these criticisms and argued that they were based on a misunderstanding of the issue. If the authorities fall into the error of saying that the ceremonies they have pre-scribed are necessary to salvation, then they are indeed guilty of imposing human doctrine. However, if they claim only that the prescribed ceremonies are a convenient and orderly method for preaching the word and administering the sacraments, no human doctrine is imposed on Christian consciences. For it is one thing to say, for example, that preaching is most effective in the morning because people are more alert in the morning than they will be after dinner, and quite another thing to say that preaching in the morning is necessary to salvation or that preaching in the afternoon is a sin.

Because of Brenz's role in the preparation and adoption of the Brandenburg-Nuremberg Church Order,[80] one must conclude that he approved of what it said 'concerning the doctrines of men.' Indeed, there was no reason for him not to approve: Osiander's statement was perfectly consonant with his own statement concerning ecclesiastical ceremonies in Schwäbisch Hall.[81] But when in the summer of 1535 he had to deal with the question on his own, in his proposed preface for the Württemberg Church Order of 1536,[82] Brenz took a different and rather harder line.

The argument was substantially as follows. St Paul says that all things in the church should be done decently and in order (1 Cor. 14:40). This means not that any particular set of ceremonies is necessary or holy – though uninformed people readily fall into this error – but that an orderly, decorous conduct of the church's affairs is 'useful and necessary' for teaching the true, saving faith and administer-ing the sacraments through which that faith is strengthened. Furthermore, since 'the elected instrument of Jesus Christ,' St Paul, calls the church order he estab-lished among the Corinthians 'the commandments of the Lord' (1 Cor. 14:37) and writes that 'God is not the author of confusion, but of peace' (1 Cor. 14:33), it follows that a church order which facilitates the preaching of God's word and the administration of the sacraments is, like a secular law established to maintain external peace, to be viewed 'not as a human ordinance but as God's ordinance.'

By arguing in this fashion, Brenz shifted the focus of attention away from the question of what is permissible because it is within the limits of secular authority to the question of what is obligatory because God commands it. This same shift of emphasis is evident in his later works on the office of Christian magistrate. Where in 1530 Brenz and his Nuremberg colleagues had been content to argue that certain magisterial actions in support of the true faith (e.g., the banishment of false preachers) do not violate the boundary between secular and spiritual authority, Brenz in the 1540s and 1550s ignored that consideration to argue instead that the actions which he wanted the magistrates to undertake in support of the true faith had been specifically commanded by God in Scripture. He was willing to concede that there was indeed a legitimate distinction between secular and spiritual government. But he no longer defended the state church in those terms because he had come to the conclusion that clear commands straight from God were more likely to get magistrates to act and subjects to obey than were rather abstract discussions about a boundary that was a best difficult to define. It was better, in other words, to be able to say, 'God commands it,' than to have to say, 'If you examine the matter carefully, you will see that the action in question does not violate the boundary between secular and spiritual authority and is thus not a violation of God's kingdom.'[83]

This was, of course, a new version of the old idea that the magistrate must use his authority according to the word, law, and command of God. What was new was the much broader understanding of what God's word, law, and command required of the magistrate.

It was in this connection that Melanchthon's ideas proved useful. The influence of Melanchthon on Brenz's theology (the doctrine of justification) is evident as early as 1531, following the establishment of close personal contact between the two men at the Diet of Augsburg in 1530.[84] But there is no evidence that Melanchthon exerted a similar influence on Brenz's conception of the Christian magistrate at that early date. We do not know if they discussed the matter during their private conversations at the diet, and it did not come up in their ensuing correspondence. However, by the time he wrote his Election Day Sermons, Brenz had had the chance to read several works, published between 1535 and 1543, in which Melanchthon elaborated his defence of the authority of the magistrate in ecclesiastical affairs.[85] That Brenz did indeed read them is attested by the wholesale incorporation of much of their content into the Election Day Sermons. Melanchthon was, in fact, the single most important influence on the formulation of Brenz's mature thought on the subject of the office of Christian magistrate.

One of Melanchthon's principal arguments was that it is the duty of the magistrates, as foremost members of the church, 'to have a regard for the interests of the church and see to it that errors are removed and consciences are healed.'[86] But this argument, which Brenz would use extensively in a later context,[87] did not really suit his purposes in the Election Day Sermons, where it occurs only once and in a variant form.[88] For what he was trying to prove, now as ever, was that the magistrate *as magistrate*, not just as individual Christian, has been commanded by God to protect and defend the true church. Certain of Melanchthon's other arguments, however, were admirably suited to this purpose.

Where the Nurembergers had said that secular authority was established 'for the sake of God's kingdom,' Melanchthon said that secular authority had been established 'for the sake of the churches' (*propter Ecclesias*), in order that it be possible to preach the gospel.[89] It was basically the same idea in both cases but more concrete and directly to the point in Melanchthon's formulation. Furthermore, Melanchthon added some supporting arguments which the Nurembergers had not used. The chief goal of human society, he said, is that men come to know God, glorify him, and gain eternal life. Thus the chief duty of the magistrate, whom God has ordained as the guardian of human society, is not simply to preserve peace and order, as though he were no more than a herdsman or a protector of men's bellies, but to use that peace and order for its proper purpose, namely the establishment and preservation of discipline, good morals, and true religion.[90] The office of magistrate is to be understood as that of guardian, with regard to external discipline, of both tables of the law. This means that the magistrate is responsible for the public observance of man's duty to God (the first three commandments of the Decalogue) as well as of man's duty to his fellow man (the remaining seven commandments). Thus the first two commandments require that the magistrate establish true preaching and worship among his subjects and abolish all false preaching and worship.[91] God has specifically commanded the secular authorities to use their office in this way (Ps. 2:10–12). Those who fail to do so will bear the chief guilt for all the souls that are seduced and lost, and the wrath of God will surely be upon them.[92]

For the sake of brevity and simplicity, all but one of the many scriptural texts which Melanchthon used to support his arguments were omitted from the foregoing summary. It should be pointed out, however, that both Melanchthon and, to a lesser extent, the Nurembergers relied heavily on texts which Brenz had either not used at all in his earlier writings,[93] or else had not used in quite the same way,[94] but which, beginning with the Election Day Sermons, became standard proof-texts in his defence of the state church as well. The most important of these texts will be cited as the appropriate places in the following pages, for the simple reason that they were essential to the persuasiveness of his argument that magisterial responsibility for true religion and good morals was not just convenient and permissible but the inexorable will and command of God.

THE LATER WORKS, 1541-59

No one of the four Election Day Sermons[95] presents Brenz's mature view of the Christian magistracy in its entirety. However, if taken together and supplemented with material from other works, a fairly complete picture of that view emerges from them.

The first point to be made in discussing secular authority, said Brenz, is that it is not something dreamed up by ambitious men eager for power but is, rather, an institution established by God for his own purposes. If Adam had remained in his original state of righteousness, all men would have been free. There would have been no strife over rank or property. Every man would have been, as it were, a monarch, a terrestrial god. Every family would have honoured its head as pope and emperor, and the heads of all families would have honoured one another as earthly gods. But Adam's fall caused human nature to be so corrupted by sin that there was no longer any mutual respect, peace, or tranquillity among men. Instead there appeared strife over rank, property, and everything else on earth. In the midst of such corruption of human nature, secular power was instituted in the days of Noah, not by men, who were too degenerate and anarchical to do any such thing, but by God (Gen. 9:6; Dan. 2:21; Prov. 8:15–16, 16:11–12; Rom. 13:1).[96]

What, then, is the chief purpose of secular government? The conventional answer is: the preservation of external peace and order. Secular government must indeed preserve peace and order, but that is not its chief purpose. For Scripture says that secular authority was established because man was created in the image of God (Gen. 9:6) and St Paul has commanded that we pray for all in authority 'in order that we might lead a quiet and peaceable life *in all godliness and honesty*' (1 Tim. 2:2). This means that 'secular authority was established in order that man, who was created in the image of God, might be able to lead a tranquil life on earth, and thus be able to know and serve God ... and attain through him true and eternal life.' After all, if man were not created in the image of God and destined for immortality, neither secular authority nor political tranquillity would serve any purpose. What would be the harm in men living like beasts if the soul died with the body? But since man was created for immortality, secular authority was instituted to preserve tranquillity among men in order that they might acquire true knowledge of God and thus achieve the end for which they were created.[97]

Now, since the source of this true knowledge of God is the gospel, which is preached in the church, it follows that secular authority was instituted 'for the sake of the church' (*propter ecclesiam*), in order that it might be possible to preach the gospel in all the earth (Is. 45:1–4). The Psalmist says (117:1): 'Praise the Lord, all ye nations: praise him, all ye people.' This means that all nations were ordained by God in order to provide for the praise of God and the glory of his name. But in all the nations the foremost position (*praecipua pars*) is held by the magistrates. Thus the magistrate must provide above all for the glory and the praise of God. And David says in the second psalm (v. 10–12): 'Be wise now therefore, O ye kings: be instructed, ye judges of the earth. Serve the lord with fear, and rejoice with trembling. Kiss the Son, lest he be angry, and ye perish from the way ...' This, too, means that the chief care of the magistrate should be the glory of God and his church. But the briefest description of the whole calling of the magistrate is found in Isaiah's prophecy concerning the Christian church (Is. 49:23): 'Kings shall be thy nursing fathers, and queens thy nursing mothers.' This meaning of 'nursing fathers' (*nutricii*), said Brenz, is 'protectors and defenders' (*tutores et patroni*).[98] In what ways, then, ought the magistrate to protect and defend the church?

When magistrates speak of themselves they tend to make a great noise about 'majesty' and 'dominion.' Scripture, however, speaks more of servitude than dominion. St Paul says (Rom. 13:3–4) that the magistrate is a servant (*minister, diaconus*) of God for the good of those who do good and the terror of those who do evil. St Peter teaches the same thing (1 Pet. 2:14). Now, the nature of good and evil is most clearly and conveniently set forth in the Decalogue. Since, therefore, secular authority has been instituted to defend good and punish evil, it is clear that whoever holds office as magistrate must not only observe the Ten Commandments himself but also see to it that his subjects do the same. If through his negligence his subjects fail to do so, God will hold him responsible.[99]

Just as there are two tables in the Decalogue, so the office of magistrate is twofold. The first table gives instructions concerning the true knowledge of God, and true worship and doctrine in the church. Thus the magistrate must establish true preaching and worship in every church in his territory and abolish all false doctrine and worship. If he does this, he serves God and shares in all the blessings that are in the church. But if he fails to do so, he is an accomplice in all the iniquities that are committed and is responsible for all the souls under his jurisdiction that are lost.[100] The second table of the Decalogue gives instructions for the love of one's neighbour and for public morality, which the magistrate must also establish among his subjects. If he does not, he is an accomplice in all the vice and immorality that result. It is not enough that morality be legislated, the legislation must be enforced. It was in these terms that Brenz chided the council for its too tolerant attitude toward the goings-on at the local brothel, for example.[101]

Thus it was that in his later writings Brenz made the magistrate's duty to preserve peace and order, to promote the common weal, clearly subordinate to his duty to serve the church. The magistrate, he argued, does not establish true preaching and worship in the hope of furthering the peace and order of his territory; on the contrary, he establishes peace and order to the end that orderly and effective preaching and worship be possible. It is the service of the church which God has commanded; peace and order are bestowed in order that it be possible to perform that service.[102] The appeal of this view was not to the magistrate's narrow self-interest as a secular ruler but to his sense of duty as a Christian. Indeed, since Brenz wanted the magistrates to do far more than the preservation of secular peace and order required, there was no other basis of appeal.

In this context, the old arguments hinging on the magistrate's duty to the common weal no longer had any place. Brenz no longer praised true preaching and worship for their prophylactic effect on peasant rebellions or Turkish invasions, and he no longer provided lists of Old-Testament kings whose tenure in office was prolonged by the persecution of idolators. Nevertheless, Brenz had not ceased to believe that there was a connection between magisterial support of the church and the stability of secular rule. After all, if God has established secular authority for the sake of the church, he can scarcely be expected not to prefer rulers who serve the church to those who persecute it. Thus, in the last of the Election Day Sermons, Brenz argued that those states which benefit the church endure for a long time and begin to decline only after they start doing injury to it (1 Sam. 2:30; Is. 60:12; Ps. 105:14–15; Ecclus. 10:8). The great kingdoms of Egypt and Babylon, for example, both gave shelter to the church for a considerable time and went into decline only after they started to persecute it. Similarly, the Roman Empire served the church unwittingly under Tiberius and certain other princes, but once it began to persecute the church the Empire was transferred from nation to nation until the emperors themselves acknowledged Christ. In our own time, Brenz added, the Roman pontiff and the bishops have great dominion, and until recently (*hactenus*) they served the church. But now they cruelly persecute not only true doctrine but also those kingdoms and republics which shelter the church. 'Thus the end of their rule is at hand; their decline has begun.'[103]

On the other hand, Brenz's main concern in the Election Day Sermons was not with tyrants who persecuted the true faith but with Christian magistrates who tended to be lax in the performance of the more onerous aspects of their job, such as enforcing their own laws against public immorality. Brenz evidently thought that in such cases the wrath of God threatened the individual magistrate more than it did the polity as a whole. In any case, the emphasis in the Election Day Sermons is on the unhappy eternal fate of the negligent magistrate, not on the rise and fall of empires. 'Whoever is elected to the city council and does not take pains that public offences be avoided and the glory of God endure, is many steps closer to hell than he was before.' Indeed, said Brenz, there is nothing more dangerous than public office in state or church. In the words of the old saying: 'Hell is paved with priests' tonsures and panelled with city councilmen's hats.'[104]

It is clear from the Election Day Sermons that Brenz was, on the one hand, anything but complacent about what the Reformation had, with the aid of the magistrates, accomplished so far. Much hard, materially unrewarding, and often unpopular work remained to be done, and Brenz's use of the words *onus* and *servitus* to describe the Christian magistracy[105] was not just conventional rhetoric. On the other hand, it is equally clear that Brenz's experiences in the 1520s, 1530s, and 1540s, with the Hall city council, Margrave George of Brandenburg-Ansbach, and Duke Ulrich of Württemberg, had not made him as cynical as some later historians about the motives of secular rulers in religious matters. He perceived the existence, in at least some rulers, of a measure of piety sufficient to make them willing to take up the burden and attempt to bear it worthily.

The worthiest bearer of that burden was Duke Christopher of Württemberg, whose view of the office of Christian magistrate was identical to Brenz's, no doubt because Brenz had been the decisive influence in the formation of that view. In some of his more private utterances, Christopher revealed a conscience burdened with precisely that sense of personal responsibility to God for the spiritual welfare and moral discipline of his subjects which Brenz had advocated in his Election Day Sermons.[106] And in his public utterances – that is, in the prefaces to some of his major pieces of ecclesiastical legislation – Christopher made Brenz's doctrine of the Christian magistracy the official justification of the Württemberg state church. First, the Württemberg Confession of 1551:

Since we [i.e., Duke Christopher] are aware that we have been called and appointed to the government of our principality and community by the grace of God, we have deemed nothing more worthwhile than to display before God ... and before his whole church our zeal to implant and uphold true godly doctrine with every possible service. For, although we know full well that there is a distinction between secular and spiritual government, nevertheless, because the Psalm [2:10–11] earnestly admonishes us and says: 'Be wise now therefore, O ye kings: be instructed, ye judges of the earth, serve the Lord with fear, and rejoice with trembling,' we have not despised the divine voice but rather have devoted all our effort and zeal to aiding the true church of the son of God.[107]

Second, the Church Order of 1553:

Whereas we dutifully acknowledge ... that we should to the best of our ability support the holy Christian church, which is the kingdom of the son of God, and his gospel; and whereas we firmly believe that all secular authority, as well as the temporal prosperity of the same, has been established, ordained, and given primarily for the purpose of upholding and furthering the true Christian church of God; therefore, we wish to leave nothing undone whereby we might give proof of our zeal and service to the son of God ... and his church, in the office and authority entrusted to us.[108]

Third, the Great Church order of 1559:

We acknowledge (notwithstanding the false opinion of some that only secular rule pertains to secular authority) that it is our duty to God ... before all else to provide the subjects entrusted to us with the pure teaching of the holy gospel ... and thus zealously and earnestly to support the true church of Christ. Only then and in addition to this [are we] to establish and maintain in temporal rule useful ordinances to secure that temporal peace, quiet, unity, and prosperity which God gives for the sake of the foregoing [support of the church] ...[109]

However, Brenz was not merely the author of the theoretical justification of the Württemberg state church; he was the principal architect of its institutions as well. Moreover, it was those institutions rather than the theory behind them that were Brenz's most original contribution to the Reformation.

4

The Organization of the Church
in Württemberg

In the first years of his reign, Duke Christopher established in Württemberg a system of church government which was to spread far beyond the boundaries of his domains and endure far past the age of the Reformation. Historians call it the consistorial system (*Konsistorialverfassung*) because, as we shall see, its central feature was a commission called the consistory. Organized much like the duke's secular administration but distinct from it, the consistorial system was highly centralized and bureaucratic, but it was also clear and simple, and it worked extremely well. As a result, it quickly became the model church polity for much of the rest of Protestant Germany and remained an important part of German institutional life until the end of World War I. Thus the consistorial system was perhaps the most important, certainly the most lasting, achievement of the Reformation in Württemberg.[1]

As a matter of fact, several other German principalities had consistories before Württemberg. But they were not the same thing. The *Konsistorien* first established in Saxony in 1539 and subsequently in other areas of northern and central Germany were courts whose main responsibility was the enforcement of the new evangelical law of matrimony. Although in some instances certain administrative duties (e.g., the examination of prospective pastors) were added to their competence, the North-German consistories were not bodies with full responsibility for ecclesiastical administration. The state churches of North and Central Germany did not in this period have bureaucracies of their own distinct from the secular administration.[2]

The Württemberg consistory, on the other hand, had a different origin and competence. Whereas the North- and East-German consistories had grown out of the need for ecclesiastical courts, and had their analogue in the prince's secular courts, the Württemberg consistory was an outgrowth of the visitations which Duke Ulrich had used to inaugurate the new church order (1536) and which had subsequently been used from time to time to inspect the state of the parishes. It had its analogue in the prince's privy council, the *Oberrat*, the central organ of the secular bureaucracy. Although for certain purposes (e.g., the imposition of excommunication) the consistory could function as a court, it was essentially an administrative organ, the summit of the ecclesiastical bureaucracy through which the prince exercised his responsibilities as *nutricius ecclesiae*.[3]

For quite some time this difference in origin and competence was reflected in a different terminology. When first established in 1553, the central organ of ecclesiastical administration in Württemberg was called the *Visitationsrat* (visitation council), but this quickly gave way to *Kirchenrat* (literally, 'church council'), which is the designation used in the Great Church Order of 1559. Later, beginning with the *Kanzleiordnung* of 1590, the term *consistorium* established itself as the designation for the clerical bench of the *Kirchenrat*, while *Kirchenrat* remained the designation of the political bench (i.e., those secular officials who managed church income and property).[4] Since the English term 'church council' is normally used to refer to something entirely different from the Württemberg *Kirchenrat*, 'consistory' is used here to translate *Visitationsrat* and *Kirchenrat* as those terms were used in the legislation of the 1550s, and the distinction between *consistorium* and *Kirchenrat* observed after 1590 is ignored.

Within weeks of its establishment in Württemberg, the consistorial system began its gradual conquest of the rest of Protestant Germany. In August 1553 Brenz himself inaugurated the process of its introduction into the Neuburg Palatinate.[5] In 1556–8, again with Brenz's personal participation,[6] many elements of the Württemberg system were introduced into the Rhenish Palatinate, and much of the Württemberg heritage survived the introduction of Calvinism into the Palatinate in 1559.[7] Meanwhile the cities of Ulm and Reutlingen (1554), and the principalities of Baden-Durlach (1556) and Oettingen (1557), adopted the Württemberg model. The process continued through the rest of the century and into the next. Among the territories affected were Braunschweig-Wolfenbüttel (1569), Henneberg (1574), Saxony and Brandenburg-Ansbach (1580), Hessen (1610), and electoral Brandenburg (1614).[8]

If Württemberg was the first Protestant territory to acquire such an exemplary ecclesiastical administration, it was in large measure because the circumstances there were unusually favourable. In contrast to Saxony, for example, there was in Württemberg no powerful nobility who, as wielders of ecclesiastical patronage, stood in the way of ecclesiastical centralization. On the contrary, ecclesiastical patronage in Württemberg was, as we have seen, largely concentrated in the duke's hands.[9] Moreover, since the time of Duke Eberhard the Bearded (1459–96), Württemberg had enjoyed a particularly good secular administration. After his return to Württemberg in 1534, Duke Ulrich undertook further improvements.

Before 1534 the duke's advisers had lived scattered about the duchy on their family estates or in ducal fortresses. Now Ulrich, applying the principles of centralized administration introduced by Maximilian I into Austria from his Flemish-Burgundian territories, called a number of noblemen and jurists to his chancellery to serve as a permanent privy council, the *Oberrat*. The administration of finances was assigned to a separate treasury department, the *Rentkammer*.[10]

Duke Christopher, the real founder of the modern state in Württemberg, improved on the work of his father, giving these administrative institutions the form they would retain for the next two centuries.[11] The emergence of the Württemberg consistorial system was once thought to be the result of a decision by Duke Christopher to reconstruct the ecclesiastical administration of his territory on the model of his secular administration. Thus the old, unstable visitation commissions were turned into a *Kirchenrat* on the model of the *Oberrat*, all church income was gathered into a central *Kirchenkasten* modelled on the *Rentkammer*, and a system of superintendents was established to supervise, with the cooperation of the local officials, the clergy in the local districts.[12] While Duke Christopher's contribution to the establishment of the consistorial system is not to be underestimated – an attempt to estimate it fairly will be made in due course – this explanation is badly oversimplified on two counts. First, it overlooks what Duke Ulrich had already achieved in the field of ecclesiastical organization. Second, it completely ignores the role of Brenz, who had wielded an important influence in Duke Ulrich's reign, and who was the leading churchman in Württemberg during Christopher's reign. For we now know that the institutions of church government which made Duke Christopher's church order unique had their origins in proposals which Brenz had put forward – sometimes in Württemberg, sometimes elsewhere – long before he entered Christopher's service.[13] The purpose of this chapter is to examine those proposals from the earliest beginnings in Schwäbisch Hall to their final realization in the Great Church Order for Württemberg.

DEVELOPMENTS BEFORE THE INTERIM

From the beginning of his career to its end, Brenz was not only an advocate of the state church but also a consistent centralizer, a determined foe of all attempts by individual congregations or their pastors to win for themselves an active role in the government of the church. His reasons for this were more practical than theological: St Paul had commanded that all things in the church be done decently and in order (1 Cor. 14:40); everyday experience taught that the congregations were seedbeds of discord and disorder; the deep-seated social attitudes of the humanist and burgher decreed that the remedy was strict control from above.

The earliest evidence of this outlook is found in Brenz's comments on the first two of the peasants' Twelve Articles (1525).[14] He rejected outright the first article, which asserted the right of each community to elect and dismiss its own pastor (a right which Luther acknowledged in principle). The Bible, said Brenz, only prescribes what sort of person a pastor must be (1 Tim. 3:2ff.; Tit. 1:5-9), not how he must be chosen. For the sake of good order, it would be best if the prince were to appoint and dismiss the pastors with the consent of the officials of the town or village in question. For if the prince alone were to choose, the people might be burdened with pastors whom they disliked, while if the local communities themselves were to choose, disorder and strife would often be the result. Above all, Brenz insisted, a Christian prince with a proper regard for the welfare of his subjects must see to it that no papist or other person without proper credentials be allowed to exercise the cure of souls in his territory. In order to consolidate his control over the appointment of clergymen, the prince should endeavour to acquire the patronage of any parishes not already under his control.[15]

In discussing the peasants' second article, Brenz argued that the Christian magistrate, again out of concern for the welfare of his subjects, should take over and reform the collection and disbursement of tithes rather than abolish them as the peasants demanded. Disorder would result if the pastors themselves were to collect and disburse the tithes, as was the practice in the ancient church, when pastors were more pious and less self-seeking than they are today. Moreover, if the subjects were left to do with the tithes as they pleased, the needs of widows and orphans would likely be neglected and, as time passed, the payment of tithes would diminish. Therefore the government, in cooperation with the officials of each community, should establish a common chest into which the tithes would be deposited and used locally to pay the pastor's wages, to provide poor relief, to support widows and orphans, or perhaps even be used 'for the need of the entire land.'[16] But entrusting the administration of church funds to the government had its own dangers: Brenz soon found it necessary to admonish the authorities not to appropriate church funds for purely secular purposes but rather to apply them exclusively to the religious and charitable purposes for which they had originally been intended. Otherwise the wrath of God would be aroused, as it was, for example, against King Balshazzar, who at his impious feast used the gold and silver vessels which King Nebuchadnezzar had taken from the temple in Jerusalem (Dan. 5).[17]

As this comment on the use of church funds indicates, there was an important qualification attached to Brenz's enthusiasm for the centralization of ecclesiastical authority in the hands of the magistrate. He was no more willing that secular officials should exploit the wealth or authority of the church for worldly purposes than he was that pastors and congregations should inject disorder and strife into the conduct of its affairs. In his view, the church had its own distinct interests which required not only a separate treasury but also, as we shall see presently, a separate administrative machinery. The magistrate was indeed to govern the church but the church was not, if Brenz could help it, to be subjected to the tender mercies of the magistrate's ambitious, worldly, and sometimes anticlerical officials.

Brenz's first proposals for a separate organ of ecclesiastical administration occurred in the context of his early struggles with the problem of ecclesiastical discipline.[18] By Brenz's day, primary responsibility for the enforcement of Christian morality in the community had long since been taken over by the secular rulers. Brenz approved of this. But he found the authorities' efforts in this area inadequate, for many sins that rendered a person culpable in the eyes of the church were either not punishable under secular law or else the relevant laws were laxly enforced. So in the 'Hall Reformation' of 1527 Brenz proposed to the city council the establishment of a church court called the synod (*synodus*). Composed of the city's pastors plus several laymen appointed by the council, the synod was to exercise ecclesiastical discipline in the case of moral offences not punished by the secular courts. The maximum penalty was to be excommunication.[19]

Brenz used the term 'synod' for two reasons: first, because the procedures followed were to be modelled on those of the old synodal courts (*Sendgerichte*) of the pre-Reformation period; and second, because he wanted to vest his proposal with the authority of the ancient church, which had possessed an institution called the synod (i.e., meeting or assembly). This ancient synod, said Brenz, had consisted of pastors and presbyters coming together to conduct church business, which had fallen under two headings: 1 / administrative matters involving the provision of the congregation with the word of God and the sacraments, and 2 / the quasi-judicial process of ecclesiastical discipline. Holding the mistaken view that the medieval synodal courts were a continuation of the synods of the ancient church in so far as the latter had functioned as organs of ecclesiastical discipline, Brenz wanted them revived in order to function as a complement to the discipline of morals by the secular authorities.[20] Moreover, he wanted to restore to the revived synod at least some of the administrative responsibilities it had supposedly had in the ancient church. So in the 'Hall Reformation' he proposed that the synod also serve as the body through which special matters not covered in the church order would be referred to the city council for its consideration and decision.[21]

The opposition of the secular authorities to such 'popery' brought Brenz's campaign for a synod to a halt, but only temporarily. In January 1531 he drafted a synodal ordinance for Schwäbisch Hall and by the beginning of the following month had proposed it for inclusion in the Brandenburg-Nuremberg Church

Order as well. The Protestant synodal court outlined in the draft ordinance[22] was modelled more closely on the old Catholic courts of the same name than the synod of 1527 had been.[23] Unlike its Catholic prototype, the synod of 1531 was to be a government-appointed commission of theologians and lawyers, but, like its Catholic model, the commission was to visit each rural parish once a year to hold court and to impose punishments (including fines and, in obstinate cases, excommunication) on moral offenders. The Ansbach theologians readily agreed to the demand for a synod and also joined Brenz in calling for the establishment in Ansbach of a *senatus presbyterorum*, a committee of ten or twelve prominent clergymen charged with administering the church order and with handling all questions concerning doctrine and ceremonies which might arise. A *senatus presbyterorum* was necessary, they said, because the margrave's chancellery was too burdened with secular matters to pay adequate attention to church business, and because in any case a church order created the need for 'an ecclesiastical administration and polity.'[24]

In May the Nurembergers responded to these proposals in a memorandum drafted by Osiander.[25] They rejected the idea of an ecclesiastical morals court, which they saw as an infringement of secular jurisdiction. On the other hand, they expressed their approval of an annual visitation of the rural parishes, not to hand out judicial punishments for moral lapses but rather to expose and correct all shortcomings and abuses in the life and doctrine of the pastors and their flocks. The theologians went on to recommend that a commission be appointed for this purpose, and that the day-to-day supervision of the pastors be entrusted to superintendents who would report serious matters to the government or, in the case of purely theological matters, to a special committee of theologians which might be given the name *senatus presbyterorum*.

By December, Brenz's efforts to secure the establishment of a synodal court, as outlined in the January ordinance, had been permanently defeated. But Brenz remained convinced that some order of public excommunication had to be established for the sake of good order in the church. He was also convinced that the new church order would remain a dead letter unless actively enforced. So, in a memorandum which he drafted in consultation with the Ansbachers,[26] he proposed the establishment in every *rifier* (*revier* = district, region) of a commission of distinguished pastors and capable laymen to serve as 'visitors, superintendents, *presbyteros ecclesiae, judices rerum ecclesiasticarum*,' or whatever else one wanted to call them. The task of these commissions would be to impose excommunication in appropriate cases, to enforce observance of the church order, to function as a marriage court, and in general to deal with all aspects of ecclesiastical administration.[27]

The interpretation of this proposal involves some risky guesswork. *Revier* is an extremely imprecise term which can refer to administrative districts of any size, even (occasionally) to an entire territory. Here the reference is apparently to a relatively small unit such as a deanery.[28] If, then, the proposal is for subordinate organs of church government, why is there no mention of the superior organ, the *senatus presbyterorum?* Presumably because that was a matter on which everyone had already agreed. Finally, why did Brenz prefer to assign local supervision of church order to commissions rather than to individual superintendents and to annual, centrally dispatched visitations, as the Nurembergers had recommended? Evidently because of the overriding desire for a body which could perform the judicial task of imposing excommunication.[29]

Whether these guesses are accurate or not, one thing is clear: the *judices rerum ecclesiasticarum* of December 1531 were the synod of 1527 in revised form. The composition (pastors and laymen) and the dual function (ecclesiastical administration and moral discipline) were the same. But where the synod of 1527 had been a church court to which certain administration duties were to be entrusted, the commission of 1531 was a state agency with both administrative and judicial functions. Moreover, the offensively 'popish' name had been dropped. Nevertheless, the proposal of December 1531 met the same fate as those of 1527 and January 1531. The opposition of the secular authorities to excommunication in any form was so strong that no formal provision for it was made in any territory with whose reformation Brenz was associated before the Interim. After the Interim, on the other hand, the notion of a body competent both in the area of ecclesiastical administration and in that of moral discipline would reassert itself, and so would the name *synodus.*

Meanwhile, the problem of enforcing church order continued to preoccupy Brenz. In the summer of 1535, while in Stuttgart for consultations on the church order that was to be issued in Württemberg in 1536, Brenz submitted to Duke Ulrich a draft visitation ordinance which was to become the point of departure for the Württemberg system of church government.[30] In the draft ordinance Brenz outlined a scheme of ecclesiastical administration far more sophisticated and centralized than anything he had previously recommended. Its central features were the same as those in the response of the Nurembergers to his synodal ordinance of 1531: an annual, centrally dispatched visitation of all the parishes, and a system of centrally appointed superintendents. The similarity can scarcely be accidental: one suspects that ecclesiastical administration was a topic which Brenz and the Nurembergers discussed thoroughly during Brenz's sojourn in Nuremberg in the autumn of 1532.[31]

In the draft ordinance for Duke Ulrich, Brenz argued that the proposed church order, like any comparable secular law, would remain ineffective unless diligently enforced. Individual clergymen would follow their own lights, producing doctrinal and liturgical confusion, unless conformity to the church order were imposed by means of regular visitations. Therefore, the duke should establish a commission of several theologians (*gelerten*) and several of the gentry (*Ritterschaft*) to conduct a special visitation for the purpose of inaugurating the new church order. Thereafter the same commission should conduct an annual visitation in every prefecture (*vogtey*).[32]

The visitors were to examine the legal and financial status of the parishes, the physical condition of the churches and parsonages, as well as the life, doctrine, and competence of the clergy. They were also to examine the schools and the schoolteachers, and to ascertain whether or not the local officials (*Amptleute*) punished public immorality. On the basis of this information they were to take the required steps to put everything on a sound basis. For example: they were, where necessary, to combine small parishes or divide large ones; to apply the surplus income of rich parishes and other foundations to the needs of inadequately endowed parishes as well as of schools and the poor; and to order the repair of church buildings so that they would no longer be like 'pigsties.' Further, the visitors were to present each pastor with a copy of the new church order and admonish him to observe it strictly; to transfer unpopular pastors to a more hospitable parish; to dismiss pastors found morally or doctrinally unsound; and to order the local officials to punish public immorality.[33]

Finally, in each prefecture the visitors were to appoint, in place of the old rural dean, a superintendent whose job would be the supervision of all the pastors in the prefecture. The income of the rural chapters, which the clergy had hitherto held 'to no good purpose,' was to be used to defray the expenses of the superintendents.[34] Unfortunately, Brenz did not say how the superintendent was to supervise the pastors. Did he, despite the slighting reference, expect the chapters to go on meeting under the chairmanship of the superintendent? Or, as seems more likely, was the superintendent simply to keep an eye on the life and teaching of the pastors under his supervision and report difficult matters to the duke's officials? Moreover, who was to function as *senatus presbyterorum*, advising the duke on doctrinal and liturgical issues raised by the visitation or reported by the superintendents? Presumably the theologians on the visitation commission, though Brenz did not mention this either.

Evidence concerning the immediate response to Brenz's draft visitation ordinance is sparse. There is no known ducal order inaugurating a visitation. On the other hand, in September 1535 Brenz, who was still in Stuttgart, wrote to a friend that he expected to be asked to return to Württemberg early in the new year to participate in a visitation of the churches.[35] This seems to indicate that a visitation along the lines of Brenz's proposal was already being planned. A visitation did in fact begin in January 1536. Although Brenz apparently did not participate, the visitation proceeded in accordance with his proposal. A mixed commission of theologians and high government officials went through the duchy, district by district, surveying and regulating the financial and spiritual affairs of the church.[36]

Moreover, the Church Order of 1536 contains several references to 'visitors and superintendents' which indicate that supervision of the churches by means of visitations was to be continuing process as Brenz had recommended. The superintendents were to examine and approve the hymns used in church services.[37] The visitors and superintendents were to establish a uniform catechism for the whole duchy.[38] And, at the conclusion of the order the pastors and other clergymen were informed that the visitors and superintendents would advise them of any further measures adopted for the good of the church.[39] (Incidentally, the term 'superintendent' here refers not to the superintendents Brenz wanted appointed in place of the rural deans, but presumably to the theologians on the visitation commission, 'visitors' being the lay members.)[40] Although it proved impossible to carry out an annual visitation as Brenz had suggested, the institution persisted and there is scattered evidence of its activity from 1540 to 1547, when the Schmalkaldic War brought it to a temporary end.[41]

During this time the visitation gradually developed into a stable system of ecclesiastical administration. In March 1538 Duke Ulrich ordered Blarer and Schnepf, the theologians on the visitation commission, to assume the task of examining prospective pastors.[42] However, an undated *Instruction for the Visitors*, probably issued sometime between 1540 and 1544,[43] shows that there was still no central organ of church government: not only economic matters but even certain ecclesiastical matters (i.e., evidence of Anabaptist or other sectarian activity) were to be reported to the treasury for appropriate action.[44] But by May 1547, when a new Visitation Ordinance was issued,[45] things had changed markedly.

The first section of the ordinance, entitled *Inquisition*, is substantially identical with a Visitation Instruction published in 1544.[46] Moreover, the structure, content, and purpose of the visitation are essentially the same as those in Brenz's proposal of 1535. A commission of at least three visitors or 'inquisitors' (one theologian, one noble, one burgher) was to visit all the prefectures one by one to determine all the defects and shortcomings that needed correction in the ecclesiastical life of the duchy. Clergymen and schoolteachers were to be examined concerning their doctrine, morals, and the conduct of their office. They were also to be asked whether the local officials were faithful in church attendance and diligent in the punishment of public immorality. The officials, in turn, were to supply information about the conduct of the clergymen. The financial situation of the churches and the condition of church buildings were also to be examined. Upon completion of the visitation of each prefecture, a written report was to be sent to the chancellery in Stuttgart.

The real novelty in this ordinance is the second section, entitled *Consultation*,[47] which set up a body competent to deal with the problems uncovered by the visitation. The inquisitors were to come to Stuttgart every four to six weeks for a consultation on the contents of the visitation reports. The participants in this consultation, known collectively as the 'visitation councillors' (*Visitations-Rethe*), were, besides the inquisitors, one theologian, one jurist, two nobles, and two burghers. These councillors were to discuss the problems uncovered by the visitation and to determine the appropriate remedy in each case. The standard of judgment for their deliberations was to be the Bible, the Augsburg Confession and its Apology, the *Loci communes* of Melanchthon, and the relevant princely ordinances and decrees. The times of these consultations, which were expected to last about a week, were to be published so that pastors and officials could refer any pressing problems to the visitation councillors for appropriate action.

The third and final section of the Visitation Ordinance (*Execution*) deals with the implementation of the decisions made in the consultation.[48] Certain matters were reserved for the duke's personal decision, e.g., the dismissal of ducal officials for irreligion, immorality, or popery. Financial matters had to be arranged with the treasury. In all other matters the visitation councillors had authority to issue orders in accordance with the relevant ordinances. If they determined that the extant ordinances needed to be changed, they were to send their recommendations to the duke and await his decision.

Thus, by the eve of the Schmalkaldic War, the visitation in Württemberg had developed into a system of ecclesiastical administration which in important respects anticipated the later consistorial system. There was at the centre a stable body operating on the basis of systematically gathered visitation reports and competent to deal with all aspects of the ecclesiastical life of the duchy. Moreover, the whole development had started with Brenz's proposal of 1535.

At the intermediate levels of ecclesiastical administration, however, Brenz's proposal was not so immediately fruitful. No action was taken in response to his recommendation that superintendents be appointed in place of the old rural deans. Indeed, before 1547 no effort was made to establish any organ of church government between the local parishes and the central administration.

Meanwhile, in Schwäbisch Hall, the old rural chapter, which had not met for over a decade,[49] was revived in 1541. The initiative for reestablishing the chapter came from some of the rural priests themselves, and Brenz's only extant statement on the matter is a memorandum for the city council suggesting what its response to that request ought to be.[50]

The original purpose of rural chapters, Brenz said, was that all the priests of one district come together once or twice a year in 'a small synod or council' to study Scripture, to correct any abuses in their churches, and to censure any of their number guilty of public offences such as concubinage, gambling, or drunkenness. But things eventually got to the point where the priests brought their mistresses rather than their Bibles to chapter meetings and, after a hasty mass, devoted themselves to gluttony and drunkenness, thus causing great scandal and setting a disgraceful example for their flocks. Therefore the priests should be told that the city council will not permit the revival of the chapter if their intention is simply to restore such abuses. But if they are willing to hold chapter meetings for the purpose of improving their churches and correcting their own moral lapses, and if they will accept the city's church order, then the council will not only permit the chapter to meet but will also provide every assistance and 'appoint certain persons' to see to it that such a godly undertaking be carried out in an appropriately dignified manner.

One may doubt that the recent history of rural chapters in general was the only motive for Brenz's insistence that a revived Hall chapter be controlled by agents of the city council. His low opinion of the quality of the men available for appointment as pastors was another consideration, perhaps the more important one.[51]

In any case, the chapter was reconstituted on the terms which Brenz had laid down.[52] Meeting once a year,[53] it had the authority to install pastors, to supervise their doctrine and conduct, and to initiate parish visitations. However, these activities were subjected to the control of the city council and the city clergy. The town pastor, Eisenmenger, was appointed superintendent in place of the old elected dean, while Brenz (as town preacher) and two members of the city council became 'chapter visitors' (*visitatores bey dem capittel*).[54] No pastor, regardless of who his patron might be, could officiate in Hall's territory until he had appeared before the council, presented trustworthy credentials concerning his past teaching and life, and passed an examination administered by the superintendent and visitors. Furthermore, while the chapter was to elect from its own membership those who would conduct the visitation of the parishes, the council had to confirm the election and give its permission for each visitation, in which one or two council members were to participate.[55] The Church Order of 1543, which established common ceremonies and a uniform standard of dcotrine (the Augsburg Confession and its Apology), became binding for the deliberations of the chapter and for the conduct of the visitation.

Thus the newly organized chapter in Hall had lost the truly synodal character of its medieval predecessor. Though the external form of a synod was retained, the actual substance was the embodiment of Brenz's predilection for the concentration of authority at the centre, in the hands of a commission of theologians and laymen (in this case the superintendent and the chapter visitors) especially appointed to deal with ecclesiastical matters.

A similar development took place in Württemberg a few years later. In a number of places groups of clergymen had begun holding chapter-like meetings on their own initiative, without the knowledge or participation of the government. The Visitation Instruction of 1544 directed the visitors to gather information about any such meetings.[56] By 1547 the duke and his advisers had decided to regulate this activity and thus make chapters a device for raising the level of life and doctrine among the clergy of the whole duchy. To this end, the Visitation Ordinance of 1547 stipulated that a number of 'synods and assemblies of the preachers' were to be established in the duchy and to meet at least once a year. The duke was to be represented by one of his advisers or by the nearest district prefect. The synods were to have no authority to make decisions in matters of doctrine but only to forward their suggestions via the ducal adviser or prefect to the visitation councillors in Stuttgart.[57]

The Visitation Ordinance also stipulated that the visitation councillors were to draw up an ordinance for the synods.[58] The resulting Synodal Ordinance was issued in August 1547.[59] The duchy was divided into twenty-three deaneries (*decanat*). The first deans were to be designated by the visitation councillors; thereafter new deans were to be elected by the chapter, subject to the approval of the visitation councillors, for an indefinitely renewable one-year term. The dean's oath of office was administered by the superintendent, that is, by a theologian who was the duke's representative at chapter meetings (no mention of the local prefect here). The dean's duties were to visit every parish in his charge at least once a year to examine the life and doctrine of the local pastor, to investigate any complaints against the pastors, and to install new pastors once they had been examined and approved by the visitation councillors. The chapters, summoned by the dean with the approval of the superintendent, were to meet twice a year. The life and doctrine of all the members, from the dean on down, were to be discussed under the leadership of the superintendent and serious faults censured.

No more than in Schwäbisch Hall was the chapter a genuine synod. It was an instrument not of local self-government but of increasing centralization. While some of the features of the Synodal Ordinance tending toward greater centralization, e.g., the dean's parish visitations, would be absorbed into the consistorial system in altered form, all the remnants of synodal polity, i.e., the chapters, would disappear.

Scarcely had the ecclesiastical constitution outlined in the two ordinances of 1547 been proclaimed when the Interim, imposed in Württemberg in July 1548,[60] undid it all. So the real achievement of an effective system of church government had to wait until more favourable times. Those times had not yet arrived when Duke Ulrich died in 1550.

THE ESTABLISHMENT OF THE CONSISTORIAL SYSTEM

When Duke Christopher succeeded to the throne (November 1550), the Interim was still in force and the future of Protestantism in Württemberg, as in the rest of

Germany, was uncertain. Government and people were loyal to the Protestant faith, and a Protestant ministry of sorts was being exercised, but the Protestant church as an institution had been destroyed. Not only had Duke Ulrich's ecclesiastical consitution been abolished, but much church property had also been restored to the priests and abbots who once again were in control of the churches and monasteries of the duchy.[61]

At the same time, however, most of the prerequisites for the exemplary institutional development of Protestantism in Württemberg in the 1550s were already present. In Johannes Brenz, Duke Christopher had a theological adviser who was the one organizer of genius among the Lutheran reformers. With more than a quarter century of experience already to his credit, Brenz knew exactly what he wanted and was able to provide invaluable advice for just about any contingency. In Duke Christopher, on the other hand, Brenz had a prince who saw eye-to-eye with him on nearly all important issues, who was extraordinarily eager to carry out Brenz's reforms, and who was himself an organizer and lawgiver of the first rank. Moreover, because the Interim had destroyed Duke Ulrich's work before it had had a chance to take root, the institutional slate had been wiped clean. Once the restraints of the Interim were removed, Brenz and Christopher would be free to revive as much or as little of Duke Ulrich's work as suited their purposes.

As a matter of fact, the first important measures of reorganization were taken while the interim was still in effect, and they were departures from Duke Ulrich's policies. In 1551, sixteen years after Brenz had recommended it to Duke Ulrich, Duke Christopher replaced the old elected deans with centrally appointed superintendents. Morover, the task of conducting visitations, hitherto shared by the roving inquisitors (Visitation Ordinance) and the deans (Synodal Ordinance), was now assigned to the deans' successors, the superintendents. As a consequence, roving visitation commissions disappeared as a routine measure of ecclesiastical administration. Chapters, too, disappeared, having been rendered superfluous by the superintendents' visitations. At this stage there was, of course, no Protestant church order for the superintendents to enforce; the purpose of the visitations envisioned in 1551 was apparently to provide the government with reliable information about the confused confessional situation which the Interim had produced.[62]

In 1551 Duke Christopher also took the first steps toward the establishment of a special church treasury, later (1559) called the common church treasury (*gemeiner Kirchenkasten*), under ecclesiastical control and with funds earmarked *ad pias causas*.[63] This was in marked contrast to the policy of Duke Ulrich, who had kept church property under the control of the state treasury and had reserved the income from three-quarters of it for the payment of his state debts.[64]

With the repeal of the Interim in the summer of 1552, the pace of change quickened, and the first phase of ecclesiastical reorganization had been completed by the next spring. The consistory, called the *Visitationsrat* at this stage, was formally established in the Visitation Ordinance of 26 May 1553.[65] This was the culmination of the tendency, already evident in Duke Ulrich's Visitation Ordinance of 1547, of the visitation in Württemberg to produce a stable, central organ of ecclesiastical administration.

At about the same time, that is, in the spring of 1553, a new Superintendence Ordinance was issued.[66] This provided the superintendents with new instructions, appropriate to the post-Interim situation, for the conduct of their visitations. It also outlined the duties of the newly created office of general superintendent. While one of the tasks of the inquisitors of 1547, that of visitation, had fallen to the superintendents (now called special superintendents), the other task, that of periodic consultation with officials in Stuttgart on the contents of the visitation reports, now fell to the general superintendents. Moreover, the 1547 superintendent's job of supervising the deans now became the general superintendent's job of supervising the superintendents.

Finally, by the time the Visitation Ordinance of 1553 was issued, the development of the church treasury had also been completed.[67]

With the establishment of the consistory, the general and special superintendents, and the common church treasury, the Württemberg system was complete. After it had been in operation a few years and some needed adjustments had been made, its component ordinances – revised, much expanded, and with supplementary material added – were published as part of the Great Church Order of 1559.

Because so many of the archival sources for the history of the Reformation in Württemberg have been lost,[68] the Great Church Order is our only source of information about many aspects of the consistorial system. While some of the ordinances of 1551–3 survive intact, others survive only in fragmentary form or not at all.[69] Moreover, there are virtually no records of the day-to-day operations of the consistorial system during the first several decades of its existence. Thus it is only on the basis of the Great Church Order that one can attempt a complete description of the system. Furthermore, since there are almost no records of the conferences, the memoranda, and the drafts that preceded the ordinances of 1551–3 or 1559, it is only by comparing the ordinances themselves with Brenz's ideas and recommendations in the pre-Interim period that one can determine the extent to which Brenz was the author of the consistorial system. The influence of Brenz's draft visitation ordinance of 1535 is already clear. But Brenz's other pre-Interim ideas and proposals on church polity bore fruit in Württemberg only after 1550, and these influences must now be documented. Fortunately, the Great Church Order provides an adequate basis for doing so.

THE PROVISIONS OF THE GREAT CHURCH ORDER

The members of the consistory, called visitation councillors (*Visitationsräte*) in 1553 and ecclesiastical councillors (*Kirchenräte*) in 1559, were divided into two groups, four 'political' councillors (*politische Räte*) and three theologians.[70] There was a corresponding division of labour which will be discussed presently. The Visitation Ordinance of 1553 assigned superintendence of the consistory to the court chamberlain (*Landhofmeister*) while superintendence of the theologians was assigned to the provost of the Stuttgart Collegiate Church (i.e., Brenz).[71] Thus the provost appeared, at any rate, to be subordinate to the chamberlain. In the Church Order of 1559, on the other hand, chamberlain and provost were clearly assigned equal rank, 'supreme superintendence' over the consistory being their joint responsibility.[72] For Brenz to have accepted anything less than full equality with the chamberlain would have been to concede that the clergy in their spiritual office were subordinate to the secular bureaucracy, a concession clean contrary to Brenz's principles as a church organizer.

Routine supervision of the day-to-day operations of the consistory was the responsibility of a secular official known as the director. He made sure that meetings were held on time, that business was dealt with promptly by the appropriate persons in the prescribed manner, that proper records were kept, and so forth.[73] He also played an important role in the work of both the political councillors and the theologians.

Under the chairmanship of the director, the political councillors handled the economic and financial affairs of the church.[74] Chief among these were the management of church property and the collection and disbursement of the income from that property. The income of all ecclesiastical institutions, save only that of the fourteen monasteries that were turned into schools (1556), was paid into the common church treasury. Officials known as stewards (*geistliche Verwalter*), appointed and supervised by the political councillors, managed the treasury depositories which were maintained in each district capital (*amptstatt*). In each district the steward paid the salaries of all clergymen and schoolteachers, and saw to the upkeep of parsonages, churches, and schools.[75] These arrangements were the perfect embodiment of the principles of church finance which Brenz had laid down in 1525.[76]

Also in harmony with Brenz's known views were the reasons given in the Great Church Order for the establishment of the common church treasury. One reason was the view that clergymen should not have to spend their time managing property but should be able to devote themselves exclusively to their pastoral office.[77] Provided with free housing and with a fixed income independent of the fluctuating yield of benefices, pastors of the Württemberg church were expected to devote themselves to study, preaching, and other pastoral functions, and to refrain from all attempts to supplement their incomes by practising some secular occupation on the side.[78]

The other reason for the establishment of the church treasury was the conviction that church income must be used for the church's purposes. In terms reminiscent of Brenz's statements in the 1520s and 1530s, the Great Church Order solemnly declared that church property and income, which had originally (i.e., under the papacy) been established to support the church and its work, must continue to be used exclusively for the same purpose. If it were used for secular purposes, to the detriment of the church and its ministry, the wrath of God would surely be aroused.[79] In actual practice, Duke Christopher did not strictly adhere to this principle. The income of the church treasury exceeded the immediate needs of the church, and Christopher regularly dipped into the surplus to supplement his state revenues. However, since the needs of the church, as determined by the consistory, came first, and since the church and its ministry benefited greatly as a result, the charge of plundering the church, often heard in Ulrich's day, could not be levelled against Christopher.[80] Evidences of the wrath of God were sometimes noted in Württemberg, but Christopher's use of church funds was never held to be the cause.[81]

While the political councillors managed the material aspects of church life, the theologians of the consistory supervised its doctrinal and pastoral aspects. Together with the director and two political councillors, they met twice a week under the chairmanship of Brenz. They had the power to appoint and dismiss all clergymen (including general and special superintendents) and schoolteachers, and to supervise their life and doctrine according to the criteria laid down in the Württemberg Confession and the relevant ecclesiastical ordinances. Since the theologians had pressing duties as preachers and scholars in addition to their duties in the consistory, care was taken that they not be burdened with political matters. The director was to screen all reports and other communications and make sure that only 'ecclesiastical [i.e., theological or pastoral] or scholastic matters' were referred to the meetings of the theologians. However, the theologians could be summoned to special meetings called to deal with matters neither purely political nor ecclesiastical but 'mixed.'[82]

The procedures to be followed in the appointment of clergymen[83] were those which Brenz had proposed in 1525 and, as far as we know, incorporated into the Hall church order.[84] No one was to be appointed to any clerical office in the duchy until he had presented reliable credentials and passed an examination administered by the theologians of the consistory. The first part of the examination was a private interview to determine whether the candidate was orthodox in doctrine, blameless in life, and of suitable age (i.e., not too young). If he met these requirements, he next delivered a trial sermon in public in the presence of the three theologians. If this proved satisfactory, he could then be installed in office. Normally no one was to be appointed to a pastorate until he had served for a time as a deacon (i.e., assistant pastor), learned the liturgy, and demonstrated his ability to handle pastoral duties.[85]

In the case of pastorates or other offices under the patronage of persons other than the duke, it was provided that the patrons could exercise their right of appointment if they wished, on the condition that the pastor-designate appeared in Stuttgart, passed the above examination, and thereafter abided by the provisions of the duke's ecclesiastical ordinances. If the patron could not or would not appoint a suitable pastor, the duke would exercise his right under the provisions of the Peace of Augsburg to do so.[86]

Once a prospective clergyman had been declared fit by the consistory, he had one more hurdle to negotiate before taking office. No clergyman was to be imposed upon a congregation against its will unless there were especially compelling reasons to do so. So the candidate had to deliver several trial sermons with the local superintendent and subprefect (*amptmann*) present. If the congregation found the candidate acceptable, the superintendent and subprefect were to report this to the consistory and the superintendent was formally to install the new pastor or deacon in office. If, on the other hand, the congregation had honest and valid objections to the candidate, he was not to be installed. But if the objections were 'trivial and without valid grounds ... based on ignorance or obstinacy,' the consistory was not to countenance them but to instruct the congregation in the error of its ways.[87]

In order effectively to supervise the life and doctrine of the clergy thus appointed, the theologians of the consistory needed full and accurate information about local conditions. (So, for that matter, did the political councillors in order to do their job.) For this they depended on the reports of the visitations conducted by the superintendents. The system of 'Visitation Superintendence of the Church' outlined in the Great Church Order was,[88] of course, the culmination of the development inaugurated by Brenz's draft visitation ordinance of 1535.

The stated purpose of the system was the maintenance of the purity of doctrine and worship in the duchy, and of honourable, Christian conduct among all officials of church and state. To this end, 'learned, God-fearing, serious, and resolute men' with 'special zeal' for the true faith were to be appointed general and special superintendents.[89] There were four general superintendents, and by 1559 it had become customary for the prelates of the monasteries in Adelberg, Bebenhausen, Maulbronn, and Denkendorf to hold the office.[90] The number of special superintendents was not specified, but it appears that initially (1551) one was appointed in each of the twenty-three districts established in the Synodal Ordinance of 1547, with subsequent modifications bringing the number up to twenty-eight.[91]

The (special) superintendent's principal duty was to visit each parish in his district twice a year. He was to give the local subprefect advance notice of the visitation, and the subprefect, in turn, was to ensure that all affected persons were available at the time of the visitation and that they gave the superintendent their full cooperation. Guided by prepared lists of points to be investigated, the superintendent was to interview each clergyman, the local magistrates, and 'several good-hearted, honourable' residents, to determine whether the pastor and deacon were orthodox in doctrine; whether they conducted services and performed their other duties diligently and according to the relevant ordinances; whether they were zealous in the pursuit of their daily private studies; whether they led upright, Christian lives; and whether they practised any secular occupations on the side. Further, whether the local magistrates and residents attended services regularly, received the sacrament, sent their children to catechism, and led blameless lives; and whether any Anabaptists or other sectarians were present in the area. Finally, whether the poor and sick were properly cared for, and whether clergymen were paid and church buildings maintained as prescribed. At the conclusion of each visitation, the superintendent was to submit a full written report to his general superintendent.[92]

Besides conducting visitations, the superintendent was to help each clergyman to correct whatever defects of life or teaching he might have, and also to assist in the solution of any other problems in the life of the local congregation. Problems which could not thus be resolved – a pastor's obstinate persistence in a 'strange opinion' or in public immorality; serious disputes among the clergy, or between clergymen and members of the lay community; refusal of the steward to pay a clergyman his proper salary; and the like – were to be reported directly to the central authorities for action. Finally, the superintendent was to install new clergymen in office, find substitutes for clergymen who were ill, and report the death of any clergyman to the consistory.[93]

If any clergyman, schoolteacher, or lay person had a grievance concerning any ecclesiastical matter, he was first to bring it to the attention of the special and general superintendents. If they could not help, a supplication could be addressed to the consistory, provided it were countersigned by the superintendents in matters affecting the life and doctrine of the clergy, or by the local secular officials and church steward in matters concerning pay, church buildings, or other politica.[94]

The four general superintendents were the connecting link between the superintendents and the consistory. They were to supervise the superintendents, passing on to them any special instructions from Stuttgart and giving them help and advice in cases too difficult for them to handle alone. The general superintendents were also to receive the visitation reports of the superintendents and go to

Stuttgart twice a year (down from four times in the 1553 ordinance) to join with the members of the consistory (provost, chamberlain, political councillors, and theologians) in a consultation on the contents of the reports. Under the chairmanship of Brenz (and his successors as provost) in his capacity as 'supreme superintendent of ecclesiastical affairs in the chancellery' (*Oberster Superattendent unserer Kirchensachen in unser Cantzley*), this group was to consider all the errors and deficiencies revealed in the visitation reports and to render to the duke a written recommendation concerning appropriate measures of correction, prevention, or punishment. When approved by the duke, these recommendations became church law. This group also had authority to deal with especially important cases of public misconduct or doctrinal aberration on the part of a clergyman, and it was, finally, the only body authorized to impose the penalty of excommunication.[95] In this last capacity it was part of a system of ecclesiastical discipline, the origins and nature of which are the subject of the next chapter.

Practically speaking, this group of ecclesiastical councillors and general superintendents meeting semi-annually was simply an enlarged consistory. However, both its function (legislative and judicial rather than administrative) and Brenz's special authority in it (sole superintendent rather than co-superintendent) indicate that, strictly speaking, it was something other than the consistory. The Visitation Ordinance of 1553 describes its functions but gives it no name.[96] The Great Church Order, on the other hand, calls it the *conventus*,[97] which, as Brenz had long before pointed out, is the Latin equivalent of the Greek *synodus*.[98] And *synodus* rather than *conventus* is the name that became common usage after 1559.[99] Thus it is clear that we are, so to speak, right back where we started: with Brenz's original proposal for a body, composed of clergymen and laymen, competent both to govern the church and to impose excommunication. The synod of 1527 and the *judices rerum ecclesiasticarum* of 1531 have become the consistory / synod of 1553/9.[100]

The Württemberg consistorial system was as fine an instrument of ecclesiastical administration as could have been devised at the time for the circumstances under which it had to operate. Extending without a break from the consistory at the centre through the system of superintendents into the remotest parish in the duchy, it had everything necessary for its proper functioning: authority, personnel, a clear chain of command, and sound finances. We have seen that all its essential features can be traced back to Brenz, to ideas that he had advocated, with or without success, during his years in Schwäbisch Hall. The consistorial system was the fulfilment of his career as a church organizer and his great contribution to the institutionalization of the Reformation.

On the other hand, Brenz did not work alone or issue church orders on his own authority. What was the contribution of Duke Christopher, himself a gifted organizer and eager participant in the process of ecclesiastical reconstruction? The question cannot be answered with precision or in detail: the sources are too few; Christopher had no pre-Interim career to serve as a reference point; and it is in any case notoriously difficult to distinguish between a reigning prince's own ideas and those of his advisers, of which there were many besides Brenz. One general observation can, however, be made. The Württemberg consistorial system, well thought out in every detail, had a clarity, coherence, and completeness unprecedented either in Duke Ulrich's ecclesiastical legislation or in Brenz's various pre-Interim proposals. To put it another way, Christopher's ecclesiastical legislation had the same qualities as his secular legislation. Thus, while the basic ideas incorporated into the consistorial system were Brenz's, the superior design of the system is surely to be attributed to Duke Christopher and his experienced secular officials.

At this point there is a loose end that has to be gathered up. The ecclesiastical visitation described above is not the only visitation provided for in the Great Church Order. In fact, there are two others, the political visitation (*Politische Visitation*)[101] and the territorial visitation (*Lands Visitation*).[102] For the moment only the political visitation need concern us.[103]

The immediate origin of the political visitation was the same as that of the ecclesiastical visitation. As we have seen, visitations under Duke Ulrich had been conducted by commissions of theologians and high state officials. Moreover, as was not emphasized earlier, those commissions had had a threefold task: first, the enforcement of doctrinal and liturgical uniformity; second, the control of property set aside for ecclesiastical use; and third, the supervision of public order and morality on the basis of the Territorial Ordinance. The first function was pastoral-theological in nature, the second ecclesiastical-political. But the third was, strictly speaking, purely secular in nature. Early in Duke Christopher's reign these functions were separated. The first two went to the new scheme of visitation superintendence that was part of the consistorial system. The third went to the political visitation, which retained the old form of a roving commission and was, to a certain extent at least, secularized. Whereas the ecclesiastical visitation was now conducted exclusively by clergymen and had as its primary aim the investigation of the life, doctrine, and official performance of the local clergy, the political visitation was carried out by secular officials and had as its primary purpose the determination of how well local officials were carrying out the provisions of certain secular laws, chiefly the Territorial Ordinance and the Welfare Ordinance.[104]

Nevertheless, despite its basically secular composition and jurisdiction, the political visitation was not entirely freed from the ecclesiastical context of its origins. The commissioners were responsible to both the privy council and the consistory.[105] Furthermore, while the visitation concerned itself in part with things remote from religious life (e.g., local firefighting arrangements), it concentrated heavily on those aspects of the duke's secular legislation that were intended to supplement the church's efforts to achieve a Christian society: regulations governing church attendance and public morality (Territorial Ordinance), as well as the care of the poor and sick, widows and orphans (Welfare Ordinance).[106] Finally, the political and ecclesiastical visitations were made to overlap widely: whereas, for example, the ecclesiastical visitation included numerous questions about the implementation of the Territorial and Welfare Ordinances by the local officials,[107] the political visitation included questions about the life, doctrine, and official performance of the local clergy and schoolteachers.[108] It might well have made more sense to have disentangled the two visitations from one another and to have relegated the political visitation to the Territorial Ordinance. But Duke Christopher liked the idea of the ecclesiastical and political visitations complementing, reinforcing, and even checking up on one another. So they remained side by side, overlapping, in the Great Church Order.[109]

For the purposes of this study, the political visitation as such is not particularly important. It was not part of Brenz's scheme of church government. Moreover, in contrast to the ecclesiastical visitation, it was relatively short-lived and exercised no important influence during its existence. Apparently never held with the stipulated frequency (annually),[110] it seems to have faded quickly and was omitted from the 1582 edition of the Great Church Order.[111] The reason seems fairly clear: the political visitation was something which, in the long run, no one needed. The church had its own visitation, entirely adequate for its purposes, and the state had other means of control, long established, which made church-style visitation superfluous.[112]

However, the thinking behind the political visitation does have some importance for this study. The aim of the visitation was not simply to ensure the efficient enforcement of certain laws, or to get local officials to tattle on clergymen and schoolteachers. Rather it was to ensure that the duke's officials functioned as effective instruments for elevating the standard of public morality and religious zeal in the duchy. They were themselves to set a good example for the common man by faithful attendance at church and frequent reception of the sacrament; by decent, sober, and honest behaviour in their private and public lives; and by Christian zeal in the care of widows and orphans, as well as in the punishment of immorality and neglect of religious duties. In the conclusion of the ordinance for the political visitation Christopher warned his officials that they owed this not only to him as their prince but also to God, who would demand of them in the last judgment an accounting of their conduct in office.[113] This was, of course, the same view of the responsibilities of secular authority that Brenz had expressed in the Election Day Sermons and elsewhere.[114]

All this suggests one final observation. It has been said several times in this chapter that the Württemberg system of church government worked well. That is true in the sense that the machinery functioned efficiently: visitations were held, reports were submitted, consistory and synod met and handed down thoughtful, well-informed decisions. It is not true, however, that the measures taken necessarily produced the desired results. Indeed, they often did not. There was much cause for dismay over such things as ignorance, incompetence, negligence, and doctrinal error among the clergy; the unchecked spread of sectarianism among the people; and acrimonious disputes between clergy and secular officials. But most of all, there was the failure of the combined efforts of church and state to stem the tide of public immorality and to produce anything like what Christopher and Brenz thought a Christian society ought to be. Both struggled to remedy the situation, and both ultimately failed.

5

The Discipline of Morals

Of all the problems that Brenz had to deal with as a reformer, the one that caused him the most trouble was that of moral discipline. Like all the Upper-German reformers, he fought long and hard to secure the establishment of a workable order of discipline that would include the effective use of excommunication as prescribed in the New Testament. But his struggle, like all the others, ended in failure.[1]

The major reason for that failure was the adamant opposition of the lay community to excommunication, an opposition usually (but not invariably) led by the secular authorities. Behind this hostility to excommunication were bitter memories of the church's use of that penalty in the pre-Reformation period.

Ever since the thirteenth century, canonists had distinguished between minor and major excommunication. Minor excommunication, which was 'a very minor weapon in the church's arsenal of penalties,' barred a person temporarily from reception of the Eucharist and could be imposed by an ordinary priest. Far more important was major excommunication, which was 'excommunication in its strict sense.' It deprived a person not simply of access to the Eucharist but also of membership in Christian society. The excommunicate 'was excluded from entry into church, from the company of the faithful, from pleading in secular and ecclesiastical courts, from the enjoyment of a benefice, and from all legitimate ecclesiastical acts; and after death his body was even denied ecclesiastical burial.' The power to impose this censure was reserved to certain prelates (bishops, archdeacons, deans of cathedral chapters, abbots) and to judges commissioned by them. The secular authorities were expected to accept and to uphold the church's sentence. Moreover, excommunicates who remained obdurate for a specified period (in Germany it was a year and a day) were to suffer secular outlawry. The purpose of this was 'medicinal.' It was intended 'to induce the excommunicate to seek absolution, reconciliation to the church, and restoration to his place in society.'[2]

Thus, though defined as a spiritual penalty, major excommunication had, by its very nature, grave social consequences. Furthermore, it was so widely misused by a worldly clergy to defend its financial, political, or other material interests against those of the laity that its origins as a pastoral measure for the good of the soul were forgotten. It was perceived instead as a means whereby the clergy arrogantly and irresponsibly interfered in matters properly under secular jurisdiction, unilaterally imposed secular penalties, and required the secular authorities to collaborate in the infringement of their own authority and the mistreatment of their subjects. All this created a prejudice against excommunication *in any form* so deep that the reformers could never wholly overcome it.

It was not just bitter memories of medieval practice that the reformers had to contend with. Another problem was misinterpretation of fundamental Protestant doctrine. Among adherents to the Reformation many took the view that 'Christian freedom' meant not simply freedom from the Catholic penitential system but freedom from any system whereby clergymen could impose external constraints upon moral behaviour. Consequently, the demand for any order of moral discipline, let alone the demand for the censure of excommunication, was certain to produce resentment and charges of a lamentable lapse into popery.

So Brenz's failure in the struggle for a workable order of moral discipline was by no means unique; it was part of a general phenomenon. Two things, however, give the story of Brenz's failure some claim to special importance. One is that his specific proposals not only bear the unique imprint of his mind but also form an integral part of that aspect of his career which is the subject of this book. The other is that Brenz's ultimate failure came only after winning from Duke Christopher an unusual degree of state support for his proposals. If Johannes Brenz and Christopher of Württemberg together could not achieve a workable order of moral discipline, was such a thing even possible in the territorial state church?

In this area, as in most others, the story of Brenz's career falls naturally into two periods: the pre-Interim years in Schwäbisch Hall, and the post-Interim years in Württemberg.

THE SCHWÄBISCH HALL YEARS

Brenz's earliest statement on the subject of moral discipline was a brief description of excommunication, written in the period 1524/5 and based on Luther's *Sermon on the Ban* (1520).[3] There are, Brenz wrote, two kinds of ban, an inward and an outward one, corresponding to the inward and outward fellowship of Christians. The inward ban excludes unbelievers, who may outwardly be good Christians, from the invisible church. Only God himself can impose it. The outward ban, on the other hand, excludes public sinners from the external fellowship of Christians and from the sacrament. According to Scripture (Matt. 18:16–17; 1 Cor. 5:3–5) it can be imposed by any Christian community, not just by the bishop. Moreover, it is to be imposed only on those who persist in serious misconduct – 'not for debt or other trivial things' – and only after repeated admonition.

Brenz's first detailed proposal for an order of moral discipline was included in the 'Hall Reformation' of 1527.[4] He had briefly discussed the basic features of such an order in his commentary on Ephesians of the previous year,[5] and he returned to the subject again in a sermon on penance preached a few weeks after the 'Hall Reformation' was presented to the city council.[6] The commentary and the sermon provide us with what little we know about the background of the recommendations in the 'Hall Reformation.'

It appears that Brenz was confronted not only with widespread public immorality but also with a fairly large group of people who took the libertine view that Christian freedom meant complete moral licence. Their reasoning, according to Brenz, was that since sins are so easily forgiven (by faith), they could sin as much as they pleased, provided only that afterwards they believed and repented.[7] Thus 'today almost no one lives more shamefully than those who glory in the name of the gospel.'[8] Moreover, these people, believing themselves good Christians, regularly demanded admission to the sacrament even though the genuineness of their faith and the sincerity of their repentance were at best open to doubt.

From Brenz's point of view this situation was intolerable. Like any conscientious pastor, he wished to preserve the sacrament from pollution by the participation of notorious sinners. But there was more to it than that. Like Bucer and Oecolampadius and other reformers with a humanist background, Brenz was committed to the notion of the church – the inclusive state church – as a holy community. From this point of view, a public sinner was guilty not merely of an offence against God, to whom he owed repentence, but also of an injury to the Christian community, to which he owed compensation.

This outlook is reflected in Brenz's comments on the best way to deal with the impiety described above. 'The holy fathers of the ancient church,' he said, devised an appropriate means of discipline. Public sinners who by their crimes had offended the whole church were only readmitted to communion after they had demonstrated the genuineness of their repentance by performing prescribed penances for a stipulated period of time. The public penances were not performed as satisfaction for the sins – Christ alone is satisfaction for sins – but for the sake of discipline (*propter disciplinam*). This system of moral discipline eventually degenerated into the papal penitential system with its indulgences and other follies and impieties. Now, Brenz argued, the wholesome discipline of the fathers should be restored, so that drunkards, fornicators, and blasphemers not be admitted to the sacrament until they demonstrate the sincerity of their repentance and make amends for the injury done to the church. 'Otherwise the holiness both of the church and of the sacrament of the Eucharist are profaned.'[9]

In the 'Hall Reformation' Brenz proposed that the exercise of this discipline be entrusted to a church court modelled on the old episcopal synod or synodal court (*synodus* in latinized Greek; *synod, send,* or *sendgericht* in German).

Synodal courts, whose function was to try individuals charged with violations of the church's moral code, had developed in the course of the ninth century out of episcopal visitations. The chief official of the court was not the bishop himself but an archdeacon or his deputy. Over the centuries, the courts developed elaborate procedures for collecting evidence and imposing punishments, which included a variety of penances as well as excommunication. The later middle ages brought a period of decline. Proud burghers, among others, found the penances humiliating. Besides, with the addition of money fines to the list of penalties, the synods came to be perceived more as a device for fleecing the public than for correcting sin. This aroused public support for the efforts of secular rulers to assume jurisdiction over public morality and to restrict the activity of the synodal courts. Synods tended to be denied access to major cities. In some dioceses they disappeared entirely before the sixteenth century, while in others they survived in the small towns and rural areas. The cities where Brenz spent his youth and early manhood – Weil der Stadt, Heidelberg, and Schwäbisch Hall – tolerated no synods but were located close to areas where such courts still functioned. So Brenz evidently acquired his detailed knowledge of them at first hand. And he was the only reformer of any prominence to see in them the possible basis of a Protestant order of moral discipline.[10]

When he drafted the 'Hall Reformation,' Brenz already knew that his idea of establishing a synodal court was intensely unpopular. Thus he devoted most of the relevant section of the 'Reformation'[11] to a closely argued attempt to eliminate the chief ground of opposition: the fear that the synod was a popish institution which would needlessly meddle in men's lives and interfere in the legitimate jurisdiction of the secular government.

It is the will of Christ, said Brenz, that Christians, in every place where they are gathered by his word and sacrament, lead an honourable, disciplined, Christian life, in order that evil men and unbelievers be attracted to faith and piety, and that pious believers be strengthened and improved. How, then, is one to deal with those undisciplined Christians who by their evil lives injure the church, besmirch the good name of Christianity, and profane the sacrament? One cannot simply rely on the secular authorities to deal with such people. Secular government is, to be sure, an ordinance of God for the punishment of evil and the rewarding of good, in order that public decency and honour be maintained in human society. But government action in this regard is usually insufficient from the church's point of view. Indeed, the secular authorities may not even be Christian. This was the case in New Testament times, when secular power was entirely in Jewish or pagan hands. The result was that secular authority ignored much public behaviour that the Christian community could not tolerate among its members. So Christ established the method whereby the church itself could deal with the offenders in its midst. According to Matthew 18:15–17: 'If thy brother shall trespass against thee, go and tell him his fault between thee and him alone ... But if he will not hear thee, then take with thee one or two more ... And if he shall neglect to hear them, tell it unto the church: but if he neglect to hear the church, let him be unto thee as an heathen man and a publican.'

Now, Brenz continued, it would have caused disorder and impropriety if every individual with a grievance against his brother had stood up in the common assembly of the church to lay charges against him. So the fathers of the ancient church worked out the following method of administering the discipline which Christ had established: in each congregation or parish, several 'elderly, experienced, brave, honest men' were elected, one to be pastor and the others to be elders or presbyters. When pastors and elders met to conduct church business, this was known as a synod, that is, an assembly. The duties of the synod were to arrange that the congregation be regularly provided with the word of God and the sacraments, and to administer moral discipline in cases of public misconduct by any member of the congregation. A person guilty of such misconduct was admonished. If he repented, he was forgiven after public confession and penance. But if he remained impenitent after several admonitions, he was publicly excommunicated, that is, barred from the sacrament until he regained admittance to the Christian community through improvement of life and public confession. Meanwhile, everyone was to avoid his company while praying for his repentance.

Nowadays, Brenz continued, it is much easier to maintain decent conduct among Christian people, since the secular sword is no longer in the hands of unbelievers but of Christians who use their office in defence of the honour of the Christian name. Nevertheless, there are many grievous sins which, because they cause no public disorder, are either not prohibited by law or else the extant laws are negligently enforced. For example: swearing and cursing, envy and hatred, gluttony and drunkenness, fornication and adultery, gambling and usury. Furthermore, even in cases where the government does impose penalties, genuine repentance and improvement of life do not necessarily result. Therefore, the church needs its own means of dealing with cases in which secular penalties are either not applied or are applied without effect.

Brenz took the (historically inaccurate) view that the medieval synodal courts were a corrupt survival of the ecclesiastical discipline established by the fathers of the primitive church, and argued that a 'useful, Christian' synod should be established in place of the 'useless' papal one. To this end, he said, the city council should appoint several honest and reputable persons from the citizenry who, when need arose, would join with the pastor (Eisenmenger) and the preacher (Brenz) to hold a synod. Dealing only with the cases of persons guilty of public sins that were not punished by the secular authorities, or persons still impenitent after the imposition of secular penalties, the synod was to admonish and, if necessary, to excommunicate the guilty parties according to the procedure outlined above.

Brenz's proposed synod resembled the ancient synod as he imagined it far more closely than it resembled the medieval court of the same name. For one thing, the elaborate judicial procedures of the latter, and its array of penalties other than the temporary withholding of the sacrament and formal excommunication, were omitted. Moreover, as we saw in the last chapter, Brenz wanted his synod, like its ancient model, to function also as an organ of ecclesiastical administration.[12]

Toward the end of Brenz's plea for the exercise of moral discipline by a synod, there were some melancholy echoes of the opposition to it. 'No one believes what good and what moral improvement would result from this order. Christ was certainly not drunk when he established it.' 'It would make of the city not a monastery but a disciplined citizenry.'[13]

We have no record of whatever discussion the city council may have devoted to Brenz's proposal. We know only that it did not give its consent. It did, however, respond in its own way to Brenz's demand for an effective discipline of morals. Sometime in the first half of 1527 the council reissued an old mandate against blasphemy and the excessive drinking of toasts, with several other 'statutes and regulations' appended.[14] Brenz had to announce and to elucidate these measures from the pulpit.[15]

In the new preamble to the mandate, the council admitted that its earlier, oft-repeated bans on blasphemy and excessive drinking had had little effect. But the city fathers also expressed their determination that things would be different this time.[16] The mandate established penalties for cursing and swearing, the unseemly drinking of toasts, and being found in taverns during church services on Sundays and holidays. Also banned was the practice of meeting before church services 'in certain houses' to hold elaborate breakfasts during which large quantities of brandy were consumed, to the great detriment of body and soul. Further, in an attempt to eliminate the abuse of wives and children and the loss of work and income that were the common aftermath of long drinking bouts in the evening, taverns were required to close at the stroke of ten. In all cases the punishment for violations consisted of a fine: three *pfennig* to two *schilling heller* for cursing and swearing; one *pfund heller* for the other offences.[17]

To ensure enforcement of the mandate, each of the city's four captains (*haubt-männer*) was each month to appoint in his district (*haubtmannschaft*) two inspectors who were to report violations to him. He was then to report the violations to the city council for appropriate action. The inspectors were to swear an oath that they would spare no one. However, they were not required to report their own wives, children, or servants.[18] That terms of abuse for the inspectors already existed (hangman's helper, traitor, etc.)[19] suggests that they were an old institution. In the mandate, the council ordered that no one mistreat them by word or deed, for that would touch the honour of God and the salvation of souls.[20]

Despite the council's good intentions to improve public morality, its mandate provided far less than Brenz had asked. The list of offences dealt with was far shorter than that he had proposed to place under the authority of the synod. Moreover, the church remained without a discipline of its own to be used when secular remedies failed. Above all, there was no provision for public excommunication. All pastors could do was privately *admonish* those guilty of public offences to abstain from communion until genuine repentance and improvement of life had taken place.[21] Nevertheless, in the prefatory remarks he had made before reading the mandate from the pulpit, Brenz dutifully and loyally supported the council's measure without once mentioning his own plan.[22]

In direct contrast to the mandate's claim that the honour of God and the salvation of souls were at stake, Brenz emphasized exclusively the secular well-being of the city. The security of the state, Brenz said, resides not only in a large population, high walls, or a full treasury, but above all in moral virtue (*honestas morum*). For although external virtue, government (*civilitas*), and justice count for little in God's eyes and do not give eternal life, they are his gifts in this earthly life. Just as there are two kinds of life, earthly and heavenly, so there are two kinds of justice or righteousness: civil or external, and divine or Christian. The blessings of heavenly life – peace of conscience, justification, and eternal life – are acquired by means of *iustitia christiana*, that is, by faith in Jesus Christ, concerning which we are instructed in Holy Scripture. The blessings of earthly life are general and external peace, prosperity, and pleasure. These are achieved not by a large army or strong fortifications, but through good public morals (*civili morum honestate*) and external justice. Whoever despises such things God punishes with wars, famine, plague, and general misery (Lev. 18:24–30; Deut. 28:15ff.; Is. 1:19–20, 5:11ff.; Hos. 4:1–3). Until now, God in his goodness has ignored the blasphemy, the drunkenness, and all the other vices practised in the city, and has given it undeserved peace, prosperity, abundant harvests, and good air. The citizens should now display appropriate gratitude by leading virtuous lives. The city council, whose job it is to care for civil justice, has sought to achieve this goal by means of its mandate, in order that public peace not be undermined by perverse morals, and especially that God not be provoked to wrathful destruction of the city because of its iniquity.

Despite his apparently unconditional surrender to the city council's demand for its own brand of moral discipline, Brenz had by no means abandoned the idea of a synodal court. In fact, he returned to it in January 1531 in a draft synodal ordinance (*Ordnung des Sends*)[23] written at the behest of the city council and intended as an order of moral discipline for Hall's rural territory.[24] Although the supporting arguments were exactly the same as in 1527, the 1531 synod bore a far closer resemblance to its medieval prototype than had the synod of 1527. In fact, procedures and penalties of the old courts were as closely copied as was possible in the new theological context.[25]

According to the proposed ordinance, a commission of three or four men well versed in both secular and ecclesiastical affairs and penalties (i.e., theologians and lawyers) was to hold court in each parish once each year, always giving a week's notice of its arrival. Once on the scene, the commissioners were to take the sworn testimony of three or four or more trustworthy members of the parish congregation about all serious, public, hitherto unpunished offences of which they had knowledge. Assuming jurisdiction only in cases where secular penalties did not apply, or where such penalties produced no improvement of life, the commissioners were to impose appropriate ecclesiastical penalties. Every effort was to be made to let the punishment fit the crime. Thus, for example, usurers and gamblers might be fined a certain amount to be paid to the local poor chest; gluttons and drunkards might be excluded from inns and taverns during a specified period; and those negligent about church attendance might be required to attend all services each Sunday for several weeks. These penalties were not to be construed, in popish fashion, as satisfaction for the sins, but merely as an external discipline whereby the sinner gave evidence of the sincerity of his repentance, made amends for the public scandal he had caused, and served as a deterrent example to others. Everyone disciplined in this fashion was to be barred from the sacrament for a time to be set by the synod. If anyone ignored the sentence of the court and persisted in his evil ways, the synod was, after two or three warnings, formally and publicly to excommunicate him. He was to be treated as a sundered member of the church until he mended his ways and the ban was lifted by the synod.

When the contents of the synodal ordinance became public, an old man called out to Brenz: 'You, sir, are up to something that won't work. You want to make the devil pious, but you can't do that.' In reply, Brenz denied any such utopian aim: 'One cannot prevent all sins or offences in the community, but everything is fine as long as one punishes them.'[26]

If one were to describe Brenz's two proposals for a synodal court in terms of the traditional distinction between major and minor excommunication, one would have to say that he was trying to establish a Protestant version of major excommunication. Excommunication was to be imposed by higher ecclesiastical authority (that is, by the synod). The excommunicate was to be treated as outside the Christian community and to be subjected to the kind of social pressure (e.g., being shunned as a 'heathen and a publican') that would presumably hasten repentance and reconcililation. Moreover, even the temporary, probationary exclusion from the sacrament provided for in the synodal proposals was treated as a species of the major ban. While such exclusion did not involve loss of membership in the Christian community, it did involve social pressures (public confession, public penance) analogous to those applied to excommunicates, and the authority to impose it was reserved to the synod. If even temporary exclusion from the sacrament was thus a form of the major ban, then Brenz had implicitly reduced the minor ban to the right of the pastor to admonish public sinners not to commune. Events would soon force Brenz to deal with this matter in greater detail.

As was the case with Brenz's 1527 proposal, we have no record of the city fathers' comments on the synodal ordinance of 1531. We know only that they did not adopt it.[27] In this case, however, Schwäbisch Hall was not the only community involved. At about the same time that he submitted the draft synodal ordinance to the Hall city council, Brenz sent a copy of it to Margrave George of Brandenburg-Ansbach, recommending provision for a synod in the Brandenburg-Nuremberg Church Order which was then in preparation.[28] The proposal found ready acceptance in Ansbach[29] but not in Nuremberg, where a dispute over excommunication was already in progress.

In the spring of 1530, Osiander had proposed for inclusion in the new church order an article on excommunication. The article authorized pastors temporarily to exclude public sinners from the sacrament pending repentance and the abandonment of their offensive behaviour. Osiander and his fellow theologians argued that excommunication in this form was a purely spiritual penalty instituted by Christ for the use of the church, and that it was especially necessary because the secular authorities did not punish all public sins. But the city fathers, supported by their lawyers, took the view that any public exclusion from the sacrament involved the social disgrace of the person affected and was thus a matter of secular jurisdiction which could not be exercised by the clergy.[30] In the traditional terminology, this clash of views could be expressed as follows: the theologians wanted to reinstitute the minor ban, but the council and its lawyers interpreted any public ban as the major ban, which they feared and would not allow.

If Osiander's rather modest proposal aroused fears for the integrity of secular jurisdiction, Brenz's synodal ordinance must have seemed a brutal assault upon it.

In a memorandum drafted by Osiander, the Nuremberg theologians objected that the synod would be a 'gratuitous violation' of secular jurisdiction, that no such thing had been prescribed in Scripture, and that it would perpetuate abuses familiar under the papacy.[31] Brenz did his best to refute these charges in a memorandum written mid-May.[32]

The synodal ordinance, Brenz began, had originally been drafted because 'one of the Schmalkaldic Articles' called upon the theologians to devise suitable means of discipline to raise public morality.[33] At the moment,

the way of life among the people is so dissolute and undisciplined that a person who one night gets himself so full of wine that he has to be carried home comes the very next morning, promises that he will never do it again as long as he lives, and demands the sacrament. If one withholds the sacrament from him for a week or so, he complains before God and man that he is being denied the sacrament. If one gives him the sacrament, he goes out that very night and gets just as drunk as he was the night before, but returns once more, promising never to do it again, until finally he is once again given the sacrament. So he lives perpetually in his intemperance ... perpetually demanding grace and forgiveness without sincerity.

Such sins, Brenz continued, are not very important in the eyes of secular government. Thus it does not punish them and would perhaps be ill advised to attempt to do so. But in God's eyes such sins are intolerable and the church cannot ignore them. However, to excommunicate someone as soon as he sins would be to misuse the ban, which should only be imposed on the impenitent, not on those who confess their sins. On the other hand, to admit him to the sacrament immediately upon his confession would give offence to the church and be harmful to him as well, since he would just run off and commit the same sin again. The method whereby the ancient fathers dealt with such cases was to impose for a time an ecclesiastical penalty as probation and as compensation for the public offence given, after which the offender was readmitted to the sacrament. Even though this means is not expressly set forth in Scripture, it is not contrary to Scripture either. Furthermore, Christian secular government itself has demanded order in such matters. And if the proposed order were adopted, it would surely be done with the consent and under the supervision of the secular authorities. How then can it be called a gratuitous violation of their jurisdiction? Nor is there any reason to fear the synod because it produced many inequities under the papacy. After all, every ordinance of the ancient church was abused under the papacy. The new evangelical church order itself may with time suffer abuse, but one cannot on that account dispense with it. There is no need to fear popery if erroneous papal doctrines are banished and sound Christian doctrines are maintained in their place.

In conclusion, Brenz stated that if the secular authorities themselves wished 'in the name of peace' to assume responsibility for punishing the sort of offences they had hitherto ignored, then they should by all means do so. But what, he demanded, if they are negligent in enforcing their own legislation? Must the pastors then 'cast the sacrament before swine, drunkards, gamblers, and whoremongers?' If not, then the church must have some orderly means available for use when necessary to prevent such 'filthy, swinish' misuse of the sacrament.

The city fathers in Nuremberg, like those in Schwäbisch Hall, were deaf to Brenz's pleading. As a result, Brenz abandoned as hopeless the project of a synodal court and with it the idea of reviving the 'wholesome discipline of the ancient fathers' with its penances and probationary exclusion from the sacrament. However, given his understanding of what Scripture prescribed, Brenz could not abandon the demand for some order of excommunication. The problem was to find an order that would satisfy the injunctions of Jesus and St Paul without arousing the intransigent opposition of the secular magistrates. This new departure in Brenz's search for a workable order of moral discipline manifested itself in the course of the continuing negotiations on the Brandenburg-Nuremberg Church Order.

In November 1531 the Nurembergers decided to resolve the deadlock between magistrates and theologians over excommunication by omitting the article on excommunication from the church order. In this way the pastors would at least not be expressly forbidden to apply ecclesiastical penalties (e.g., exclusion from the sacrament) in the case of especially offensive public misconduct.[34] In December the Ansbach theologians gave their qualified consent to this proposal in a memorandum written by Brenz.[35]

Brenz and his colleagues began by lamenting that so many persons unjustly viewed excommunication, established by Christ and practised by the apostles, as 'hateful and prejudicial to secular government.' But, having got that off their chests, and recognizing that further dispute was pointless, they agreed to the exclusion of the article on excommunication on the ground that 'as things now stand in the church, the orderly and useful practice of the ban is not possible.' For no one, they wrote, should be publicly excommunicated except on the basis of a free confession of public misconduct or, if the charge be denied, of a judicial finding based on the testimony of reliable witnesses. However, Christian freedom is now so thoroughly misunderstood that almost no one will submit even to private examination and admonition before communion. Moreover, the pastors have no established church courts to which they can appeal, nor can they have recourse to the secular courts, which do not take cognizance of many of the sins which render the perpetrator liable to excommunication in the eyes of the church. And it certainly would not be proper for an individual pastor, acting alone on the basis only of his personal knowledge of the case, to excommunicate anyone. 'Thus it seems to us that, in this state of disorder, an order of excommunication *in the church* is not possible.'[36]

Nevertheless, Brenz and his colleagues continued, the ban must somehow be exercised, for it is just as vital to the welfare of the Christian community as secular penalties are to the welfare of the secular community. So the authority to impose it should be assigned to *judices rerum ecclesiasticarum*, that is, to government-appointed commissions of pastors and laymen who will also be responsible for ecclesiastical administration 'in every district.' Otherwise, public excommunication simply cannot be practised. And a government which impedes the legitimate exercise of the ban will share the guilt for all the disorder and unpunished offences which result, something for which it will eventually have to answer before God.[37]

This memorandum has an importance far transcending the occasion for which it was written. It contains, in rough outline, the essential features of the order of excommunication which Brenz would finally succeed in establishing in Württemberg over twenty years later. In this connection, three features of the memorandum deserve comment.

The first is Brenz's refusal to go along with the idea of assigning the authority to excommunicate to the individual pastors. While he agreed with his Nuremberg colleagues that excommunication had been established by Christ for the use of the church, he also believed that the ancient fathers had wisely assigned the authority to impose it to a church court rather than to the pastors themselves. Publicly to exclude someone from the sacrament was, in effect, to impose major excommunication: the public inevitably saw it that way (witness the reaction of the Nuremberg city council to Osiander's proposal), and Brenz, for his own reasons, wanted it that way. He thought that the imposition of such a penalty by pastors acting alone would be intrinsically arbitrary and capricious. It would, moreover, be ineffective, since the pastors would be isolated and defenceless in the face of public hostility to excommunication. Thus, if it was to be fair, orderly, and effective, public excommunication had to be imposed by a higher authority following appropriate judicial procedures.

The second important feature of the Ansbach memorandum is Brenz's unequivocal statement that the exercise of excommunication 'in the church' was impossible and that, as a consequence, the authority to impose the ban would have to be invested in *judices rerum ecclesiasticarum*. This was as much as to say that since excommunication could not be imposed in the church, acting on the authority which Christ had given it, it would have to be imposed by the state, acting on the authority which God had given it. But while Brenz explained the necessity of this move, he said nothing in defence of its propriety. How could something established by Christ in the church be placed under the authority of the magistrate? In fact Brenz was simply pursuing the implications of the arguments he had used during his campaign for the establishment of a synodal court: The office of magistrate includes the punishment of public immorality; Christ established the means whereby the church itself could impose punishments because, at the time, there were no Christian magistrates; now there are Christian magistrates, but they (and their officials) tend to be lax in the punishment of evil and their punishments do not necessarily produce true repentance; moreover, out of fear for the integrity of their jurisdiction, the magistrates will not permit the establishment of a church court; since the church is therefore not able to use the authority which Christ gave it to expel unrepentant sinners from its midst, it will be necessary to ask the magistrate to use his authority over ecclesiastical affairs to do so. Such an arrangement was certainly second-best as far as Brenz was concerned, but it was entirely proper and legitimate nevertheless. Moreover, Brenz remained convinced for the rest of his life that it offered the only realistic hope for a workable order of excommunication.

The last of the three noteworthy features of the Ansbach memorandum is that the *judices rerum ecclesiasticarum* were the synod of 1527 in revised form. Brenz retained the notion of a single body competent in the areas both of ecclesiastical administration and moral discipline. On the other hand, he dropped the offensive name, any other reference to the hated episcopal courts, and any claim (implicit or explicit) of autonomous ecclesiastical jurisdiction. The revised synod of 1531 was, like its direct descendant, the Württemberg consistory/synod, unequivocally an organ of the Christian state.

While the Ansbach memorandum was thus rich in premonitions of developments in the still distant future, it had no effect at all on developments in the short run. All the church orders with which Brenz was associated in the 1530s and 1540s provided for a fairly strict form of the minor ban: those wishing to commune had to announce their intention beforehand to the pastor, who was to examine them carefully and admonish the unworthy not to commune.[38] But none of these church orders or related ordinances provided for public excommunication in any form.

Indeed, in the period after December 1531, Brenz, weary perhaps of hopeless struggles, seems to have called off his campaign for an order of public excommunication. For the rest of the pre-Interim period he contented himself with attempts to move the secular authorities to enact more comprehensive moral legislation and to enforce that legislation more diligently. Already in August 1531 Brenz had advised Margrave George that his 'eminently Christian mandates' against cursing, swearing, immoderate drinking, and other public offences would have little effect unless he saw to it that his officials were more zealous in enforcing them.[39] Similarly, in 1535 Brenz recommended to Duke Ulrich, who, like his predecessors, had assumed responsibility for punishing public immorality,[40] that one of the aims of the proposed annual visitation ought to be to determine how well his officials were carrying out that responsibility.[41] Finally, in the Schwäbisch Hall election sermons of the 1540s, one of Brenz's main themes was the magistrates' duty to serve the glory of God by punishing all public deviations from Christian morality, as summarized in the Decalogue, regardless of whether the particular offence constituted a threat to public order.[42]

The results of all this exhortation were, at best, meagre. In 1543 the city council of Schwäbisch Hall still tolerated public prostitution and indecent dances.[43] And in 1546 Brenz was still pointing to the need for governmental action against 'blasphemy, drunkenness, fornication, etc.'[44] In other words, the situation as Brenz had perceived it in 1527 was fundamentally unchanged: the state was still negligent and the church was still helpless. Only when he entered the service of Duke Christopher did this situation change for the better.

Before proceeding to the consideration of developments after the Interim, one last feature of the developments in the pre-Interim period should be noted. Even though Brenz's first utterance on the subject of excommunication had been a definition of it taken over from Luther, the views on the proper exercise of excommunication which he developed in the following years were much at variance with Luther's. In the Schmalkaldic Articles of 1537 Luther rejected the greater ban as a purely secular penalty inappropriate in the church, and acknowledged only the lesser ban, i.e., the barring of obstinate sinners from the sacrament and from other fellowship of the church until they changed their way of life.[45] While in the articles themselves Luther assigned the exercise of this lesser ban to the pastors, he later argued that they ought to practise it only in consultation with the congregation.[46] He also expressed strong disapproval when secular authorities attempted to assert control over the exercise of excommunication by the church.[47] Brenz, along with the other leading Lutheran reformers, signed the Schmalkaldic Articles, even though his views on excommunication were not accurately reflected in them: harmony on so many other points more than outweighed the difference of opinion on this one.

THE YEARS IN WÜRTTEMBERG

Duke Christopher had a deep sense of personal responsibility to God for the moral behaviour of his subjects. Throughout his reign, therefore, he took an active interest in promoting efforts by church and state to curb public immorality. Christopher's Territorial Ordinance of 2 January 1552,[48] the fifth and by far the most comprehensive of a series which had begun with Duke Eberhard's ordinance of 1495, prescribed fines and/or jail sentences for a fairly long list of violations of

Christian conduct: negligence in church attendance; cursing and swearing; magic, exorcism, and fortune-telling; fornication, prostitution, and adultery; drunkenness; gambling; usury.[49] However, the duke's officials were no more zealous than their counterparts elsewhere in the enforcement of such legislation. Thus Brenz found himself faced with an old problem when, at one of the first meetings of the new synod, the general superintendents asked what was to be done if lax enforcement of the Territorial Ordinance resulted in many unworthy persons seeking admission to the sacrament.[50]

The Church Order (order of worship) of 1553 provided one possible answer to this question. The section on admission to the sacrament stipulated that those who intended to commune must report to the pastor beforehand for examination and counselling, and that the pastor was both to admonish unrepentant sinners not to commune and also 'to *exclude* them until their betterment.'[51] But the idea of a pastor's excluding anyone from the sacrament on his own authority was completely contrary to Brenz's strongly held views on the subject of moral discipline. How such a provision found its way into a key ordinance of the church which he led is a mystery. At any rate, at the above-mentioned synod meeting, which took place sometime before September 1554,[52] Brenz seized the opportunity to nullify the offending provision and to establish his own views as church law.

In response to the general superintendents' query, Brenz argued that the Superintendence Ordinance of 1553 required each pastor to report any unrepentant sinner to the superintendent who, if his added admonition did no good, would report the sinner through the general superintendent to the synod for further admonition and, if necessary, excommunication. Brenz insisted that this was in accordance with the rule of Christ, who, when he said, 'tell it to the church' (Matt. 18:17), deprived any pastor of the authority publicly to exclude anyone from the sacrament *privato suo arbitrio*. Finally, Brenz directed that the superintendents impart this interpretation of the Superintendence Ordinance to the pastors during their visitations.[53]

Two important additions to Württemberg church law resulted from this synod meeting. One was an addendum to the Superintendence Ordinance which 'explained' the provisions of the Church Order of 1553 concerning admission to the sacrament.[54] The requirement for prior announcement, examination, and counselling remained in force. However, if a notorious, unrepentant sinner were nevertheless impiously and maliciously to demand the sacrament, the pastor was not *privato judicio* to deny it to him but was to report the matter to his superintendent and await his instructions. Or, if such a sinner preferred simply to abstain from the sacrament rather than abandon his evil life, and would not heed the pastor's admonitions to repent, this too was to be reported to the superintendent.

The further steps through the general superintendent to the synod and excommunication, only briefly indicated in the addendum to the Superintendence Ordinance, were fully set forth in the new Order of Ecclesiastical Censure,[55] which was the second addition to church law to come out of the synod meeting discussed above.

The order provided that cases in which the imposition of the prescribed secular penalties produced no 'true, Christian improvement' were to be dealt with 'in the pastoral and preaching office' according to procedures modelled on those laid down by Christ in Matthew 18. First, the culprit's pastor was to admonish him to abandon his evil ways. If this had no effect, the pastor was to report the matter to his superintendent, who, accompanied by the pastor and two judges of the local court, was to visit the sinner in question and admonish him once more. If this in turn had no effect, the superintendent, pastor, and judges were to report the offender through the general superintendent to the consistory so that he (the sinner) could be haled before the next meeting of the synod to be given a final admonition. If this failed, the synod could, with the knowledge and approval of the duke, excommunicate him.

The excommunicated person had to stand before his home congregation while the pastor read out the synod's sentence. He was barred from the sacrament and from all other Christian ceremonies except the sermon, during which he had to stand in a specially reserved pew. If he died without repenting, he was not to receive Christian burial. Furthermore, the local subprefect was to bar him from all weddings, taverns, and other public gatherings, while all social intercourse with him, save only those business dealings necessary to keep him clothed and fed, was banned. If the excommunicated person led a virtuous life until the next visitation and then asked for pardon, the superintendent and pastor, together with the local subprefect and judges, were to inform the consistory, which could, again with the knowledge and consent of the duke, lift the ban and order the pastor publicly to proclaim the person's restoration to full church membership.

In the case of public misbehaviour so outrageous that the delays involved in the above procedure could not be tolerated, the admonitions could be dispensed with and a report sent via the superintendent and general superintendent to the consistory, which would advise the duke on the appropriate action to be taken.

Finally, pastors were instructed to teach their congregations not to despise excommunication but to remember that 'orderly and legitimate excommunication is the deprivation of all temporal and eternal well-being.'

Thus, by the summer of 1554 Brenz had at last achieved an order of moral discipline which met the requirements that he had formulated over two decades earlier. Broadly speaking, the order consisted of a carefully coordinated system of secular and ecclesiastical penalties designed to preserve the purity of the sacrament and the holiness of the community. The ecclesiastical penalties consisted, first, of an attenuated form of the minor ban exercised by the pastors and, second, of the major ban exercised by a central *senatus presbyterorum* acting *ex permissu et concessione principis*.[56]

Hardly had this system been established when, in the autumn of 1554, two clergymen came forward with an alternative proposal. The two were Caspar Lyser, pastor in Nürtingen, and his brother-in-law Jakob Andreä, pastor and general superintendent in Göppingen.[57] For some time Lyser and Andreä had been the leaders of a group of pastors who, incensed by the number of drunks and other reprobates who demanded admission to the sacrament without showing any signs of genuine repentance, were eager to 'restore' excommunication in the Württemberg church.[58] It was probably Andreä who had raised the question of moral discipline in the synod of 1553–4.[59] However, he and Lyser were more attracted to a congregational discipline on the Genevan model than to the centralized system imposed by Brenz. They were attracted in particular by Pierre Viret's plan for a congregational consistory of six or eight persons, chosen in part from the ministers and in part from the laity, which would meet each week to admonish public sinners and to excommunicate those who failed to heed admonition.[60] Convinced that this plan was 'indeed pious and in accordance with Scripture' (Matt. 18), Lyser, on 6 September, personally submitted to the duke a letter asking permission to put it into practice in his congregation.[61] At about the same time Andreä had a meeting with the duke and presented the same request orally.[62]

Duke Christopher was himself favourably disposed toward the Lyser-Andreä proposal[63] but, as a matter of course, asked Brenz for his written opinion of Lyser's letter.[64] For Brenz it was not simply his order of moral discipline that had been challenged but his view of the church as well. Lyser and Andreä thought of the church primarily as the local congregation,[65] but Brenz, as always, thought of it above all as the centralized territorial church. From this point of view it made no sense at all to decentralize ecclesiastical discpline while doctrine, liturgy, church finances, and personnel all remained, for the sake of good order, under centralized control. So in his memorandum on Lyser's letter,[66] Brenz the theologian proved himself a far more consistent and uncompromising centralizer than Christopher the prince.

Brenz began by praising Lyser's zeal for moral discipline, but went on immediately to express wonder at his apparent ignorance of the Superintendence Ordinance of 1553, 'as though he were a stranger in Your Grace's domain.' It is true, Brenz continued, that in Matthew 18 Christ established the exercise of excommunication in the church. But since everything in the church must be done decently and in order, the administration of this penalty is not permitted to just anyone or by just any means. Indeed, in the ancient church it was exercised not in every little town or village but only in the more important cities where bishops and their chapters resided. Accordingly, the Superintendence Ordinance (with the provisions summarized above) has been established in order that nothing respecting the exercise of excommunication be rashly undertaken by the pastors or their congregations, and also that nothing be lacking in the church's ministry. The Superintendence Ordinance and the Territorial Ordinance together constitute a system of moral discipline that is not only completely adequate but also perfectly consonant with the rule laid down in Matthew 18. The corruption and wickedness which unfortunately persist are the result not of any fault in the ordinances themselves but of the failure of the secular officials and the pastors (often not immaculately moral themselves) to implement them properly.

Heedless of the legitimate and useful order already established, Lyser wants, Brenz continued, to entrust the imposition of excommunication to the 'private whim' of this or that pastor. Brenz pointed to the excessive severity of Lyser's own attitude toward moral offenders as an example of the danger inherent in such a scheme. In his letter to the duke, Lyser had referred approvingly to Chrysostom's statement that he would rather lose his life than give the sacrament to the corrupt, and had cited Jesus's admonition not to cast pearls before swine.[67] To this Brenz replied that a man who drinks too much one day but promises improvement the next is not immediately to be judged a swine. Better to run the risk of an occasional case of unworthy communion than to risk despising a contrite and humble heart.[68] It is never the office of a pastor to search the reins and hearts, to judge a man's repentance insincere, and to deny him the sacrament *privato suo arbitrio*. Lyser had, of course, not requested the right to make such judgments on his own authority but only in consultation with the local consistory, a procedure which would, he said, prevent the kind of tyranny that had characterized excommunication under the papacy. But Brenz trusted local congregations even less than he trusted their pastors, and the notion of a congregational consistory was to him so redolent of disorder and injustice that he did not scruple to charge Lyser with popery.[69] His urgent recommendation to the duke was to stay with the established order and to require Lyser to observe it. Christopher accepted this advice and notified Lyser accordingly.[70]

But Andreä, hoping that Duke Christopher was still favourably disposed even if Brenz was not, made one last effort in behalf of a decentralized ecclesiastical discipline. In a letter to the duke dated 2 November, he raised the spectre of God's wrath upon the duchy if moral offences were not removed, and requested a meeting of the synod for the purpose of a 'serious, renewed discussion of the matter.'[71] Christopher, however, remained firm in his resolve to support the views of his provost. On 24 November, Lyser and Andreä had to appear before a special session of the consistory, where a formal remonstrance, written by Brenz, against their attempt to inaugurate a 'special *censura ecclesiastica,*' was read to them. They were then required to indicate whether or not they would obey the duke's command that they desist from all 'innovations' and observe the established order. Both submitted, and that was the end of the Lyser-Andreä affair.[72]

Three things make the above-mentioned remonstrance particularly interesting. First, Brenz did not simply repeat the arguments he had used in the memorandum against Lyser; he added to them. Second, echoes of the Ansbach memorandum of 1531, already audible in the memorandum, are even stronger in the remonstrance. Third, Brenz used the traditional terms *excommunicatio minor* and *excommunicatio major* for the first and last time, and in a rather arbitrary way as well.

It is true, Brenz began, that every pastor is to exercise ecclesiastical censure in his church. But there is a major difference between the censure appropriate to the office of pastor and that appropriate to the church as a whole (*der gemeinen Kyrchen*). Pastoral censure comprises, besides preaching, what used to be called *excommunicatio minor*, that is, the private examination of communicands and the admonishing of impenitent sinners not to commune. This form of excommunication is adequately provided for in the Church Order of 1553. The censure appropriate to the church as a whole consists of what used to be called *excommunicatio major*, that is, the public imposition of the ban on an impenitent sinner. This is a much more complicated and difficult matter than the minor ban. In the past a person publicly excommunicated was disgraced and could neither testify in court, inherit property, nor hold any honourable office. Such a penalty cannot be imposed by a pastor. It requires, rather, an orderly, judicial process on the basis of special laws or canons defining the offences to be dealt with and the procedures to be followed. There would also have to be a *Summum et generale Consistorium* to hear appeals.

However, Brenz continued, 'owing to the condition of these times,' the *excommunicatio major* (i.e., public excommunication in the church by church courts) cannot successfully be inaugurated. Any attempt to do so would cause great dissension and disorder. Therefore, in order that scandalous vices not go unpunished, the duke, as *Nutricius Ecclesiarum*, has established in his Superintendence Ordinance an order of ecclesiastical discipline culminating in the imposition by the synod, acting on the order of the duke himself, of public excommunication (i.e., a penalty tantamount to the major ban, but imposed by the state rather than by the church). The duke has also established a Territorial Ordinance with secular penalties for public immorality. Admittedly, the secular officials have been somewhat lethargic in enforcing the ordinance, but the duke can be relied upon to provide the necessary remedy for that. Meanwhile, it is his will that all clergymen peacefully and obediently adhere to the order of moral discipline established in his ecclesiastical and secular ordinances.

In the same year as the Lyser-Andreä affair, 1554, Brenz included in his commentary on Matthew yet another discussion of excommunication.[73] In dealing with the *locus classicus* for such discussions (chap. 18, vss. 15–18), he addressed himself to the question of how a New Testament precept could appropriately be applied in different times and altered circumstances. His answer was clearly a justification of the established Württemberg order of excommunication,[74] though neither it nor the controversy with Lyser-Andreä was mentioned. This particular defence of the established order is interesting chiefly for two reasons. The first is that it provides fresh evidence of Brenz's conviction that, in some respects at least, developments since New Testament times have been to the good. The other is that Brenz here gives his clearest, most precise statement of where the magistrate gets the authority to excommunicate.

The rule laid down in Matthew 18, Brenz began, is, if rightly understood and applied, of great benefit to the church. If falsely understood and applied, however, it causes great disruption in the government of church and state, as was the case with the exercise of excommunication under papacy. In the present day, he went on, the Anabaptists view the absence from our churches of a literal observance of this rule as evidence that we do not have a true church. To this Brenz replied that the rule was never intended to be applied literally at all times and in all circumstances. When Jesus said, 'tell it to the church,' he was speaking to his immediate disciples and referring specifically to the small, isolated assemblies (*coetus*) of the ancient church, which were deformed (*pravi*) in that they had to manage their affairs without the help and support of the secular magistrate. In such circumstances, the procedure beginning with direct individual complaint against a brother, and culminating in excommunication from the assembly, was appropriate because it could be carried out with decency and order. But in the modern state church, whose assemblies sometimes number in the thousands, literal application of this procedure would result in great confusion and disorder. In the midst of so many conflicting wills, in such uproar of the multitude, there would be no hope of honest counsel or judgment, and there would be no end of strife. Consequently, the rule laid down in Matthew 18 has to be adapted to fit the conditions of the church as it exists today, that is, to a great assembly of which the magistrate, whose office includes the correction and punishment of evil, is both member and governor. In such a church, public excommunication is to be exercised by specified judges selected from the whole church by the prince in his role as governor and orderer of ecclesiastical affairs. It is thus not necessary to establish a new ecclesiastical court (*novum Ecclesiasticum senatum*); one should use that which has already been established *in Politia* (i.e., the synod).

Thus, Brenz said, the state church has two forms of excommunication at its disposal: public and private. Private excommunication (i.e., the minor ban) is simply the private admonition of the pastor to the sinner that the latter not commune until he has repented. Public excommunication, on the other hand, is that magisterial penalty (*ea Magistratus poena*) whereby criminals are expelled from society, thrown into jail, and put on bread and water. It is, in other words, the magistrate's authority over public morals. This public excommunication is exercised in the church when anyone legitimately condemned of wrongdoing is expelled from the church by order of the magistrate and banned from all social intercourse or honest employment. Excommunication by order of the magistrate is no less valid than excommunication imposed by the church: it is not simply the judgment of man but the judgment of God, binding in heaven as well as on earth.

The order of excommunication which Brenz had successfully defended in 1554 had to face one more challenge. In 1557, during discussions among the evangelical estates concerning unity on various matters, including ecclesiastical discipline, Duke Christopher was favourably impressed by Count Palatine Wolfgang of Zweibrücken's Disciplinary Ordinance (June 1557), which provided for a congregational discipline substantially like that which Lyser and Andreä had proposed.[75] The duke's senior advisers, however, strongly opposed the introduction of the Zweibrücken order into Württemberg. One group of advisers, Brenz among them, submitted a memorandum[76] pointing out that the established system of ecclesiastical censure was working adequately. The superintendents were doing their job, and the offenders reported to the synod were being punished. What was needed, the councillors implied, was more cooperation from the secular officials in administering moral discipline. At this point Brenz and his fellow councillors still had reason to hope that the elaborate system of visitations (see below) would produce the desired cooperation between pastors and local officials.

In another memorandum, an anonymous adviser (probably a Tübingen jurist) struck a more ominous note.[77] He argued that the duke's courtiers and officials would never submit themselves to censure by a local, congregational body, and that the common people, too, might well rebel rather than submit to such a discipline. Thus, if the duke wished to reign in peace and be served by loyal officials, he had best stick to the established order of ecclesiastical censure.

This negative reaction to his proposal made Christopher angry. He complained that, at the local level, the established order placed too much reliance on fines and jail sentences, with the result that his secular officials were being burdened with 'spiritual matters.' It was not that he wanted his officials relieved of their duty to punish moral offences: quite the contrary. But he did believe that 'a more *Ecclesiastica Censura*' (i.e., excommunication by a congregational disciplinary authority) would have a strongly deterrent effect on the public immorality that he felt obligated to eliminate.[78] Still, he had no answers to the objections raised by his advisers, so he had to yield to their judgment.

Brenz's centralized *excommunicatio in politia* may well have been more orderly, peaceful, moderate, just, and altogether more politic than the decentralized *censura ecclesiastica* that Duke Christopher and others had hoped for. But, whether imposed from above or by a committee of one's friends and neighbours, excommunication was still excommunication, difficult to impose on a hostile and resentful public. In Brenz's scheme, the enforcement of the sentences handed down by the synod rested primarily with the local secular officials, who were, as we have already seen, no more diligent in the performance of that duty than they were in enforcing the provisions of the Territorial Ordinance.

Duke Christopher did his best to correct this. Indeed, he attempted, by means of visitation piled on top of visitation, to achieve the worthy but hopelessly utopian goal of a godly society in which immorality would not simply be punished, but largely eradicated.[79] In February 1557, annoyed by the failure of the ecclesiastical and political visitations to eliminate deficiencies in the administration and enforcement of his secular and ecclesiastical legislation, Christopher established a special, supplementary territorial visitation (*Landvisitation* or *Landinspektion*), one of the principal aims of which was 'to prevent and punish immorality.'[80] Two years later, the territorial visitation was elevated to the status of permanent institution by being included in the Great Church Order,[81] though it was stipulated that this particular visitation was to be employed only to deal with 'failures, crimes, or deficiencies' too serious to be dealt with by other means. In such cases, two commissions of three visitors each (one noble, one theologian, and one secular councillor) were to inquire into the observance of the duke's ecclesiastical and secular ordinances, punish offences, and eliminate abuses. In the process they were to make special efforts to produce harmony and cooperation between clergymen and secular officials 'in the extirpation of evil and vice.' The visitors were also to instruct the local officials that whoever, on the same day that he took communion, got drunk or participated in licentious dancing or other wantonness, was to be put in the local madhouse (*Narrenheüsslin*) on bread and water for fourteen days (eight days for women).

In the absence of any record of its activities, it is impossible to say to what extent the territorial visitation established itself in actual practice.[82] One suspects that it faded as quickly as the political visitation.[83] At any rate, it did not lead to the extirpation of evil and vice. In August 1562 there was in Württemberg a terrible storm which destroyed crops and led to famine. Christopher saw in this God's punishment for the disorderly lives of so many of his subjects, and especially for the spreading vices of gluttony and overdrinking. So he established yet another special visitation, the so-called territorial visitation or general visitation of 1562–4. Conducted by several commissions equipped with extraordinary powers of correction and punishment, this visitation consisted of an inordinately detailed inquiry into every aspect of ecclesiastical and political administration with the aim of rooting out evil and imperfection of every sort. The duke's senior advisers, including Brenz, tried to persuade him that this was more than God expected or flesh could bear, and that he was only undermining the authority of his officials and arousing discontent among his subjects. This advice only angered Christopher, who persisted with the visitation until the plague of 1564 and projects undertaken in the following years pushed it into the background.[84]

Not even all this heroic effort could produce adequate execution of the Order of Ecclesiastical Censure. In 1565 Brenz complained that the sentences imposed by the synod were never enforced. As a consequence, the sentenced persons persisted in their evil lives and were reported to the synod time after time for the same offence. Thus the synod was so overburdened with matters of moral discipline that it could scarcely get to its other business and was becoming 'a pointless spectacle.' In these circumstances even Brenz was prepared to contemplate a degree of decentralization. He recommended to the duke that responsibility for the initial determination of who should be excommunicated be transferred from the synod to a local committee composed of the pastor, superintendent, subprefect, and several judges, with the proviso that this determination would have to be confirmed by the duke on the advice of the consistory before it became operative.[85] While this proposal would have lightened the synod's burdens, it did not touch the central problem, that of enforcement. Moreover, Duke Christopher, acting on the advice of his secular advisers, rejected Brenz's proposal on the ground that there would never be any rest from the litigation over appeals from the hasty and ill-considered judgments which such a local committee would surely render.[86]

This was the sorry end of Brenz's long struggle to achieve a workable order or excommunication. It was at last clear that no such thing was possible in the territorial state church, not even with the wholehearted help of an exemplary Christian prince. There was nothing to do but leave things as they stood and hope that, by the grace of God, better times would come.

Few modern readers will shed any tears over this defeat for ecclesiastical inquisition and princely absolutism. Which is fair enough. But it should be remembered that, by the criteria according to which Brenz had to judge his own work, the defeat was well-nigh tragic. It meant that the church to which he had devoted over four decades of creative labour could not adequately perform one of its elementary tasks: it could preach the true word and administer the true sacraments, but it could not discipline its own members as Jesus and St Paul had commanded. The church could not persuade, the state could not force, an unwilling community to accept that discipline. The Word was evidently not as powerful, the Sword not as potent, and the Reformation not as hard a blow to Satan's dominion, as Brenz and his fellow reformers had supposed in the heady days of their youth.

6

Resistance and Toleration

The organized territorial churches which began to emerge from the reform movement in the mid-1520s had two chief adversaries. One, armed Catholicism, was external; the other, Anabaptism, was internal. The efforts of Protestant governments to deal with these threats to their newly established ecclesiastical order raised serious questions. For example, what could the Protestant estates legitimately do if the emperor, as seemed increasingly likely, made war on them because of their religion? Did not the same gospel which denied the right of peasants to take up arms against their overlords, the princes, also forbid princes to do the same against their overlord, the emperor? Again, did secular rulers, whose authority did not extend to the spiritual realm of conscience, have the right to take action against the Anabaptists? And if they did, was it necessary and legitimate indiscriminately to impose the death penalty on them all, as imperial law prescribed?

Both secular rulers and fellow reformers repeatedly asked Brenz for his opinion on these and related questions. His answers, though scarcely unique, were individual and, from 1530/1 on, at variance with those of the Wittenberg reformers. On the issue of resistance to the emperor, Brenz was a 'Franconian conservative,' that is, a spokesman for the ultra-cautious policy which prevailed in Brandenburg-Ansbach and in Nuremberg as well as in some smaller cities such as Schwäbisch Hall. He agreed with the early Luther that the Protestant estates could not take up arms against the emperor, even in defence of their faith against unprovoked attack, and refused to espouse the more positive attitude toward active resistance which Luther and the other Wittenbergers adopted in the autumn of 1530. By so doing, he placed himself outside the mainstream of sixteenth-century Protestant thought on the subject of resistance to authority.

On the issue of the treatment of Anabaptists, Brenz allied himself with those who favoured a more tolerant and humane approach than custom and law allowed. He was not by any means an advocate of toleration in the modern sense of the term. Quite the contrary: his doctrine of the Christian magistracy required that the magistrate take steps to eliminate Anabaptism or any other form of 'false doctrine and worship.' On the other hand, Brenz thought it neither necessary nor proper that these steps should include the indiscriminate use of fire and sword. He agreed with the early Luther that the death penalty was inappropriate and maintained that view even after Luther, under the influence of Melanchthon, reluctantly abandoned it in 1531. In this case it was Brenz who was in the mainstream of Protestant thought, at least in the Holy Roman Empire.

THE RIGHT OF RESISTANCE

During the 1520s, territorial governments friendly to the Reformation increasingly had to deal with the questions posed by the emperor's implacable hostility to it.[1] Thus, in the 'Hall Reformation' of 1527, when Brenz called upon the city council of Schwäbisch Hall to abolish mass throughout its territory, he realized that he was placing the city fathers in a difficult position. If they did as he recommended, they ran the risk of trouble with the emperor; if they did not, they and their subjects faced the wrath of God in this life and the danger of damnation in the next. So in urging the course which would avert the wrath of God, Brenz offered the council an argument which it might use to stay the wrath of the emperor should he demand an explanation for the changes it had made in public worship.[2]

First of all, Brenz began, every imperial city has received from the emperor certain privileges or freedoms which permit it to take whatever action is necessary to preserve peace and good order. Moreover, the popish mass is a detestable form of worship contrary to God's word and to the usage of the churches in the time of the Christian emperors Constantine and Theodosius, for which reason God is aroused to wrath and inflicts destruction and disorder on the offending land. Therefore, the government of Schwäbisch Hall, in order to avert the wrath of God and to preserve peace and order, has felt constrained to establish in the churches attended by its subjects a form of worship in harmony with the word of God and similar to that used in the first Christian churches. Since all the ceremonies hitherto used in the churches were established over a long period of time 'without the mandate or confirmation of His Imperial Majesty,' the council intended no disobedience toward the emperor when it undertook to improve public worship. On the contrary, it deemed its action to be in accordance with the imperial mandate, issued at the recent diet in Nuremberg (1523), ordering the estates to assure that only the pure gospel, according to the approved interpretation of the holy Christian church, be preached in their territories.[3] This pure gospel is being preached in Hall, and the city council only wanted to bring public worship into conformity with it. Furthermore, the imperial mandates also speak of a future council which will reform the order of worship for all Germany,[4] but this intention has not been carried out. Meanwhile, therefore, in order to avoid the scandal of making the gospel appear to be a lie, it has been necessary to establish a suitably reformed church order in the city. Even though the Edict of Worms (1521) could be interpreted as an endorsement of every ordinance and regulation previously used in the churches, everyone knows that the emperor, as a good Christian, undertakes nothing contrary to the word of God. Furthermore, the imperial estates confirmed the Edict of Worms at the Diet of Nuremberg (1524) only after protesting that they did so merely to avoid a display of disobedience in this matter.[5] Finally, should the emperor himself undertake to establish ceremonies that are 'more Christian and godly,' he will find the government of Hall and its subjects obedient children of God and subjects of the emperor.

Protesting loyalty to the emperor while denying his will was a hoary tradition of German political life, and the self-serving interpretation of the deliberately ambiguous imperial recesses of the early 1520s was the standard practice of Protestant territorial governments. Moreover, the territorialism implicit in Brenz's argument would eventually provide the basis for religious peace in the Empire. But meanwhile, what if the emperor rejected the arguments of the Protestant estates and attempted to force the restoration of Catholicism in their lands?

Brenz's earliest known discussion of this issue was part of a memorandum which he wrote in the autumn of 1527 in response to an inquiry from the Schwäbisch Hall delegation at a congress of cities in Nuremberg.[6] The question was whether the Swabian League had the authority to uphold the ecclesiastical as well as the temporal jurisdiction of its members who were prince-bishops. In other words: did the League have the right to force the imperial cities back into subjection to episcopal jurisdiction? In his response Brenz noted 1 / that there is no episcopal or other human jurisdiction over the word of God, the sacraments, or men's souls; 2 / that the prince-bishops were members of the League as princes, not as bishops; and 3 / that the League was a purely secular union to maintain the temporal rights and privileges of its members. Thus it had no authority whatever in religious matters, and any attempt by the League, acting on its own, to usurp such authority could legitimately be resisted, by force if necessary. But what if the League, acting on special orders from the emperor, should attempt to force the imperial cities back into submission to episcopal jurisdiction? In this case the cities would have to suffer injustice without resisting, for the gospel does not permit the cities to resist their sovereign, the emperor, for the sake of the gospel. They can appeal for justice; they must continue to confess the true faith and must refrain from active participation in its suppression; but aside from that their only option is to suffer. In the years which followed, Brenz would adhere steadfastly to this position and elaborate upon it.

In 1529 the Protestant estates, convinced by the Diet at Speyer and its aftermath that the emperor was indeed planning to use force against them soon, undertook intensive efforts to establish a defensive alliance. These efforts were impeded by divisions in the Protestant ranks over two issues. One was the long-standing disagreement over the Lord's Supper between the Zwinglians and the Lutherans. The other was the disagreement, which only now became apparent, among the Lutherans themselves over the right of armed resistance to the emperor. In Hessen the landgrave and his advisers had long since persuaded themselves that the imperial estates had the constitutional right to resist an emperor who violated their rights.[7] In Saxony opinion was for a time divided. The elector's jurists argued that the law upheld the right of anyone unjustly attacked to defend himself.[8] Luther, however, argued that the Bible forbade anyone to resist the emperor, the highest political authority in the Empire, by force.[9] Not until the autumn of 1530 were the Saxon theologians and the elector persuaded of the validity of the jurists' arguments (see below). Meanwhile the governments of Nuremberg and Brandenburg-Ansbach, which Hessen and Saxony wanted as allies, had adopted the stand originally taken by Luther, a position from which they steadfastly refused to be budged by the arguments found persuasive in Hessen and Saxony. Through his close contacts with both the Nurembergers and the Ansbachers, Brenz became involved in the debate.

It was Lazarus Spengler who, in November 1529, in a memorandum for the Nuremberg city council, penned the classic statement of the 'Franconian' position on resistance to the emperor.[10] He began by formulating with great care the question at issue: whether God's word (not reason or human law) permitted the city council of Nuremberg (or any other imperial estate) forcibly to resist any effort by the emperor (not some lesser authority) to reimpose Catholicism by force of arms. Spengler readily conceded that if the emperor made such an effort he would thereby exceed his authority and become a tyrant. Spengler also conceded that the Protestant estates were duty-bound to offer passive resistance to such tyranny: to cooperate in it would be to deny the gospel. At the same time, however, he argued forcefully and at length that the Bible absolutely forbids any Christian territorial ruler to resist with force any attack upon him by the emperor, no matter how unjust it may be. The crux of his argument was that vis-à-vis the emperor an imperial estate does not have the status of government. In relations with other estates or with its subjects, an estate does have such status and can in good conscience repel force with force. But the relationship of imperial estate to emperor is that of subject to lord. In such a relationship a Christian ruler must, like any private person, obey legitimate authority and suffer injustice without seeking revenge. The proper way to deal with a tyrannical emperor is to dethrone him and elect another. If that is not possible, and if petitions do no good, then one must simply suffer passively if one wants to remain a Christian. In any case, as the history of the church from earliest times shows, mere force cannot deprive a Christian of the gospel or salvation.

In Nuremberg the city council accepted Spengler's arguments. Then Spengler set out to win over Margrave George, who at this stage still inclined toward the view that armed resistance in defence of the gospel was permissible. Spengler sent a copy of his memorandum to Georg Vogler, the Ansbach chancellor, who also opposed resistance. Vogler, in behalf of the margrave, sent a copy to Brenz, requesting his opinion.[11] In his reply (27 November 1529),[12] Brenz called Spengler's memorandum 'most godly and Christian,' singling out for special emphasis the argument that the imperial estates were subjects of the emperor and thus owed him the obedience which the Bible commands all Christians to render to authority. The estates, he said, have no more right to take up arms against the emperor than their subjects had to rebel against them in the Peasants' War. Princes or cities that resist the emperor by force are rebels, not Christians, and can expect no help from God. Nor can they expect much help from man, either. For the great majority in any city or principality are conventional Christians, who, if the test came, would be unwilling to risk life or property for the sake of the gospel. On the other hand, princes and cities who do right, confess Christ, and suffer injustice for it may call on God for help.

The combined efforts of Spengler, Brenz, and Vogler were enough to persuade Margrave George that it would be wrong to resist the emperor by force of arms.[13] When Philip of Hessen found out about this, he wrote a long letter to the margrave (21 December 1529),[14] attempting to win him back to the cause of active resistance. Philip readily conceded that Scripture forbade 'ordinary individuals or mere subjects' to resist authority by force. But he insisted that this ban did not apply in the case of Protestant princes who defended the adherents of the true faith against unjust attack by the emperor. The magistrates whom Paul and the other apostles forbade to resist the Roman government were 'mere governors,' whom Rome could appoint and dismiss at will, to whom secular affairs alone had been entrusted, and who thus had no subjects for whose eternal salvation they were responsible. The German princes, by contrast, are hereditary rulers whom the emperor may not dismiss, and it is their God-given duty not only to provide for their subjects' temporal welfare but also to promote the glory of God and the salvation of their subjects' souls as well. Besides, relations between emperor and princes are governed by the terms of a contract (i.e., the electoral capitulation) which both sides have sworn to uphold. The princes' duty to obey the emperor ceases when he violates the contract by exceeding his authority. In secular matters he has no authority to make or alter laws without the consent of the estates; much less does he have authority to use force in divine matters, and that without a hearing. Thus if the emperor should attempt to suppress the gospel and force the restoration of popery, the princes should sacrifice 'love, life, honour, goods, land, and people' in order to stop him. To do less would be to become a party to tyranny and the eternal destruction of innumerable souls. An emperor who makes war on the gospel and its adherents is at least as much an enemy of God as a Turk. If it is permissible to fight against the Turks, why should it not be permissible to fight against 'this more than Turkish tyranny'?

At the end of December 1529 the margrave communicated the landgrave's views, without revealing the identity of their author, to both Spengler and Brenz, and asked for their comments. Both emphatically rejected the contention that the biblical ban on resistance to authority did not apply to princes who defended the true church against armed attack by the emperor.[15] Brenz's memorandum, apparently dashed off in great haste in the first days of the new year, was unusually long-winded and repetitious.[16] Its essential content was as follows.

Brenz readily conceded that the Protestant estates must not consent to the suppression of the gospel or become a party to such suppression but must, as Christian governments, resist it by every legitimate means and at the risk of 'body, life, land, and people.' But at the same time, he said, several important considerations must be borne in mind. First, the Empire and its constitution are, like all legitimate secular governments, an ordinance of God. Therefore, whoever is legitimately elected emperor remains the supreme governing authority in the Empire until God removes him or the electors depose him. The Protestant estates, on the other hand, are the emperor's subjects: all their rights and privileges come from him, and their titles[17] bespeak their subjection to him.

Second, God has not given to subjects the right to use the sword against their government in defence of the gospel, which does not require human protection in any case (Matt. 26:53). Indeed, when Peter tried to defend Jesus at the time of his arrest, Jesus told him to put his sword away, 'for all they that take the sword shall perish with the sword' (Matt. 26:52). To take up arms against the emperor in defence of the gospel is itself a violation of the gospel: it is to deny with the hand what one confesses with the mouth. A subject may take up arms against the emperor only if he (the subject) receives a special call from God, as was the case when Jehu slew King Joram (2 Kings 9), or if the emperor is legally deposed. In the case of the present emperor, deposition is impossible because the majority of the estates are content with him and even support his ungodly, tyrannical persecution of the gospel. And if the Protestant estates have received a special, divine commission to remove him, they must provide clear, convincing proof, including miracles. Otherwise they must not resist him by force, just as David refused to lay hands on Saul, even though Saul persecuted the word of God (1 Sam. 24 and 26).

Third, to suffer the unjust persecution of the gospel without resorting to illegitimate means of resistance is not by any means to approve of that persecution or to become a party to it. One can still resist by publicly confessing one's faith, protesting the persecution, petitioning for redress, refusing to carry out orders contrary to the word of God, and so on. Such things are in part commanded by God, in part permitted. But God has forbidden the use of force against legitimate government in defence of his word. If the peaceful, Christian means of resistance do not work, then the only option available to a Christian ruler is to suffer, even if 'body, life, land, and people' are lost as a result.

Brenz was also willing to concede that there was between the emperor and the estates a sworn contract which obliged the emperor to leave the estates unmolested in the enjoyment of their rights and privileges. But he would not admit that the contract entailed the right of the estates to resist tyranny by force. For all governments, he said, have a contractual relationship with their subjects, and are bound by it to render them justice. If it were true that the estates might forcibly resist an emperor who violates their rights, then every prince's subjects might also forcibly resist him under similar circumstances, such as the imposition of unjust taxation. 'What an extraordinary state of uproar we would have in the Empire' in that case! However, the truth of the matter is quite different. In a contract between equals, violation of it by one party releases the other party from it. But in the relationship between a government and its subjects, the contract is supplemented by God's command forbidding subjects to resist even tyrannical government by force. Thus the Protestant estates may not in good conscience take up arms against the emperor 'even if he be a Turk twice over.'

In 1530 the intransigent attitude and threatening demeanour of the emperor and the Catholic estates at the Diet of Augsburg (June-November) made it seem more likely than ever that the emperor would make war on the Protestant estates. Nevertheless, Brenz held unflinchingly to his opposition to armed resistance. While the diet was still in session, Brenz, who was in attendance as theological adviser to Margrave George, wrote a brief memorandum on what a Christian prince should do if the diet adopted a recess 'contrary to the gospel.'[18] First, he should join with the other evangelical estates in a protest against the recess and in an appeal to a free council. Second, if the emperor should ignore all appeals and attempt by means of war to force acceptance of the recess, a Christian prince must not resist his legitimate sovereign by force but rather must suffer as befits a Christian. Third, the prince must not flee his lands but must remain both to confess the true faith and to live it by refusing either to resist or to assist the emperor in his attempt to restore the old religion. Fourth, the prince should maintain the dismissed pastors and preachers in his land 'until God once again grants his mercy, which he will not withhold for long.' Fifth, should other princes and lords resist the emperor by force, a Christian prince must refuse any call from the emperor for military aid against them. To render such aid would be to become his accomplice in evil. Princes who follow these rules of Christian conduct may indeed suffer misfortune in the short run, but in so doing they will win God's favour and in the long run they will fare better in this world than those who take up arms against authority in defiance of God's word (biblical and historical examples are given).

In Saxony, meanwhile, Luther and the other Wittenberg theologians were under heavy pressure to abandon their opposition to resistance by force. The pressure came from Philip of Hessen, who argued his case in a letter to Luther (21 October 1530),[19] and from the Saxon jurists, who confronted the theologians at a three-day conference in Torgau (26–8 October).[20] The jurists shared the landgrave's general point of view but, in a memorandum witten shortly before the Torgau conference, they argued their case in terms of legal procedure rather than those of constitutional law. Citing both canon and secular law, they argued that in order to escape irreparable loss or injury, one may forcibly resist a judge whose sentence is under appeal; who proceeds contrary to law or justice, whether an appeal has been lodged or not; or whose judgment is notoriously unjust. The Protestant estates, so the argument went, have appealed to a general council. Thus whatever jurisdiction the emperor ordinarily has in the matters in dispute is suspended pending the outcome of that appeal. Moreover, to obey the emperor's edicts and mandates contrary to the word of God would cause irreparable injury. And in matters of faith, one must obey God rather than man. Besides, the emperor has no jurisdiction whatever in matters of faith. He may summon a council if the pope is negligent, and he may carry out the decisions of a council once they have been adopted. But with respect to the determination of matters of faith, he is just an ordinary private person, subject to the decisions of the council like everyone else. If, therefore, it is legitimate to resist a judge who has jurisdiction over the matter in question but proceeds unjustly, or whose decision has been appealed, it is all the more legitimate to resist a judge who does not have such jurisdiction. Moreover, the injustice of the emperor and his advisers is more than notorious, for in matters of faith they are manifestly our enemies, antagonists, and rivals.[21]

In their response Luther and his colleagues admitted that they had finally been persuaded that the secular law did indeed permit resistance to the emperor in the circumstances described by the jurists. On the principle that the gospel does not nullify the secular law, and in the light of their teaching that the law must be obeyed, they now dropped their previous objections to armed resistance in the event that the emperor made war on the Protestants for the purpose of suppressing the gospel.[22]

This change of mind in Saxony opened the way for the formation of a Protestant defensive alliance in Schmalkalden two months later. The recess issued by the estates attending the meeting in Schmalkalden expressed the hope that Brandenburg-Ansbach and Nuremberg, whose agents had not had the authority to make any commitment on behalf of their governments, would soon join the alliance.[23] It was against this background, in February 1531, that the Ansbach theologians, with Brenz in attendance, took up the question of resistance to the emperor.[24] Under Brenz's leadership they turned out the memorandum which was to be his last statement on the question of resistance until the Interim.[25] It consisted largely of a catalogue of objections to the arguments used by the participants in the Torgau conference.[26]

First of all, they said, the emperor is no ordinary judge, subject to higher authority in the exercise of his office, but rather the supreme secular magistrate, from whom all other governments in the Empire have their authority. Thus, while it may well be that the law permits armed resistance to an ordinary judge, it is by no means clear that it permits such resistance to the highest magistrate, the emperor. For one of the commentaries on the law says that we ought to endure unjust violence committed by legitimate authority.[27] Furthermore, while it may be the case that the jurisdiction of an ordinary judge against whom one has appealed is suspended, it does not follow that the jurisdiction of the emperor, the highest in the Empire, is suspended by an appeal to a council. For the emperor is the supreme magistrate in the administration of the secular sword. The council, on the other hand, has only the spiritual sword, the word of God. Thus it can hardly hear appeals against the emperor's use of the other sword. Even if such an appeal were possible and did suspend the emperor's jurisdiction over the matter in dispute, it would still be wrong to resist his unjust use of force by force. For it is never proper to use the sword against the sovereign from whom flows the authority to bear the sword.

Second, one is dealing here not simply with the person of the emperor himself but with 'the entire imperial majesty,' that is, the emperor, the electors, the princes and estates of the Empire, who together constitute the *senatus et summus magistratus Romani imperii*. In this group the Protestant estates are a minority. It is only in their eyes that the emperor's injustice is notorious. To the Catholic majority, on the other hand, the emperor's actions against the Protestants, whom they regard as rebels and despoilers of monasteries and churches, are notoriously just. The law, to be sure, provides that court assessors ought to resist the unjust actions of a judge. But if the majority of the assessors support the judge, should the minority who judge justly and wisely arouse the populace to rebellion against the majority? The gospel says of Joseph of Arimathea, who was a councillor in Jerusalem, that he did not consent to the actions of his fellow councillors against Jesus. It does not say, however, that he aroused the populace against the other councillors on account of their unjust actions (Lk. 23:50–3).

Third, armed resistance to the emperor assuredly involves a *mutatio imperii*. Therefore, since the aim of the imperial law is surely to maintain the Empire in its present condition, one must conclude that that law permits no armed resistance to the emperor. That the papal law allows such resistance is no surprise, for it 'despises government presumptuously and is not afraid to speak evil of dignities' (2 Pet. 2:10). But even if the civil law does permit armed resistance in certain cases, the emperor, who is *viva et animata lex*, may forbid such resistance in those cases or in any others as he sees fit. And it is clear that in the event of war with the Protestant estates, the present emperor would, with the support of the majority of the estates, do just that. Anyone who nevertheless took up arms against him would thereby violate God's ban on resistance to legitimate authority and fall under Christ's dictum that those who take up the sword shall perish by the sword (Matt. 26:52).

Fourth, even if it were established beyond doubt that the civil law permits resistance to the emperor, and that the emperor may not rescind the right to do so, the fact remains that Scripture forbids any Christian to resist legitimate authority by force. Thus it is no good for the Saxon theologians to argue that the secular law must be allowed to run its course. For human law allows many things which are forbidden to Christians by God's law (e.g., divorce on grounds other than adultery). But where God's law and human law are in conflict, the Christian must obey God rather than man.

At this point Brenz and his colleagues turned their attention to an argument that had not been used at the Torgau conference. They had before them an anonymous memorandum in which the author, apparently a theologian, contended that the divine law banning armed resistance to authority ought to give way to the higher law of Christian love, which obligated Christian rulers to defend their subjects and fellow Christians from the unchristian violence of the emperor.[28] Left unanswered, this argument would have undermined Brenz's case against armed resistance to the emperor, not by refuting it but by rendering it irrelevant in the light of the highest principle of Christian morality. Thus challenged, Brenz and the Ansbachers had recourse to arguments which, strictly speaking, condemned *all* armed resistance to attack on grounds of religion but were clearly intended only to shore up the case against resistance to the emperor.

The current situation, they insisted, is such that Christian love demands the suffering of persecution far more than it does resistance to it. For most of the subjects of the Protestant estates are still godless, despising the gospel, or are at least inconstant under persecution. The minority who are true Christians, constant in time of trial, should, out of Christian love, prefer to die themselves rather than subject the greater part of the population to the horrors of war against their will. Such a war would not only bring the 'misery, conflagration, rapine, licentiousness, destruction of land and people, killing,' and all the other evils which go with any war, but would also cause the gospel to be perceived as seditious and destructive. If, on the other hand, the Protestants offered no resistance, war would be avoided, persecution would in all likelihood affect only a few persons, and God would soon send an appropriate means of deliverance. Furthermore, as every true Christian knows, the passive suffering of unjust persecution would not bring irreparable harm to the Christian churches, for the church has always flourished in times of persecution, as Scripture testifies of the Israelites (Ex. 1:12) and as Tertullian wrote of the early Christians (Apol. 50.13).[29]

Brenz and the Ansbachers summed up their case against armed resistance as follows: since the right forcibly to resist the emperor is not sufficiently established in secular law; since such resistance is contrary to God's law in any case; and since Christian love will not permit resistance in the present circumstances; no Christian can in good conscience take up arms against the emperor in the cause of the gospel. Then they concluded with a brief resumé of 'the earlier memoranda' which Brenz had written on the subject of resistance. In particular they emphasized that the gospel does not require human protection, and that the Christian princes, as subjects of the emperor, were bound by the biblical injunctions against armed resistance to authority.[30]

The memoranda of 1530/1 succeeded in keeping Margrave George in the company of those who thought it unchristian to take up arms against the emperor. Although George cooperated closely with members of the Schmalkaldic League in non-military measures in defence of the Reformation, he never did join the League itself.[31]

The arguments which Brenz used in the memoranda summarized above only partly reveal the motives for his opposition to armed resistance to the emperor. So the task of explaining that opposition remains.

Brenz's attitude toward the Empire was one of veneration, an attitude nourished by both religion and politics. In the first place, he regarded all government as an ordinance of God, as one of the instruments – the others being nature and the external word – through which God rules the world. To oppose God's ordinance was, he thought, to behave satanically.[32] This applied in special measure to the Holy Roman Empire, which Brenz identified with the Roman Empire, the fourth and last of the monarchies foretold by the prophet Daniel (chap. 7), and the one destined to remain as an ordinance of God till the Day of Judgment. Thus, even if the emperor were a heathen twice over, every God-fearing Christian would owe him obedience in all things under his authority.[33]

In the second place, Brenz viewed the Empire and the question of resistance to the emperor with the eyes of a conservative townsman.[34] The argument in favour of armed resistance, in both its Hessian and Saxon forms, reflected the political interests and constitutional theories of the princely courts which had produced it. But the imperial cities had a set of interests and a view of the imperial constitution which made it extremely difficult for most of them to embrace the cause of armed resistance to the emperor under the leadership of the princes.

The German princes had just spent more than two centuries establishing their *Landeshoheit* and their predominance in the Empire at the expense of (among others) the emperor. In 1519 they had for the first time imposed upon the emperor an electoral capitulation which required him to acknowledge and uphold their accumulated rights and liberties. Implicit in this process of constitutional development, as certain of the Protestant princes and their lawyers interpreted it, was the idea that the imperial estates, or at least the princes, were not mere subjects of an absolute emperor but independent co-sovereigns with rights that could be defended, by force if necessary, against infringement by the emperor. The successful armed defence of these rights could, of course, become the occasion for the further consolidation of the princes' authority at the expense of the emperor's, a prospect which the princes could contemplate with emotions ranging from equanitmity to enthusiasm. Thus, if they took up arms to defend their subjects in the exercise of the true religion against unlawful armed attack by the emperor, their political and religious interests would be in harmony.

Things were not so simple in the imperial cities. The greatest single threat to their political independence and economic prosperity had been, and remained, the greed and ambition of the very same princes who had so severely reduced the power of the emperor. Thus the cities could not contemplate with equanimity the prospect of a further devolution of power from the emperor to the princes. On the contrary, they needed an Empire and an emperor at least strong enough to protect them from the aggressive designs of their princely neighbours. Recent emperors had usually been unreliable allies, but Charles V, at the outset of his reign, had pointedly (and effectively) sided with the cities in a number of cases where princely and urban interests clashed. The cities entertained high hopes that this promising collaboration would continue. Consequently, urban magistrates had compelling reasons for carefully cultivating good relations with the emperor; for clinging to the view that the imperial estates, princes included, were subjects of the emperor, to whom they owed 'proper obedience'; and for holding fast to an imperial status quo which guaranteed their continued freedom and well-being.

Unfortunately, the emperor's hostility to the Reformation injected an unwelcome element of tension between the religious and the political interests of a majority of the imperial cities. The political ally on whom they were so dependent became their religious adversary, while their potential confessional allies among the princes harboured political ambitions and constitutional views which they could not but fear. This was a dilemma from which there was no easy escape.

For several years (ca. 1526-9) the cities tried to have it both ways, i.e., religious cooperation with the Protestant princes (short of an armed alliance) and at the same time good political relations with the emperor. But from the diets of 1529/30 onwards they were under growing pressure to seek in alliance with the Protestant princes military protection for the Reformation against an increasingly bellicose emperor. Eventually, most of the cities – the most noteworthy exception being Nuremberg – chose alliance with the princes, their theologians and jurists fashioning or borrowing arguments to overcome whatever scruples there were against armed resistance to the emperor. For some cities, Schwäbisch Hall among them, this choice was particularly difficult and came only after years of hesitation and soul-searching.

In addition to the general considerations summarized above, the city fathers in Schwäbisch Hall had their own special reasons for wishing to maintain good relations with the emperor despite their determination to maintain the Reformation at home. They were still involved in the consolidation of their rural territory, a process the successful completion of which required the cooperation of the imperial government. Furthermore, Hall was among those cities which, as members of the Swabian League, had relied most heavily on military alliance with the Habsburg emperors to keep them from falling prey to the ambition of the territorial princes. So anxious was the Hall city council not to offend its precious Habsburg ally that it even refused, despite Brenz's scolding, to join in the Speyer Protestation of 1529 or to sign the Augsburg Confession of the following year.[35] Only after the breakup of the Swabian League did Hall move to join the Schmalkaldic League (see below).

Brenz, offspring of the governing class in one imperial city and leading public servant in another, could scarcely have avoided being influenced by the political and constitutional views which prevailed in his urban environment. Against this background alone, leaving loftier theological motives out of account, it is easy to understand certain of the themes which pervade his memoranda on armed resistance: the distinctly old-fashioned reverence for the Empire and its institutions, the fear of a *mutatio imperii,* and the conviction that the imperial estates were subjects of a sovereign emperor. It was, above all, the conviction that the estates were ordinary private subjects vis-à-vis the emperor which made it impossible for Brenz to sanction armed resistance. For even if human law permitted such resistance (something which Brenz conceded only for the sake of argument), God's law as the reformers understood it clearly did not.

Now, important as all this is, the crucial thing requiring explanation here is not Brenz's view of the constitutional relationship between emperor and estates but rather his obstinate refusal to accept any of the arguments for abandoning or modifying that view. After all, that decidedly non-urban reformer, Martin Luther, had started off believing that the imperial estates were the emperor's subjects and therefore forbidden by Scripture to take up arms against him,[36] but had eventually changed his mind. Moreover, Brenz's reverence for the Empire as an object of divine prophecy does not explain the obstinacy of his opposition to armed resistance, for that reverence, too, was something which he had in common with Luther[37] who, however grudgingly, accepted the legal argument that imperial law itself permitted the estates under certain circumstances to take up arms against a tyrannical emperor. The most plausible explanation for the steadfastness of Brenz's opposition to armed resistance is that his political environment insulated him from the sort of pressure to modify his views that the Saxon jurists exerted on the Wittenberg theologians. The city fathers of Schwäbisch Hall obviously had no interest in bringing such pressure to bear on Brenz; quite the opposite. Neither did Margrave George of Brandenburg-Ansbach, for whom, it will be remembered, Brenz wrote the majority of his memoranda on the topic of armed resistance. Indeed, the margrave had excellent reasons, in addition to native caution and religious scruples, for being extremely wary of the cause of armed resistance to the emperor. His greatest political ambition was to make good his claim to two Silesian principalities, Oppeln and Ratibor, which were fiefs of the Habsburg crown of Bohemia. This made him and his advisers as eager as any city magistrates to avoid all actions which might jeopardize political cooperation with the Habsburgs, and therefore just as receptive to Brenz's arguments against armed resistance.[38] Thus the princely environment as Brenz knew it at first had offered no challenge to the religious or constitutional presuppositions of his position on that issue. The trouble with this explanation is that one cannot know for sure what Brenz would have said or done in the event of such a challenge. It is entirely conceivable that, as on so many other occasions in his career, he would have stuck obstinately to his own personal opinion while yielding in silence to magistrates who rejected it. But in this case it never came to that, and the fact remains that a combination of religious precept, constitutional tradition, and political interest caused him and the magistrates whom he advised to agree on the proposition that the eternal and temporal risks of armed resistance to the emperor far outweighed the risks of non-resistance.

It is an ironic footnote to all this that when Schwäbisch Hall finally joined the Schmalkaldic League, Brenz supplied the arguments which justified its doing so.

The circumstances, briefly, were as follows.[39] During the first few years of the Schmalkaldic League's existence, the city council in Hall pursued the ambivalent policy of maintaining close contacts with the League while refusing to join it for fear of offending the emperor. But with the dissolution of the Swabian League in February 1534, Hall and other non-Schmalkaldic cities were suddenly without the security which only membership in a potent alliance could provide. In the period 1535–7 Hall, in consultation with the other Franconian cities of Nördlingen, Heilbronn, and Dinkelsbühl, debated whether to seek that security by joining the new alliance which some cities, including Nuremberg, had formed with the emperor, or by joining the Schmalkaldic League as Philip of Hessen repeatedly urged them to do. The members of the Hall Council were wary of joining the League because of their scruples about armed resistance to the emperor, and because they feared becoming entangled in the political adventures of some of the League's members. Brenz intervened in the discussion with two memoranda, one in 1536 and the other in 1537,[40] urging that Hall join the League, and using essentially the same arguments both times.

It is true, Brenz said, that the Christian faith and the gospel cannot be upheld or protected by the secular sword and that no alliance should be undertaken with that aim in mind. On the other hand, the city council is obligated to protect its subjects against unjust force, in matters of faith as well as in secular matters. By joining the Schmalkaldic League it can perform this obligation without in any way violating its duty to God or the emperor. The emperor may personally dislike the League and the religious views of its members, but that does not make membership in it an act of disobedience. For one thing, the emperor does not have unilateral authority to decide whose understanding of God's word is the true one. For another, the terms of the League treaty contain nothing contrary to the obedience owed God or the emperor.[41] In fact, the real purpose of the League is to help the emperor maintain peace in the German Nation, specifically the Religious Peace of Nuremberg (1532), proclaimed by the emperor himself and intended to preserve the peace of the Empire 'against the malicious designs of the papists.' (The Peace, also known as the Nuremberg Standstill, promised that all proceedings against the Protestants at the *Reichskammergericht* would be suspended, and that no estate of the Empire would make war on another over matters of faith and religion.)[42] So membership in the League is 'more an act of obedience than of disobedience' toward the emperor. And any armed resistance by the League to an attack on one or more of its members contrary to the terms of the Nuremberg Peace would obviously be legitimate self-defence, sanctioned by both God's word and natural law. Should it ever come to pass that the League did engage in unjust disobedience toward the emperor, the League treaty would automatically become null and void and the city council would be absolved from all obligations under it.

Joining the Schmalkaldic League, Brenz continued, is not only 'a godly undertaking' but also a most necessary one from the political point of view. If the enemies of the gospel did not fear the Elector of Saxony and the Landgrave of Hessen, they would make short work of Hall and other Protestant cities. The bishop and his officials would be emboldened to institute proceedings before the *Reichskammergericht*, with its papist judges, to recover lost property or jurisdiction. And some robber baron (*schnaphan*) would soon make the loss of some trivial ecclesiastical endowment the excuse to start a feud with the city. As a consequence, the city council would never be able to deal effectively with the rural pastors and impose religious uniformity on the rural parishes. To a certain extent Hall already enjoys the protection afforded by the papists' fear of the might of the League, but the full protection of the League can only come with membership in it. To be sure, not all members of the League are desirable allies. Some, for example, would like to use it for purposes inconsistent with its strictly defensive aim of resistance to attack on grounds of religion. But there are safeguards against this in the League constitution. And the danger arising out of the shortcomings of some League members is nothing compared to the danger of facing the fury of the papists alone.

Thus did Brenz fashion for himself the rather fanciful picture of a Schmalkaldic League which had no need and no intention to engage in armed resistance to the emperor. The emperor himself had proclaimed a religious peace. The League, whose charter contained nothing inimical to the authority of the emperor, was the champion of that peace. The only threat to the peace and to the security of Schwäbisch Hall came, obviously, not from the emperor but from malevolent papists among the imperial estates, armed resistance to whose assaults was permitted by the laws of both God and man. By engaging in such wishful thinking about the League, the Nuremberg Peace, and the intentions of the emperor, Brenz was able to urge the city council to join the League without thereby departing from the position he had taken in his earlier memoranda on armed resistance to the emperor.

Their scruples overcome at last, the city fathers did as Brenz advised. Schwäbisch Hall, along with Heilbronn, was formally admitted to the League in the summer of 1538.[43] Thus secure against bishops and robber barons, the council was able to complete the reformation of its territory and to establish a church order which managed to survive the crises of the Schmalkaldic War and the Interim.[44]

If the surviving sources are an accurate indication, Brenz was silent on the subject of armed resistance to the emperor until 1548, when Duke Christopher, still heir apparent in Württemberg, put to him some questions arising out of the imposition of the Interim there. Among the things Christopher wanted to know were whether the Christian faith or the 'liberty' of the magistrate might be defended against the emperor by force of arms, and whether an inferior magistrate (i.e., a territorial prince) might in good conscience rule over subjects whom his superior (the emperor) deprived of the true worship of God and forced into idolatry.[45] In his reply, the last of his memoranda on armed resistance, Brenz addressed the second question directly, answering the first one largely by implication.[46]

The office of Christian magistrate, he began, has two parts. One is to support the church, so that the true worship of God is preserved and handed on to posterity. The other is to maintain external peace and civic virtue. While it is always preferable that these two parts, which form one office, be kept together, it sometimes happens that the superior magistrate reserves the first part (ecclesiastical governance) to himself and allows the inferior magistrate to retain only the second. Therefore, if the superior magistrate abolishes true worship and establishes idolatry in the jurisdiction of the inferior magistrate (by imposing and enforcing the Interim), the inferior magistrate is obliged, if he is a Christian and if he cannot maintain his control of ecclesiastical administration by ordinary and legitimate means, to bear witness to the true faith by his public confession, to withhold his approval from the emperor's impiety, to bear patiently what he cannot change, and to hope for aid from heaven. He is not, however, obliged to give up the other part of his office, the administration of civic peace and virtue.

The reason for all this, Brenz continued, is that the inferior magistrate, having been deprived of the first part of his office, is no longer a magistrate as far as ecclesiastical administration is concerned but rather a private person. Consequently, his duties are those of a private person, namely: not to resist evil, except by lawful means; to leave vengeance to God; and to support the church, not with the sword but with prayers, exhortations, confession of true doctrine, and other services of that sort. At the same time, however, the inferior magistrate, having been left in possession of the other part of his office, is still magistrate as far as the maintenance of civic peace and virtue are concerned, and he must continue to exercise that authority. His models should be Joseph, Daniel, and others who refused to lay down their external rule even though the subjects they governed were idolatrous, and who, meanwhile, helped the church in whatever way they could, bringing many to the knowledge of the true God by their confession of true doctrine and their pious example. If the magistrate were to reliquish the part of his office remaining to him, he would thereby abandon his calling, expose his subjects to even greater dangers, and deprive them of all hope of the restoration of pure doctrine in the church.

Brenz's advice to Duke Christopher was thus no different from that he had given in earlier years to the Hall city council and to Margrave George. Nevertheless, the final paragraphs of the 1548 memorandum demonstrate how deeply the experience of the Interim had affected Brenz and how strongly tempted he was to say yes to armed resistance.[47]

What has been said above, he wrote, about enduring the tyranny of a superior magistrate who abolishes true worship and imposes idolatry, refers to the general rule governing the conduct of ordinary individuals toward authority and to the usual office of the inferior magistrate. It does not refer to those special cases in which certain men of inferior rank are divinely inspired by 'the heroic impulses and extraordinary gifts of the Holy Spirit' to take up arms against the tyranny of their superior in order to restore the glory of the name of God. Such a case was that of Mattathias, who led the Jewish revolt against the paganizing program of Antiochus IV (1 Macc. 2). Another was the revolt of the Armenian Christians against persecution by pagan Rome. Even though such special cases do not constitute a universal rule or establish general precedents, the Holy Spirit can, nevertheless, pour out his gifts whenever and on whomever he pleases. (That is, he could inspire some prince or hero to take up the sword and rescue the true church from the Interim.) But since the human heart is inclined to make the glory of God and the safety of the church the cover for its carnal ambitions, one must always 'try the spirits whether they are of God' (1 John 4:1). In other words, we should adhere to the general rule and to the usual office until we know for certain that the Holy Spirit has called us to something else. Otherwise, someone of inferior rank might rashly undertake something against his superior and turn *zelus pietatis* into *scelus seditionis*.

Thus to the very end Brenz remained a prisoner of his hierarchical conception of political authority. Much as he wanted to see divine justice visited upon the emperor who had driven him into exile and who threatened to overturn all that he and his fellow reformers had accomplished in the previous quarter century, he could not bring himself to advise Duke Christopher or anyone else to take up arms against his sovereign. If God's ban on armed resistance to the emperor was to be set aside, God himself would have to issue the call, not Johannes Brenz or any other human agent.

When Duke Christopher succeeded his father in November 1550, the Interim was still in effect, but Duke Maurice of Saxony had already begun to plan the alliance that would cut short the period of the emperor's uncontested mastery in the Empire. Wooed by both sides, Christopher joined neither. King Ferdinand's plans to exclude him from the succession in Württemberg made Christopher far too dependent on the good offices of Emperor Charles even to contemplate joining Maurice's alliance. On the other hand, Christopher was too conscientious a Lutheran to yield to the considerable pressure put on him to become simply a tool of the emperor's political and religious policies. Encouraged by Brenz, he pursued a policy of friendly neutrality.[48] As it turned out, Duke Maurice's successful campaign against the emperor in the spring of 1552 led to the abrogation of the Interim sooner than anyone had expected and, eventually, to the Peace of Augsburg.

It is not known whether Brenz regarded Maurice of Saxony as an authentic Mattathias, but he had no difficulty in accepting gratefully the fruits of Maurice's victory over the emperor. Because the establishment of religious peace eliminated the danger which the emperor had for so long posed to the Protestant estates, theoretical discussion of the question of resistance to him could cease. Meanwhile, another issue, one that had been on the agenda almost as long as that of resistance to the emperor, was still very much alive, to wit: the appropriate response of Protestant governments to the resistance offered them by religious dissidents, chiefly the Anabaptists. In his approach to this issue, Brenz was just as reluctant to sanction violence as he was in his approach to the issue of resistance to the emperor. At the same time, however, he was far more willing to break with tradition and to quarrel with the law. A 'conservative' on the issue of resistance, he was a 'liberal' on the issue of toleration.

THE ANABAPTISTS

Between July 1528 and February 1531 Brenz produced a series of memoranda on the subject of the treatment of Anabaptists. The first of the series was written in response to a request that originated in Nuremberg.[49]

On 4 January 1528 the imperial government issued a mandate, based on the decree of the emperors Honorius and Theodosius against Donatist rebaptizers, prescribing the death penalty for Anabaptists.[50] A few weeks later the Swabian League called upon its members, which included Nuremberg, to employ the death penalty against Anabaptists who would not abandon their heresy.[51] The motive for these harsh measures was the assumption that Anabaptism was in reality a conspiracy to overthrow the existing order of society and government.[52] From May onward the Nuremberg city council jailed several Anabaptists who subsequently refused to recant despite repeated instruction by the city's preachers. In the previous year an Anabaptist had been put to death, though for sedition rather than for heresy. Now, in the first week of July 1528, the council received conflicting advice from its theologians and jurists on how to proceed. The theologians, who all along had favoured the death penalty for avowed rebels, counselled milder treatment for non-revolutionary Anabaptists: pardon for those who recanted, branding and banishment for the obstinate. The jurists, on the other hand, favoured compliance with the imperial mandate.[53] Meanwhile, some of the theologians had, at their own initiative, sought the support of outsiders. Wenceslaus Linck wrote to Luther, seeking his advice.[54] A similar request appears to have gone out to Brenz, probably from Lazarus Spengler, a strong opponent of the death penalty for Anabaptists and a good friend of Brenz, to whom he was to return for support in later disputes over the treatment of religious dissidents.[55]

Brenz's memorandum, which was completed on 7 July 1528, bore the title 'Whether a Secular Government May, in Conformity with the Laws of God and of Reason, Condemn Anabaptists to Death by Fire or Sword.'[56] The only one of Brenz's memoranda on this subject to be widely circulated in print, it is the work which established his reputation as a relatively tolerant man. Sebastian Castellio included a substantially complete Latin translation of it in his pioneering work on religious toleration, *Concerning Heretics, Whether They are to be Persecuted* (1554).[57] Moreover, Castellio dedicated his book to Duke Christopher of Württemberg, giving as one of his reasons for doing so the following:

Finally, I have dedicated this book to you because the opinion of your doctor Joh[an]n[es] Brenz is included among the others. Immediately after the publication of this work, as I hear, the cruelty of persecution was diminished and not so many were put to death thereafter. Such was the force of the opinion of one man of sound judgment even in times so corrupt. Keep on, Brenz, and advance in this Christian clemency in which you have commenced. You have already staunched much blood by your little book.[58]

This was indeed rare praise for a Protestant theologian. It was also, on the whole, well deserved praise, as we shall see.

In the memorandum, Brenz posed two questions. The first was whether the magistrate may, according to Scripture, 'punish Anabaptists or other heretics with the secular sword.' In his answer, which was divided into three parts, Brenz condemned not only the death penalty but also, by clear implication, any other secular penalties (e.g., banishment) for unbelief per se.

To begin with, he applied the doctrine of the two kingdoms in a manner betraying the influence of the early Luther. There are, Brenz said, two types of offences, spiritual and secular, for which God has ordained two types of sword and punishment. Spiritual offences – unbelief, heresy, misunderstanding of Scripture, and things of that nature – are punished by the word of God. Secular offences – treason, murder, robbery, and whatever else disturbs the common peace – are punished by the secular sword. Heresy always has a certain plausibility and clothes itself in Scripture. The secular sword is powerless against such things. Indeed, unbelief and heresy are strengthened by mere civil persecution. The word of God, on the other hand, quickly puts them to flight and is thus the only appropriate weapon against them. If heresy could be driven out by force, what point would there be in studying Scripture, for the hangman would be the most learned doctor. 'Before the world, heretics and unbelievers may very well live as uprightly as true believers.' As long as they do, the secular sword has no cause to punish them. Their punishment will come in the next world, if they have had no change of heart (Matt. 13:30). In this world one should do no more than impose the ban on them (Tit. 3:10–11). To put a man to death for heresy or unbelief is not simply to deprive him of his bodily life but of his soul as well. For, had the tyranny of secular government not deprived him of the chance, he might with time have turned from unbelief and error to the true faith.[59]

Next Brenz turned to a consideration of Deuteronomy 13:1–10, the section of the Mosaic law prescribing death for false prophets and the favourite text of those who advocated the death penalty for Anabaptists and other heretics. Brenz tried to render the text irrelevant by emphasizing the fundamental difference between Christianity and Judaism. Among the Jews there were physical promises and blessings, a physical land, kingdom, and priesthood. There was also a physical slaughter of enemies. All these things were but signs of the truth to be revealed in Christianity. Just as the physical blessing of the Jews corresponds to the spiritual blessing of Christians, and the physical kingdom to a spiritual kingdom, so also the physical extermination of the Canaanites, Jebusites, and false teachers signifies the spiritual extermination of the enemies of the Christian: sin in the body is to be surpressed by the spirit of God, and false teachers are not to be followed in faith but shunned.[60]

To the objection that, while the physical punishment of heretics might be inappropriate to the spiritual office, it is appropriate to the office of secular government, Brenz first repeated his earlier argument that the function of secular authority is to maintain external peace and that it has no jurisdiction over unbelief or heresy. Then he added the argument that the magistrate who suppresses any faith by the sword establishes an extremely dangerous precedent. He may indeed persecute only false faith, but his successors, having acquired the habit of persecution, may persecute the true faith. This actually happened when certain Roman emperors, habituated to persecution by the treatment of the Arians, themselves turned Arian and began to persecute the orthodox. 'Thus the safest and surest course is that secular government remain in its own sphere and let spiritual sins receive spiritual punishments. For it is much better to tolerate a false faith four or ten times than it is to persecute the true faith only once.'[61]

Finally, Brenz dealt with the contention that Anabaptists are guilty not merely of heresy but also of accompanying views which make them liable to civil punishment. One of these was their teaching that goods should be held in common. One cannot, Brenz insisted, justifiably put them to death on that score. Just as they do not teach that others should be forced to hold goods in common and do not themselves force anyone to do so, so force should not be used against them. Until now the religious orders always practised the community of goods and were thought to be the most perfect Christians because of it. Why then must the poor Anabaptists now be slaughtered for exactly the same teaching? Their error is not the result of evil or malice but of simplicity and ignorance in the understanding of certain passages of Scripture. If a man is immediately to be put to death because he misunderstands one or two passages of Scripture, no one, not even the most saintly doctors, would be safe from the sword. 'Therefore the proper treatment for this misunderstanding [of the Anabaptists] is friendly, Christian instruction and not the secular sword.' If they will not be instructed, then let them be shunned as heathen and publicans, but let the government keep hands off unless some civil offence is added to mere doctrinal error.[62]

If it be objected, Brenz continued, that there might well be an insurrection if the Anabaptists become sufficiently numerous and decide to impose their communistic views by force, then it must once more be asked why we fear from the Anabaptists what we did not fear from the monks. 'Furthermore, if everything out of which sedition might conceivably at some time arise must be suppressed by the sword, then one would have to prohibit rigorously all public drinking and banquets, market-days, and church gatherings. For experience shows that insurrection has been hatched at many a drinking bout, that many a market-day has produced a riot, and that in many a church a conspiracy has been conceived.' There may well be among the Anabaptists some individuals who plot rebellion or other crimes. There is no faith, no class, without its black sheep. Let any secular punishment fall on them, not on the simple and the ignorant.[63]

A further ground for demanding civil penalties against the Anabaptists was their tenet that no Christian can be a magistrate, and their refusal to swear the customary oath of allegiance. This is indeed their teaching, Brenz replied, but if they are to be put to death because of it, then a beginning should be made with the priests and monks, who have been guilty of the same offence. Instead of executing the Anabaptists, one should treat them exactly as one used to treat the religious: if they will not swear the oath, then deprive them of their civic privileges. Anything more than that is tyranny.[64]

The second question which Brenz posed was whether the decree of Honorius and Theodosius, the prime authority to which the advocates of the death penalty appealed, actually demanded that penalty for rebaptism per se. Brenz's answer is a classic example of how an inconvenient but authoritative text was commonly dealt with in medieval and early modern times.

First, Brenz attempted, by means of a strained reading of the text, to show that the decree applied only to the rebaptism of clergymen and, further, only to those caught in the act. Thus, he said, the intent was more to prevent rebaptism by means of intimidation than it was to kill rebaptizers.[65] Then he went on to argue that 'even if this were not the case, the law cannot be applied to rebaptism pure and simple.' For the emperor Theodosius was a most God-fearing man who knew Scripture by heart and whose court resembled a cloister. "We may assume, therefore, that this law contemplated nothing imprudent or ungodly.' But it would have been both imprudent and ungodly to execute someone who erred simply because he erred, when he might still have been instructed, and who in any case ought to have been punished only by the gospel. Therefore, this law must certainly have been established to deal not simply with mere rebaptism but with some associated civil crime which is not mentioned, and which cannot now be determined because the original sources are lost.[66]

In support of this conclusion, Brenz called attention to sections of the imperial law which impose lesser sentences on much more serious crimes. The two emperors Valentinian and Gratian were content to deem a rebaptizing bishop unworthy of his office. Why, then, should the other two emperors have been such tyrants as to put ordinary people to death for mere rebaptism? Again, the imperial law on apostasy prescribes confiscation of goods as the maximum penalty for relapse into Judiasm. Why should the misuse of one sacrament be punished more severly than apostasy from the whole faith? And if everyone who misuses one sacrament is to be put to death, then one would have to burn or decapitate not only all those who commune unworthily at Eastertide, but the pope and bishops as well, since they have forbidden communion in both kinds. Finally, the imperial law punishes the greater heretics with nothing more severe than the loss of 'all imperial freedoms.' Why should a harsher penalty be imposed for mere rebaptism? And if people are to be executed for rebaptism, then one must start with the pope and the priests, who practise rebaptism on infants who have received emergency baptism at home 'from the women.'[67]

In view of all these considerations, Brenz continued, one must assume that so Christian an emperor as Theodosius would never have been so shameless as to impose the death penalty for mere rebaptism. Some associated secular offence must have been the real target of the decree. But if the law was in fact aimed at rebaptism pure and simple, the in it was certainly due to the instigation of 'bloodthirsty bishops,' of whom there were many in the days of Theodosius, and to whom the newly converted emperors paid entirely too much heed. Should we regard as holy a law enacted in such a fashion? Should one not rather pay more heed to what is fitting for a Christian government than to what violent tyranny can accomplish? It befits a Christian magistrate to be less bloodthirsty than a heathen, and to care more for the cure of souls than for vengeance. To instruct with the sword or the hangman poor Anabaptists with a simple-minded misunderstanding of Scripture is no cure at all.[68]

In conclusion, Brenz urged that no insurrection need be feared if the secular sword is properly employed in the protection of the weak and the dispensation of justice to all. Insurrection is caused not by evil men but by sinful rulers, as the story of King David shows (2 Sam. 11 and 15). Therefore, the magistrates should leave the chastisement of the simple Anabaptists to the gospel and concentrate on the maintenance of peace and harmony. Let anyone who disturbs the peace, be he baptizer or rebaptizer, receive the appropriate penalty.[69]

Concerning this memorandum of 1528 Melanchthon later observed that Brenz could afford to be so lenient in his attitude toward the Anabaptists only because he had had no personal experience of their pernicious influence.[70] It is true that there were, as far as we know, no Anabaptists in Schwäbisch Hall until the 1530s.[71] Only in such happy remoteness was it possible for Brenz to picture the Anabaptists as nothing more than simple, misguided individuals and to ignore the question of how one was to deal with obstinate, proselytizing sectarians who threatened the established ecclesiastical order. On one point, however, Brenz does seem to have reasonably well informed. In Nuremberg and elsewhere, the interrogation of large numbers of Anabaptists had revealed that the great majority were not the rebels and revolutionaries that Melanchthon and the imperial mandates assumed them to be. Thus Brenz's refusal to regard them as insurgents deserving the death penalty was based, it would appear, not on inexperience but on accurate (if second-hand) knowledge and fair assessment of the facts.[72]

In the context of what Protestant theologians and governments were saying in 1528, Brenz's opposition to the death penalty was by no means exceptional. The Nuremberg theologians took the same view, though only Wenzeslaus Linck did so for reasons that closely resembled Brenz's.[73] Moreover, the Nuremberg council apparently decided against imposing the death penalty for ordinary Anabaptists before Brenz's memorandum was available for its consideration.[74] The attitude of other city governments was similar: at a meeting of the Swabian League in Augsburg in February and March, the cities had opposed the ultimate penalty for Anabaptists.[75] In 1528 Luther, too, was still writing in opposition to the death penalty except for leaders of insurrection.[76] And even Melanchthon, who had denounced certain Anabaptist doctrines as seditious, still hesitated to recommend execution for those whose only offence was to have been taken in by such doctrines.[77]

The foregoing observations raise a question: if in 1528 there was, at least for the time being, a Protestant consensus against the death penalty, and if Brenz's comments had no influence on the specific situation to which they were addressed, how did his memorandum acquire the historical significance mentioned earlier? For one thing, the memorandum circulated widely in printed form. The first edition appeared in the summer of 1528 despite the efforts of the imperial govenment to prevent its publication. Several other editions in German and Latin, including that of Castellio, followed in the next thirty-four years.[78] Second, the memorandum presented a version of the position of the early Luther far longer and more elaborate than any other, including those from Luther's own pen. Moreover, it remained, as far as one knows, 'the only published judgment of a Protestant theologian which so unequivocally rejected corporal punishment or execution for Anabaptists and, beyond that, launched so fundamental an attack on the applicability of the traditional law which the mandates of Charles V always invoked.'[79] The full significance of this can only be appreciated if one remembers that in 1529 the Protestant estates formally endorsed the imperial decrees against the Anabaptists,[80] and that in 1530/1 the Wittenbergers adopted their harsh stand in favour of the death penalty for Anabaptist preachers and their obstinate followers.[81] In these circumstances Brenz's memorandum not only gave courage and support to all those who, for whatever reason, opposed such fierce punishment for heresy, but also gave pause to many who were tempted to support it.

A few instances of this influence can be documented. For example, in 1530/1 Melanchthon had a difficult time convincing his Saxon colleague, Friedrich Myconius, who had read Brenz, that Anabaptists were indeed seditious and thus liable to the death penalty.[82] In 1531 Sebastian Franck included in his *Chronica* a lengthy summary of Brenz's memorandum, along with an introduction praising him as one who 'almost alone, like a baying hound, has raised his voice against so much spilled blood.'[83] Finally, by means of the above-mentioned inclusion in Castellio's *Concerning Heretics*, the memorandum of 1528 supplied arguments for advocates of toleration clear up to the Enlightenment.[84]

Brenz's next two memoranda on the Anabaptist question were written in March and May 1530. There is strong circumstantial evidence that the March memorandum was written in connection with a disagreement in Nuremberg over the treatment of the Anabaptist preacher Bartholomäus Friedrich. Friedrich, held in custody since 1528, had successfully resisted all the attempts of the preachers to induce him to recant. Early in 1530 he went on a hunger strike in an attempt to force a final disposition of his case. There was no evidence of sedition or other crime, but the council feared that if it simply set him free, he would resume preaching and baptizing in its territory. At the beginning of March the council asked the advice of its theologians and jurists. The majority of both groups recommended either continued incarceration or banishment preceded by flogging. But a minority favoured release without further punishment and without conditions. In these circumstances someone – presumably Lazarus Spengler, who, though he opposed the death penalty, also opposed the toleration of 'idolators, seducers, [and] heretics' – asked Brenz for his opinion.[85] Brenz's memorandum, dated 12 March, had as its title the question which had been put to him: 'Whether a Government Violates Conscience when it Forcibly Banishes False Teachers.'[86]

There is incontrovertible evidence that the May memorandum was written at the request of Lazarus Spengler in reply to the memorandum in which an anonymous Nuremberger argued that governmental action against heretics violated the New Testament distinction between secular and spiritual authority.[87] Brenz's memorandum, dated 8 May, was entitled 'Answer to the Memorandum Which Deals with This Question: Whether a Secular Government May Use the Sword in Matters of Faith.'[88]

Because of their importance for an understanding of Brenz's doctrine of the Christian magistracy, both of the 1530 memoranda for Nuremberg were discussed at some length in chapter three.[89] Here they need to be examined briefly once more because of their importance for an understanding of Brenz's ideas about the treatment of Anabaptists.

From the language of the March memorandum it is clear that Brenz no longer saw himself dealing with simple, misguided souls but with 'godless evil-doers,' 'false, seducing teachers,' 'fanatics' who are 'confused and obdurate in their thinking,' 'obstinately committed to error ... disputatious and unwilling to obey the truth.'[90] It was not to be expected that Brenz, who had been a state-church man from the beginning, and who as early as 1525 had demanded governmental action against false preaching, would recommend a hands-off policy toward such people. On the other hand, in justifying action against them, he attempted to remain true to the doctrine of the two kingdoms as outlined in the memorandum of 1528. Thus he maintained that secular penalties like flogging (which he personally did not favour) and banishment constituted no violation of conscience, not even in the case of unjust persecution of true believers, because such punishments left the individual free to believe as he wished. In the case of just and carefully considered action against false teachers, banishment prevented them from seducing others and left the door open to their return to the truth, but allowed them to persist in error if they wished.[91] Since the death penalty was not being considered as an option, Brenz did not have to argue against it. But it was, by implication, the one governmental measure which he would have labelled a violation of conscience, since it closed the door to a future return to the true faith.[92]

In the May memorandum Brenz had to justify governmental action against Anabaptists (or others) who attempted to establish 'a new sect and preaching office'[93] outside the established church. Once again he tried to do this without abandoning the principles laid down in 1528. As we have seen,[94] his argument turned on the distinction between true or false faith on the one hand and the external works of that faith on the other. Personal faith, he said, is free but public teaching and worship are not, for they are external, worldly things under the authority of the magistrate as guardian of public peace and order. Thus if a few individuals are unhappy with the established church in their community, each individual can believe and even confess for himself whatever he wishes. That is no concern of the secular magistrate. But if those individuals form a group and try to establish a new sect and preaching office without governmental authorization, that is a threat to peace and order and thus very much the concern of the secular magistrate. When he takes action against such things, he by no means usurps God's authority over faith and conscience, since no one's faith is constrained. Once again, as in the March memorandum, Brenz insisted that the government's authority over the public exercise of religion was legitimate even if used by a heretical or infidel government to persecute the true church.

One of the texts that Brenz cited in support of the position he took in the May memorandum was Deuteronomy 13:1–6 (in his own condensed version): 'If there arise among you a prophet or a dreamer, who giveth thee a sign etc., saying, Let us go after other gods and serve them etc., that prophet shall be put to death, and thus shalt thou put the evil away from the midst of thee.' The first thing to note here, said Brenz, is that it is not false faith per se but the preaching of that faith that is proscribed. The text does not say 'he that believes falsely' but rather 'if a prophet says: Let us go after other gods.' The second thing to observe is that the administration and execution of this law have been entrusted to the secular magistrate, for Jewish kings were given a copy of the Mosaic law and charged to govern in accordance with it (Deut. 17:18–20). It is true that the letter of the Mosaic law is no longer binding. But since, as St Paul says (2 Tim. 3:1–6), all Scripture was given for our instruction, it is legitimate to infer from the law on false prophets that a Christian magistrate should employ just and appropriate means to protect his subjects from false preaching and worship. But what if the magistrate should conclude from the law that he has the right to put false teachers to death rather than simply to banish them? That he cannot do, Brenz insisted, for, as St Paul says (Gal. 5:1–6), if the letter of the law is binding in this case, then it is binding in all cases. It is the intent of the law, not the letter, that is essential. The intent of this particular law is the evil and disorder be prevented. It is not necessary to inflict bodily death to do this. Persuasion or, if 'fair words' fail, banishment, will do the job better.[95]

In these two memoranda of 1530 Brenz not only maintained his opposition to the death penalty but also remained true to the principle that personal faith is outside the jurisdiction of secular authority. Admittedly, he was able to maintain that principle only by using arguments with which the modern mind is extremely uncomfortable. The distinction between faith, which is free, and the external works arising from faith, which are not, seems extremely arbitrary and unnatural. And the refusal to see in corporal punishment (short of death) any constraint upon conscience seems at best psychologically naïve. But both arguments were common enough in the sixteenth century. Moreover, as Brenz's willingness to accept the possibly unpleasant implications for true believers shows, such arguments were more than merely self-serving. During the Interim, Brenz himself went into exile without ever complaining that his conscience had been violated.

Not long after completing the memorandum of May 1530, the last to be written for Nuremberg, Brenz wrote the first of two important memoranda for Margrave George of Brandenburg-Ansbach on the treatment of Anabaptists in his territory. Brenz, who frequently acted as the margrave's theological adviser in the period 1529–33,[96] had in fact become involved in the Ansbach government's confrontation with Anabaptism over a year earlier.

In the spring of 1528 it was discovered that Anabaptism had established itself in several communities in Brandenburg-Ansbach. The margrave, who was little inclined to enforce the imperial mandates against Anabaptism, pursued a mild policy. One preacher was found guilty of insurrection and executed, but most of the Anabaptists were prepared to recant and were allowed to remain unmolested in the territory. In May 1529 Brenz participated in the interrogation of the members of a newly discovered Anabaptist congregation in Schalkhausen. This may have been Brenz's first contact with real, live Anabaptists. After failing in an attempt to induce the pastor of the congregation, Johann Hechtlein, to recant, Brenz participated in the margrave's consultation with his secular and theological advisers on the measures to be taken against Hechtlein and his flock. The pastor and one other were to be banished; the rest were given a week to recant and were forbidden to discuss or disseminate their views of baptism and the Lord's Supper. Those who did not observe these provisions were to suffer the harsher punishments sanctioned by the imperial diet at Speyer that year. Since no protocol of the meeting has survived, it is not known whether Brenz approved of the threat to apply the imperial law.[97]

Nearly all the members of the Schalkhausen congregation, including even Hechtlein, were subsequently induced to recant. But the Anabaptist movement in the margraviate continued to spread. In 1530 Marx Maier, an important Anabaptist missionary, together with a group of his followers, was arrested in Creglingen. In June the regents in Ansbach sent reports of the ensuing interrogations to Augsburg, where Margrave George was attending the imperial diet. George requested a memorandum from his theologians, including Brenz, who was attending the diet in George's service.[98] The recommendations in the memorandum,[99] which Brenz wrote,[100] are exactly what one would expect from the author of the three memoranda already discussed.

Brenz first dealt with the case of Maier, who had absorbed Hut's teaching that all unbelievers and secular governments would be destroyed three and one-half years after the Peasants' War. Even though that deadline had passed and Maier had not set a new one, such views were a serious matter, for Hut's eschatology had repeatedly been cited to prove the thesis that Anabaptism was revolutionary.[101] Determined to undermine any possible basis for a death sentence, Brenz found in Maier's testimony various grounds for concluding that he was 'not an instigator but only a disciple and ally of insurrection.' Therefore, 'in order that Marx's soul not be destroyed with his body,' he should be given Christian instruction by preachers. If he recanted, the margrave could forgive all his other offences. But if he would not recant, he could be punished for insurrection, though only as a follower, not as an instigator (i.e., no death penalty). Furthermore, the sentence against him should specify that he was being punished not for heresy but for his civil crimes.

As for the other Creglingen Anabaptists, those who recanted should be reconciled with the church in ceremonies to be conducted in the appropriate local congregation. Those who refused to recant should be jailed and subjected to 'assiduous instruction.' If that failed, they should be released on the condition that they refrain entirely from propagating their views. Unspecified penalties (banishment?) might be imposed on those who failed to keep this undertaking. The reason for recommending this procedure, said Brenz in conclusion, is that 'it is not proper for any Christian government to punish false faith which is adhered to privately and without harm to others. But it may with good conscience ban unauthorized public teaching and preaching, and punish those who disobey that ban, in order that the false faith of one person not cause harm or disadvantage to his neighbours.'

The recommendations in this memorandum were evidently too mild for the margrave, who subsequently ordered the execution of Maier. The city council of Ansbach, however, refused to carry out the sentence on the ground that no charge of insurrection could be proved. As things turned out, he was not executed, for by the end of 1530 not only Maier but most of the other prisoners as well had indicated their willingness to recant.[102]

The second of Brenz's two memoranda for Margrave George was written not as part of proceedings against a particular group of Anabaptists but rather in the attempt to formulate general rules for dealing with them. In December 1530 the Protestant estates meeting in Schmalkalden had called for such an attempt, directing that their 'councillors, jurists, and theologians' were within two months to hold a special meeting to decide upon (among other things) a common Protestant policy on the Anabaptists. On 15 January 1531 Margrave George wrote to Brenz asking him to attend a meeting of the Ansbach theologians on the issues raised in the Schmalkaldic recess. Brenz accepted the invitation and took part in the discussions, which were held on 8 February.[103] The contents of the resulting memorandum, 'On the Diversity of the Anabaptists,'[104] are in some respects strikingly out of line with the position Brenz had taken previously.

Brenz and his colleagues asserted that the Anabaptists were divided into two groups, teachers and followers, and further that the members of both groups were to be classified according to whether they taught or believed 1 / mere errors, 2 / open blasphemy, or 3 / sedition. Observing that judges had hitherto always treated followers more leniently than teachers, Brenz and his colleagues recommended 'moderation' in the treatment of both. Those guilty of teaching or believing mere errors should, they urged, not be punished by the secular sword at all but should rather be instructed out of the word of God. For even though the secular law imposes a penalty on rebaptism, St Augustine has explained that the penalty applies to the violent crimes of the rebaptizers rather than to their doctrinal errors.[105] On the other hand, those who believe or teach open blasphemy (e.g., that Christ was not truly God, or that the devil and all unbelievers will ultimately be saved) may be punished according to secular law. The *jurisconsulti* will know what the prescribed penalties are. Nevertheless, Christian love demands merciful treatment of those who recant: it must be evident that one aims more at the salvation of their souls than the death of their bodies. Finally, in the case of those who teach or believe in insurrection, the secular authorities already know what the law prescribes. Above all, governments should issue edicts against Anabaptist conventicles and punish those who in violation of such edicts summon and hold conventicles.

There is an obvious and pervasive ambivalence in this memorandum. On the one hand, its concessions to the rigours of the imperial law are unprecedented in the writings of Brenz or his Ansbach colleagues.[106] Even though the principle of no secular punishment for mere doctrinal errors is affirmed, the death penalty for blasphemous doctrines is sanctioned. And where banishment had previously been the recommended punishment for obstinate preachers, conventicle leaders may now be executed for sedition. At the same time, however, no opportunity is lost to recommend moderation or mercy, and the harsh penalties of the imperial law are permitted, almost grudgingly, rather than demanded.

All this is explained by the purpose of the memorandum, which was to contribute to the formulation of a common Protestant policy. This imposed constraints from two directions. On the one hand, the imperial mandates could not be ignored without supplying the Catholic estates with new grounds for reproaching the Protestant estates with excessive mildness toward the Anabaptists. On the other hand, one had to maintain the common front with the Saxon theologians and their much harsher views. Indeed, the category of open blasphemy was borrowed from Luther out of deference to the Wittenbergers.[107] Thus the Ansbach memorandum was a compromise in the interest of the common Protestant cause, and its ambivalence was the result of the wish to persist in one's own well-established policy while yet avoiding direct conflict either with the imperial law or with one's confessional allies. The policy on the treatment of Anabaptists in Brandenburg-Ansbach remained unchanged: no death sentences were imposed. Brenz's views, too, remained unchanged, as an examination of his subsequent career will show.[108]

Only in the mid-1540s did Anabaptists, mostly Württembergers on their way to Moravia, turn up in Schwäbisch Hall's territory in sufficient numbers to constitute a problem. In 1545 the council issued a mandate, presumably written by Brenz, against them. Although the mandate appealed in a general way to 'the emperor's command' to justify action against the Anabaptists, it concluded by merely threatening with 'severe punishment' those who received or administered rebaptism or harboured Anabaptists. Neither corporal punishment nor the death penalty was ever used against Anabaptists in Hall.[109]

In contrast to Schwäbisch Hall, where Anabaptism never became a serious problem, the Duchy of Württemberg was a major centre of Anabaptism throughout the sixteenth century and after. During Duke Ulrich's exile, under the Austrian administration, the persecution of Anabaptists in Württemberg was especially severe. Between 1528 and 1534 an undetermined number were executed (thirty-two to forty-five according to the *Hutterite Chronicle*).[110] Duke Ulrich's restoration brought an abrupt change in policy. He was not inclined to tolerate Anabaptists, which the Treaty of Kaaden forbade him to do in any case. But he did put an end to executions on grounds of faith, and other corporal punishments (e.g., torture, branding), though often threatened, were but rarely imposed. In his measures to combat Anabaptism, which culminated in an ordinance of 1536, the emphasis was upon inducing individuals to recant, not only by means of jail sentences but also by means of instruction from the most learned preachers available. Those who would not recant were to be banished. Only in the case of banished persons who secretly returned were harsher penalties threatened.[111]

Ulrich's policy toward the Anabaptists conformed to the recommendations not of his jurists, who favoured the death penalty, but of his theologians who, under the lead of Erhard Schnepf, opposed it with arguments not unlike Brenz's. Although Brenz and Schnepf had worked together on the Church Order of 1536,[112] there is no evidence that they had discussed the Anabaptist problem. Schnepf would of course have known Brenz's memorandum of 1528. But both he and Duke Ulrich were also intimately familiar with current policies and practices in Hessen, which were referred to in the memorandum in which the theologians presented their views to the duke. So Brenz's influence on Württemberg policy at this stage was only one among several. Nevertheless, that policy was so thoroughly in line with his views that under Duke Christopher no fundamental changes had to be introduced.[113]

From the beginning of his reign, the need to combat sectarianism was a constant theme of Christopher's ecclesiastical legislation. The Visitation Ordinance of 1553 instructed the synod to deliberate on appropriate means for doing so.[114] Later, the Church Order of 1559 repeatedly emphasized the duty of superintendents and general superintendents to gather evidence of sectarian activity and to deal with it according to the relevant ordinances.[115] Under the heading 'sectarians' were included not only the Anabaptists but also Schwenckfelders[116] and Sacramentarians (i.e., Zwinglians). Of these, the Anabaptists were the only group that was numerically significant.

Duke Christopher's first concrete measure against the Anabaptists was an instruction to his officials dated 14 June 1554.[117] According to its provisions, local subprefects and pastors were to interview those suspected of Anabaptism, admonishing them to abandon any erroneous views and to attend church regularly. Obstinate individuals were to be jailed for up to three weeks. The names of any teachers or ringleaders, as well as the names of those who still remained obstinate after serving their jail sentences, were to be submitted to the duke. Moreover, all Anabaptists found holding conventicles were to be arrested and reported to the duke. Since the imposition of further punishments was reserved to central authority, they were not discussed in this instruction for local officials.

The results produced by the above measures evidently did not satisfy Duke Christopher, who in September 1556 planned to issue a public mandate against the Anabaptists. In the first draft of the mandate, the duke gave all sectarians until 1 January 1557 to abandon their errors and become good members of the established church. After that they were to be punished 'without mercy' according to the provisions of the imperial law.[118] If the mandate had gone into effect in this form, the policy established under Duke Ulrich would have been reversed and death sentences would henceforth have been unavoidable.

The duke's secular and ecclesiastical advisers objected to the very idea of a mandate on the ground that the instruction of June 1554 was, if properly enforced, perfectly adequate.[119] The duke, however, insisted on a mandate. Out of the ensuing discussions, which lasted into the new year, there emerged a second draft, which marked, in effect, a return to established policy. In this second version, those who had not abandoned their errors and become good church members by Pentecost 1557 were threatened with 'penalties on honour, body, and property' according to the nature of each case. There was no mention whatever of the imperial law or of the death penalty.[120] The mandate was not to be published in this form either, but the retreat from flirtation with the full rigours of the imperial law was permanent.

Given what we know of Brenz's attitude toward the imperial law on Anabaptism, and of his influence on Duke Christopher, it is logical to assume that his powers of persuasion effected the change of view reflected in the second draft of the mandate. Besides, there is exactly contemporary evidence that Brenz's nearly thirty-year-old campaign against the application of the imperial law was still in full swing. Toward the end of 1556 he was asked for his comments on the draft of the church order about to be issued by Count Palatine Wolfgang of Zweibrücken. On Christmas 1556 Duke Wolfgang's court preacher reported to him that although Brenz was pleased with the order as a whole, he thought that the provisions concerning the Anabaptists were too harsh, that all references to the imperial law ought to be expunged, and that the duke, 'as a Christian and virtuous prince,' ought not to permit human blood to be shed 'impiously or frivolously.'[121]

Meanwhile, Duke Christopher's advisers had evidently thought better of their claim that the instruction of June 1554 was entirely adequate, for they produced a new, expanded version which was included in the ordinance of 13 February 1557 for the territorial visitation.[122] The revised instruction placed even greater emphasis on winning Anabaptists over by careful instruction seasoned, if necessary, by a few weeks in jail. Banishment and confiscation of goods were prescribed for those who could not thus be persuaded to recant. Only backsliders, returned exiles, ringleaders, ministers (*Vorsteher*), and seditious intriguers were threatened with interrogation under torture and with the penalties appropriate for disobedient subjects or rebels. Moreover, obstinate ministers and ringleaders were henceforth to be imprisoned rather than banished, in order that they not be left free to spread their poison in other territories. This last provision was made in compliance with the imperial recess of 1551.[123]

While events were proceeding thus in Württemberg, Duke Christopher was energetically pursuing efforts to achieve Protestant unity in the Empire.[124] As part of that unity Christopher wanted a common Anabaptist Ordinance. Although the Protestant estates never got around to adopting such a measure, Protestant theologians attending a religious colloquy in Worms in the fall of 1557 approved a document entitled *Procedure for Dealing with the Anabaptists*.[125] The views of Melanchthon, who was the first to affix his signature to it, are so thoroughly predominant in it that it can be viewed as essentially his work.

The *Procedure* stipulated that Anabaptists whom several weeks of imprisonment and instruction did not move to recant were, after being excommunicated, to be punished by secular authority. Leaders and false teachers who refused one last opportunity to recant were to be executed as rebels and blasphemers. Followers, on the other hand, were to be kept in jail in the hope that in one to three years' time they would come to their senses. Against the objection that no one should be executed on grounds of faith, the *Procedure* insisted, first, that Anabaptist teachings contain sedition, over which secular government has undeniable authority (Rom. 12). Thus obstinate Anabaptists are executed not for their faith but for 'seditious falsehoods.' Furthermore, Anabaptist doctrines are blasphemous, and in Leviticus 24:16 God commanded the magistrate to put blasphemers to death. The Mosaic Law is not just the code of the ancient Jews but is 'natural law' binding on modern government as well. Thus Servetus was justly put to death for his blasphemous denial of the Trinity.

Brenz was one of the attending theologians who signed the *Procedure*. His motive for doing so cannot possibly have been that he found Melanchthon's familiar arguments suddenly convincing. Quite the contrary: Brenz's views remained unchanged and, as we shall see presently, the death penalty was not introduced into Württemberg. In fact, in the copy of the *Procedure* preserved in Stuttgart the passages prescribing the death penalty and approving the execution of Servetus are lined out.[126] The logical explanation for Brenz's signature is that once again, as in February 1531 and for substantially the same reasons, he made common cause with his fellow theologians while continuing to pursue his own established course in the area for which he was directly responsible. Brenz may also have reasoned that a document issued only by theologians would have little effect on actual practice in the Protestant territories. (In fact, it had none.)[127] Considering that human lives were at stake, it does Brenz little credit that he so readily compromised his principles for the sake of harmony. Nevertheless, Roland Bainton's judgment that 'Brenz's signature marks a signal departure from his earlier liberalism'[128] requires qualification: there was no such departure for Brenz personally or for Württemberg. On the other hand, to those who know his views only through his published writings, the *Procedure* must have given the impression that he had indeed forsaken the 'liberalism' of the memorandum of 1528. A desire to counteract this impression and to remind the world of his real views may well have been behind the publication in Tübingen in 1558 of a new edition of that memorandum.[129]

Also published in 1558 was the duke's mandate against the Anabaptists. In this, the third version of the measure first proposed in the fall of 1556, Anabaptists and other sectarians, as well as those who aided and abetted them, were threatened with 'the corporal punishments prescribed in the imperial recesses,' banishment from the duchy, confiscation of all their goods and chattels, 'and other grave penalties.'[130] Only after the mandate had been incorporated into the Great Church Order of 1559[131] was an ordinance with detailed instructions for its enforcement issued.[132] The provisions of the ordinance which dealt specifically with the Anabaptists were essentially an elaboration of those of the visitation ordinance of 1557.[133] A new note of harshness was added with the stipulation that even ordinary Anabaptists who refused to answer questions during interrogation were to be taken to Stuttgart and interrogated under torture.[134]

The actual treatment of Anabaptists in Württemberg was in fact milder than that prescribed in the ordinance. Ordinary Anabaptists were usually not tortured and normally not held in prison for more than a few weeks. Leaders who refused to recant were kept in prison indefinitely but treated leniently. And the theologians, including Brenz himself, exhibited remarkable patience in their efforts to win obstinate Anabaptists back to the territorial church. Even though their efforts were largely fruitless, and even though the number of Anabaptists in the duchy continued to grow, the theologians neither lost patience nor urged the adoption of the death penalty. In fact, the Anabaptist Ordinance that was issued shortly after Brenz's death (1572) abandoned the use of force almost entirely.[135] The theologians who helped prepare the ordinance justified this mildness and rejected harsher measures with the arguments that Brenz had used since 1528.[136]

There remains to be considered one last statement by Brenz on the treatment of Anabaptists. During the same period in which he was leading the reorganization of the church in Württemberg, Brenz also assisted Count Palatine Otto Henry with the introduction of the Württemberg system of church government into the Neuburg Palatinate (1553) and the Electoral Palatinate (1556–8).[137] In 1556 the superintendents in both territories were instructed to deal with Anabaptists or other sectarians according to the guidelines set forth in an appended memorandum by Brenz.[138]

In the memorandum[139] Brenz singled out the shortage of able pastors and the immoral lives of so many members of the established church as the principal reasons for the appeal and spread of Anabaptism and other sectarian movements. To check the spread of the sects, Brenz recommended the following measures. Pastors should preach quietly and clearly, without bluster or abuse, against sectarian doctrines, 'with the Christian order of the church and the eternal salvation of the erring' as their sole concern. Secular officials should enforce church attendance and punish public immorality according to the provisions of the Territorial Ordinance. Sectarian conventicles should be banned, and subjects forbidden to attend meetings or conventicles in neighbouring territories. Pastors were to take note of individuals who either habitually refrained from taking communion or who kept their children away from catechism. Any whose motives for this were seditious were to be dealt with according to the secular law. Those whose motives were merely sectarian were to be instructed, first by the pastor and the local subprefect (in the presence of witnesses), then by the superintendent, and finally by the synod. Those who remained obstinate after all this were to be reported to the prince, who would first remove them from all public offices and then, if there was no improvement, banish them.

At the end of the memorandum Brenz frankly acknowledged that the proposed measures would perhaps not achieve the eradication of sectarian error. Nevertheless, he refused to recommend harsher measures. For just as Amorites and Jebusites remained in Israel, though subject to Israel's authority; and just as all men must suffer sin to remain in their flesh and be content that the spirit has power over it; so the Christian church should be content that the true teaching of the gospel and the right use of the sacraments retain the upper hand even though many tares be found among the wheat. As Christ said, the tares should not immediately be gathered up lest the wheat also be rooted up with them (Matt. 13:24–30). It is sufficient if one work 'to deter only what is worst and most damaging.'

The most obvious difference between this memorandum and the ducal ordinances in Württemberg is that the memorandum makes no provision for incarceration, either as part of the process of instruction or as a penalty for obstinate leaders. Thus it is possible that both the use in Württemberg of imprisonment during instruction (which almost disappeared from the ordinance of 1572) and the use of prolonged imprisonment in lieu of banishment for ministers and ringleaders, were contrary to Brenz's own wishes.[140]

By refusing to put Anabaptists to death, sixteenth-century German Protestants unwittingly took a decisive step toward religious toleration. It would take another three centuries for universal religious toleration to be achieved in Germany. 'But the step from executing heretics to letting them live was an essential one, even if the death sentence was replaced by expulsion. After all, the great dividing line is that between life and death ... [and] it was during the sixteenth century that most Protestant governments in the Empire chose life for the heretic.'[141] Brenz played a noteworthy role in the making of that choice. Except for the two regrettable occasions when he deferred to the judgment of others, he consistently opposed the death penalty for heretics. That opposition, moreover, had an effect on the course of events, albeit one impossible to determine with precision. The printed versions of his memorandum of 1528 helped to publicize and to keep alive the case against the death penalty which Luther had enunciated and then abandoned. And, of course, Brenz had a direct influence on the treatment of Anabaptists in those South-German territories where he was personally active. It is true that all the governments in question had already established a policy of refusing to invoke the death penalty before Brenz arrived on the scene. On the other hand, the influence of his 1528 memorandum may in some cases have played an important or even a crucial role in calling that policy into being in the first place. More important, there was everywhere strong pressure, from within and without, to scrap the policy of moderation in favour of rigorous enforcement of the imperial law against rebaptizers. Brenz invariably assumed the leadership of those who wished to maintain and develop the policy of moderation and thus to avoid needless bloodshed. This is not to be underestimated, for Brenz could, if so inclined, have come down on the other side. Had he done so, it would have made a major difference, especially in Württemberg, where his personal influence was so strong. Had he, for example, chosen to support the policy embodied in Duke Christopher's draft mandate of September 1556,[142] the lives of many South German Anabaptists would have been even harder and shorter than they actually were. One may thus conclude by reaffirming the justice of Castellio's claim that Brenz's opposition to the execution of Anabaptists saved more than a few lives. It was not the least significant of his accomplishments.

Afterword

What concluding judgment should one pass upon Brenz's career as a reformer? For reasons only partially discussed in the preceding chapters, an entirely positive judgment is difficult.

The state church, to the establishment of which Brenz contributed so much, was, as we have seen, an institution in which there was simply no room for the 'congregationalist' or 'free church' implications of the doctrine of the priesthood of all believers. That freedom to choose and to administer the external order of the church which Luther had defined as the common possession of all Christians became, instead, the prerogative of the foremost member of the church, the Christian magistrate, whose secular authority, it was argued, had been divinely established for the purpose of governing the church. The German territorial rulers who heeded the reformers' call to exercise this prerogative thereby increased their authority over their subjects. Before the Reformation, they had acquired and exercised a significant degree of *Kirchenhoheit*, but the remnants of episcopal jurisdiction and the patronage rights of other individuals or corporations had made that authority incomplete and rather haphazard. As a result of the Reformation, however, it became not only complete but also, with the establishment of the Württemberg consistorial system, painstakingly thorough and efficient. The personnel and property of the church; education, social welfare, and the regulation of marriage and morals; and the entire public exercise of religion were, as never before, under the control of the secular magistrates. Moreover, the means whereby that control was exercised, Brenz's consistorial polity, afforded ordinary laymen no more active a role in church government than they had in secular government. Passive obedience (or, in the case of ungodly rulers, passive resistance) was all that was permitted to them in either case, a view incessantly driven home in all sermons, theological treatises, official creeds, catechisms, and church orders.

Seen in this light, the Reformation in general and Brenz's career in particular were part of that long process which produced not only the German absolutist state of the Old Regime but also the *Staatsfrömmigkeit* and the *Untertanengeist* which continued to influence German public life long after the demise of the Old Regime. But Brenz had no way of knowing that any such process was under way, and he would have had great difficulty recognizing its outcome as something to which he had contributed. For that outcome had little to do with his intentions as a reformer.

Despite his ardent championing of the authority of the secular magistrates and his encouragement of the expansion of their *Kirchenhoheit*, Brenz was himself by no means *staatsfromm*. His comments on the general run of worldly potentates were just as scathing as those of Luther.[1] Even pious, well-meaning magistrates were, he thought, no more infallible than the pope. That is why both his doctrine of the Christian magistracy and his consistorial polity contained so many features designed to prevent the exploitation of the church by the state. Moreover, Brenz clearly recognized the need for an authority which would protect society in general from governmental misbehaviour. That authority could not be the people themselves, to whom Brenz did indeed preach the duty of passive obedience, denying them even the right to engage in public criticism of government. It was, rather, the clergy who, in the exercise of the ministry of the word, were to instruct Christian magistrates in their duty and publicly to recall them to that duty if they strayed from it.[2] Like Luther, Brenz exercised this pastoral responsibility with amazing freedom and frankness, not hesitating to speak out even on issues (e.g., oppressive taxation) which were purely secular in nature.[3] In this way, he helped to establish a tradition which several generations of German pastors and theologians were able to follow.

This approach, however, had a flaw: in its relations with the state, the church was, in fact, much the weaker partner. This circumstance was at first obscured by the essential harmony of outlook and interest between clergy and magistrates. During Brenz's lifetime, and for about a century thereafter, the typical German ruler was not a high-handed, worldly-minded autocrat but a pious *Landesvater* and *auditor ecclesiae* who, like Duke Christopher, took seriously the idea that his first duty was to God and his church, and who listened with patience and respect to the counsel and the criticism offered by his theologians. In the period after the Thirty Years War, however, German thrones increasingly were occupied by worldly absolutists whose principal preoccupation was self-aggrandizement or *raisons d'état*, not the glory of God or the salvation of their subjects' souls. While such rulers were content, even eager, that the church continue to dispense true doctrine and conduct true worship, they were little disposed to heed, or even to tolerate, unwelcome criticism from their clergy. Indeed, they used the ecclesiastical authority which the Reformation had bequeathed to them in order to ensure that theologians, pastors, and teachers performed their offices in ways beneficial to the state, e.g., by preaching deference to authority, acceptance of the existing social order, a positive attitude toward military service, and so forth. In this way, the polity which Brenz had intended as a means whereby Christian magistrates were to serve the church and to be subjected to its guiding influence became instead the means whereby worldly magistrates could use the church as a handy means of social control.

Thus Brenz's achievements as a reformer had their highly problematical side. The observed disjunction between original intention and long-range consequences does not dissolve the historical link between deed and outcome. Nevertheless, the significance of Brenz's career as a reformer does not reside solely, or even primarily, in his unwitting contribution to the predicament of a later age. He had his hands full with the exigencies of his own age, and he deserves the courtesy of being judged on the basis of his response to them. That is, of course, what the foregoing six chapters were an attempt to do.

Brenz was a state-church man because historical circumstances hardly allowed him to be anything else. Like any follower of Luther, he believed that a thoroughgoing reformation was essential. Faced with the refusal of pope and bishops to provide it, Brenz, like any good Upper-German townsman and humanist, turned for help to the secular magistrates, who already exercised considerable authority over ecclesiastical and religious life. He did so in the knowledge that there was no other way to overcome the obstacles to a peaceful, orderly, durable reform, and in the belief that God had called the magistrates to the office of government in things ecclesiastical. So his first achievement as a church organizer was to persuade (or help persuade) governments in Schwäbisch Hall, Brandenburg-Ansbach, Württemberg, and elsewhere that it was their duty, both as secular magistrates and as individual Christians, to institute the Reformation and to become the administrative heads of new, Protestant, territorial state churches.

In presenting his case to the magistrates, Brenz initially (i.e., in the 1520s) emphasized that, by establishing true preaching and worship, they (the magistrates) would best achieve the chief purpose of their office: the maintenance of secular peace and order. After 1530, by which time the easy assumption of a causal link between the true faith and secular order had been undermined, he argued that the chief end of secular authority was a much loftier one than merely maintaining peace and order, namely, serving God and his church by establishing true doctrine and worship, abolishing false doctrine and worship, and enforcing a decent standard of Christian morality. Moreover, throughout his career Brenz demanded of the magistrates a high degree of restraint in the exercise of their authority over the church. They were not to interfere in the ministry of the word; they were not to exploit the wealth of the church for the relief of the state treasury; they were not to violate the rights of individual conscience by punishing mere unbelief, nor were they to use unchristian violence (i.e., the death penalty) against those who passed from mere unbelief to false preaching and worship; and, finally, they were not to use the defence of the true faith as a pretext for unchristian rebellion against imperial authority.

Although the territorial rulers who responded to Brenz's call did, to be sure, expand and consolidate their authority over the church as a result, they also accepted a view of their office which placed the glory of God, the good of the church, and the welfare of their subjects ahead of their own personal comfort or political advantage. Too many German rulers tried too hard for too long (over a century) to live up to this idea for it to be written off as mere ideological window-dressing for political self-aggrandizement.

Important as Brenz's role in winning and retaining the support of magistrates for the Reformation was, it was by no means unique. Many other reformers played a comparable role in their communities and regions. Moreover, Brenz's doctrine of the Christian magistracy, though it expressed his own deepest conviction in a cogent way, was largely derivative. His second achievement as a church organizer, on the other hand, the Württemberg consistorial system, was his own special contribution to the Reformation. No other Lutheran reformer achieved anything like it. It was a polity which allowed church and state to cooperate without interfering in one another's jurisdictions. Secular officials handled the financial affairs of the church, thus relieving the clergy of the worldly cares which had burdened their medieval predecessors. The direct exercise of the church's pastoral ministry, on the other hand, was in the hands of clergymen. The keystone of the polity, the centralized system of 'visitation superintendence,' was as effective an instrument of ecclesiastical government as was possible in sixteenth-century society. Through it, errors, abuses, and needs could be uncovered, brought to the attention of the appropriate authorities, and promptly dealt with. Orthodoxy of doctrine and uniformity of practice could be maintained throughout a principality, even in its remotest corners. The only thing the Württemberg polity could not accomplish was an effective discipline of morals, not because the polity itself was defective, but because cooperation between church and state, clergy and laity, broke down over this issue. However, as long as true doctrine could be preached and the true sacraments administered decently and in order and passed on to posterity, Brenz's polity fulfilled its primary function. Its rapid and widespread adoption outside Württemberg, and its long life in the places where it was adopted, are eloquent testimony to its worth in the eyes of contemporaries and of many succeeding generations as well.

One does not have to share Brenz's faith, be a partisan of established churches, or be blind to the problematical aspects of his work in order to form a positive estimate of his achievement as a reformer. The Reformation was a powerful, complicated, turbulent movement. Imposing order upon it was a long and difficult process. Brenz brought exceptional talents to bear on that process, and his successes in it entitle him to an honourable place in the history of the Reformation and of sixteenth-century Germany.

Notes

ARG   *Archiv für Reformationsgeschichte*

BWKG   *Blätter für Württembergische Kirchengeschichte*

CR   C.G. Bretschneider et al., *Corpus Reformatorum*, vols. 1–28 (Halle, 1834–60): *Philippi Melanchthonis Opera Quae Supersunt Omnia*; vols. 29–87 (Braunschweig, 1863–1900): *Calvini Opera Quae Supersunt Omnia*

Frühschriften   Johannes Brenz, *Frühschriften*, ed. Martin Brecht et al., 2 vols. (Tübingen, 1970 / 74)

Herolt   'Chronica zeit- unnd jarbuch vonn der statt Hall ursprung unnd was sich darinnen verloffen unnd wasz fur schlösser umb Hall gestanden durch M. Johann Herolt zusammengetragen,' in *Württembergische Geschichtsquellen*, pub. Württembergische Kommission für Landesgeschichte, vol. 1 (Stuttgart, 1894): *Geschichtsquellen der Stadt Hall*, vol. 1, ed. Christian Kolb, pp. 35–270

Köhler   Walther Köhler, *Bibliographia Brentiana* (Berlin, 1904; rpt. Nieuwkoop, 1963)

LW   *Luther's Works*, ed. Jaroslav Pelikan, Helmut T. Lehmann, et al., 52 vols. to date (St Louis and Philadelphia, 1955–   )

Opera   *Operum Reverendi et Clarissimi Theologi, D. Ioannis Brentii, Praepositi Stutgardiani Tomus Primus* [*Secundus*, etc.], 8 vols. (Tübingen, 1576–90)

Pressel   Theodor Pressel, ed., *Anecdota Brentiana: Ungedruckte Briefe und Bedenken von Johannes Brenz* (Tübingen, 1868)

Reyscher   August Ludwig Reyscher, ed., *Vollständige, historisch und kritisch bearbeitete sammlung der württembergischen geseze*, 19 vols. in 29 (Stuttgart and Tübingen, 1828–51)

Richter   Aemilius Ludwig Richter, ed., *Die evangelischen Kirchenordnungen des sechszehnten Jahrhunderts*, 2 vols. (Weimar, 1846; rpt. Nieuwkoop, 1967)

Sattler   Christian Friedrich Sattler, *Geschichte des Herzogthums Würtenberg unter der Regierung der Herzogen*, vols. 3 and 4 (Tübingen, 1771). Page references are to the *Beilagen* (appended documents), which have separate pagination.

Sehling   Emil Sehling et al., eds., *Die evangelischen Kirchenordnungen des XVI. Jahrhunderts*, vols. 1–5 (Leipzig, 1902–13); vols. 6 et seq. (Tübingen, 1955–   )

St L.   *Dr. Martin Luthers Sämmtliche Schriften*, ed. Johann Georg Walch et al, 23 vols. in 25 (St Louis, 1881–1910)

WA   *D. Martin Luther Werke, Kritische Gesamtausgabe*, 58 vols. in 73 (Weimar, 1883–   )

WA-Br   *D. Martin Luthers Werke: Briefwechsel*, 15 vols. (Weimar, 1930–78)

WA-TR   *D. Martin Luthers Werke: Tischreden*, 6 vols. (Weimar, 1912–21)

CHAPTER ONE

1 Friedrich Wilhelm Kantzenbach, 'Der junge Brenz bis zu seiner Berufung nach Hall im Jahre 1522,' *Zeitschrift für bayerische Kirchengeschichte* 32 (1963): 53–73; Hans-Martin Maurer and Kuno Ulshöfer, *Johannes Brenz und die Reformation in Württemberg* (Stuttgart and Aalen, n.d.), pp. 13–23; Martin Brecht, *Die frühe Theologie des Johannes Brenz* (Tübingen, 1966), pp. 7–22; Julius Hartmann and Karl Jäger, *Johann Brenz: nach gedruckten und ungedruckten Quellen*, 2 vols. (Hamburg, 1840), 1: chapter one.

2 Also known as the *Bursa Realium*. One of three residences where students (*Burschen*) in the faculty of arts lived under the guidance of a *regens*.

3 On Brenz's career in Hall through 1526 see Maurer / Ulshöfer, pp. 23–57; Hartmann/ Jäger 1: chaps. 2, 4; and Friedrich Wilhelm Kantzenbach, 'Theologie und Gemeinde bei Johannes Brenz, dem Prediger von Hall: Sein erstes Wirken für die kirchliche Neuordnung der Reichsstadt von 1522 bis ca. 1526,' BWKG 65 (1965): 3–38.

4 Gerd Wunder, 'Der Haller Rat und Johannes Brenz 1522–1530,' *Württembergisch Franken* 55 (Neue Folge 45, 1971): 56–66, pp. 56–9.

5 *Frühschriften* 1:5–15.

6 Ibid., pp. 17–22.

7 Herolt, p. 189: 'Nachdem Johann Brencius, prediger zu Hall, zwei jar gepredigt ... hat man im 1524. jar die papistischen ceremonien von tag zu tag fallen lassen ...'

8 Hartmann/Jäger 1:60–2.

9 Herolt, p. 43.

10 Pressel, p. 2 (Brenz to Johannes Oecolampadius, 27 June 1524).

11 Herolt, p. 114.

12 Ibid.

13 Ibid., p. 189; Pressel, p. 89.

14 'Reformation der kirchen in dem Hellischen land. Herr Jo Brentz,' Richter 1:40–9. Richter gives the date incorrectly as 1526. See Martin Brecht, 'Anfänge reformatorischer Kirchenordnung und Sittenzucht bei Johannes Brenz,' *Zeitschrift der Savigny Stiftung für Rechtsgeschichte*, Kanonistische Abteilung, 55 (1969): 322–47, pp. 324–6.

15 Richter 1:48–9. For Luther's views, see *An die Radherrn aller Stedte deutsches lands: dass sie Christliche schulen auffrichten und halten sollen* (1524), WA 15:27–53; LW 45:347–78.

16 According to James M. Kittelson, 'Humanism and the Reformation in Germany,' *Central European History* 9 (1976): 303–22, pp. 308–9, this 'broadening of the reform movement' to include, in addition to doctrinal and liturgical changes, 'the establishment of public schools for both boys and girls, public regulation of marriage and morals, and the institution of public ... welfare programs' was primarily the work of those reformers who were 'converted humanists.'

17 *Frühschriften* 1:148–9 (see n. 32 below); Herolt, p. 117.

18 Details in chapter five.

19 Herolt, p. 189; Maurer/Ulshöfer, p. 57.

20 Julius Gmelin, *Hällische Geschichte* (Schwäbisch Hall, 1899), pp. 743–4.

21 Richter 1:49.

22 In the 'Reformation' (ibid.), Brenz urged the council not to let the cost stand in the way.

23 'Das die underthonen zu ufferziehung der jugent guter predinger notturfftig vil daran gelegen und damit (sonderlich uff ir selbs bit) zu versehen seyen,' Stadtarchiv Schwäbisch Hall 4/53, fols. 121a–124b.

24 Gmelin, p. 744.

25 Herolt, pp. 189–90; Hartmann/Jäger 1:332–3.

26 Herolt, p. 190.

27 Ibid., p. 125.

28 Ibid., pp. 118–19, 133–4.

29 Hartmann/Jäger 2:78–80.

30 *Ordnung der Kirchen inn eins Erbarn Raths zu Schwäbischen Hall Oberkeit und gepiet gelegen* (Schwäbisch Hall, 1543): see Köhler, no. 122. Richter 2:14–21 provides an abridged text. This order deals exclusively with doctrinal and liturgical matters.

31 Maurer/Ulshöfer, pp. 65–70.

32 'Rhattschlag und Guttbedunckhen herrn Johann Brentii über der Bauren gestelte ... Zwölff Articul ...,' *Frühschriften* 1:136–74.

33 See, for example, *Von Milterung der Fürsten gegen den auffrurischen Bauren* (1525), *Frühschriften* 1:182–7.

34 Maurer/Ulshöfer, pp. 50 – 7. The text of the *Syngramma* is in *Frühschriften* 1:234–78.

35 Friedrich Wilhelm Kantzenbach, 'Johannes Brenz und die Reformation in Franken,' *Zeitschrift für bayerische Kirchengeschichte* 31 (1962): 149–68, pp. 150–4; Maurer / Ulshöfer, pp. 72–80.

36 H. Westermayer, *Die Brandenburgisch-Nürnbergische Kirchenvisitation und Kirchenordnung, 1528–1533* (Erlangen, 1894), pp. 68–118; Adolf Engelhardt, *Die Reformation in Nürnberg*, vol. 2, in *Mitteilungen des Vereins für Geschichte der Stadt Nürnberg* 34 (1937), pp. 108–40; Sehling 11:113–22 (eds. intro. to the text of the order).

37 Text in Sehling 11:140–205; Richter 1:176–211.

38 Details in chapter four, pp. 64–5.

39 Maurer/Ulshöfer, pp. 97–113. See also Julius Rauscher, *Württembergische Reformationsgeschichte* (Stuttgart, 1934), pp. 111–35.

40 Maurer/Ulshöfer, pp. 113–16; Rauscher, pp. 135–8.

41 Pressel, pp. 156–66: 'Vorred D. Johan Brentzen mit etlichen furnemlichen und notigen artickeln auff die Kirchenordnung im Furstenthum wurtenberg gestelt Anno MDXXXV.'

42 Traugott Schiess, ed., *Briefwechsel der Brüder Ambrosius und Thomas Blaurer* 1 (Freiburg i. Br., 1908): 630 (A. Blarer to Martin Bucer, mid-January 1534): 'Pendet [Schnepfius] ex Brentio totus.'

43 Ibid., pp. 788–9 (A. Blarer to T. Blarer, 14 March 1536): 'Mitto excusae iam ordinationis exemplar ... Erunt, scio, quae superstitiora videbuntur ... Verum bene nobiscum agi credidi, quando innumera alia, quae a Br(entio) assuta erant, resecta sunt ...'

44 The text of the order (without the catechism) is in Reyscher 8:42–59.

45 Pressel, pp. 166 – 70: 'Ordnung der Visitation. 1535.' See also Martin Brecht, *Kirchenordnung und Kirchenzucht in Württemberg vom 16. bis zum 18. Jahrhundert* (Stuttgart, 1967), pp. 23–6.

46 Pressel, p. 170.

47 Maurer/Ulshöfer, pp. 116–18; Rauscher, pp. 140–3; Hartmann/Jäger 2:42–57.

48 Maurer/Ulshöfer, pp. 113, 118.

49 Ibid., pp. 89–90; CR 4:910–11; Pressel, pp. 228, 229–32, 235–6.

50 Maurer/Ulshöfer, p. 90.

51 Ibid., pp. 90–3; Pressel, pp. 258–66; Hartmann/Jäger 2:157–64.

52 Maurer/Ulshöfer, p. 93; Pressel, pp. 268–78.

53 Maurer/Ulshöfer, pp. 93–4; Hartmann/Jäger 2:164–73.

54 Maurer/Ulshöfer, pp. 123–6, 130–1.

55 On Christopher's life up to 1548, see ibid., pp. 133–6; Bernhard Kugler, *Christoph, Herzog zu Wirtemberg*, 2 vols. (Stuttgart, 1868–72), 1:3–80.

56 Pressel, pp. 281–6, 288–92, 295–7, 307, 310, 316, 319–20; Maurer/Ulshöfer, p. 143.

57 Maurer/Ulshöfer, pp. 126–30; Gustav Bossert, *Das Interim in Württemberg*, Schriften des Vereins für Reformationsgeschichte, no. 12 (Halle, 1895), chaps. 2, 6–8.

58 '...Joannis Brentii iudicium et consilium de eodem libro Interim ... datum: Anno 1549,' in BWKG 32 (1928): 24–37. In July 1549 Brenz and two other theologians showed Duke Ulrich how to exploit the provisions of the Interim in order to defeat the intention of the Bishops of Augsburg and Speyer to conduct visitations in the duchy: Pressel, pp. 299–303.

59 Pressel, pp. 306–7, 311–13.

60 Maurer/Ulshöfer, pp. 140–3.

61 The letter of installation is in Pressel, pp. 388–90.

62 *Von Gottes gnaden vnser Christoffs Herzogen zu Württemberg vnd zu Teckh, Grauen zu Mümpelgart, etc. summarischer vnd einfältiger Begriff, wie es mit der Lehre vnd Ceremonien in den Kirchen vnsers Fürstenthumbs, auch derselben Kirchen anhangenden Sachen und Verrichtungen, bissher geübt vnnd gebraucht, auch fürohin mit verleihung Göttlicher gnaden gehalten vnd volzogen werden solle* (Tübingen, 1559; facsimile rpt. Stuttgart, 1968). A substantially complete version of the text is found in Reyscher 8:106–284; 11/1:2–9; 11/2:24–126.

63 Brecht, *Kirchenordnung und Kirchenzucht*, p. 49.

64 Reyscher 8:114–67.

65 Viktor Ernst, ed., *Briefwechsel des Herzogs Christoph von Wirtemberg*, 4 vols. (Stuttgart, 1899–1907), 1:182–8.

66 Reyscher 8:167–221.

67 Ibid., 4:85–92.

68 Fols. cxcv-ccxvii of the 1559 ed.

69 Reyscher 11/1:2–9; 11/2:24–126. Useful discussion in Maurer/Ulshöfer, pp. 160–4, and in Gerald Strauss, *Luther's House of Learning: Indoctrination of the Young in the German Reformation* (Baltimore and London, 1978), pp. 14–19.

70 Ludwig Ziemssen, 'Das württembergische Partikularschulwesen 1534–1559,' in *Geschichte des humanistischen Schulwesens in Württemberg*, pub. Württembergische Kommission für Landesgeschichte, vol. 1 (Stuttgart, 1912), pp. 468–599: 509–12.

71 Reyscher 11/2:63–91. At the university the students were taken into the *Stipendium*, a foundation for the maintenance of promising but needy theology students, established by Duke Ulrich in 1537. Its new ordinance (1557) was incorporated into the Church Order of 1559, ibid., pp. 91–123. Under the name *Tübinger Stift*, the institution still exists today.

72 Sattler 4:86–97.

73 Pressel, pp. 33–9.

74 Reyscher 11/2:2–9 (German schools); 11/2:27–62 (Latin schools).

75 Ibid., 11/2:25–6 (preface to the school ordinances in the Church Order of 1559).

76 Ibid., p. 27.

77 This statement applies only to the remaining sections of the order that are in fact ecclesiastical in nature. Four brief sections (nos. 9–12, fols. ccxvij verso–ccxx) dealing with the qualifications of surgeons and scribes have only the most tenuous connection with ecclesiastical matters (i.e., the use of church funds and/or the participation of *Kirchenräte* in supervisory committees). Three larger sections (no. 13: 'Rugordnung,' fols. ccxxi–ccxxxi; no. 14: 'Politische Visitation,' Reyscher 8:256–60; no. 15: 'Land Inspection,' ibid., pp. 260–5) are, strictly speaking, secular measures for the enforcement of public morality, included in the Great Church Order because they complement and overlap the ecclesiastical measures to the same end. Sections 15 and 16 will be discussed briefly in chapters four and five.

78 Details in chapter four.

CHAPTER TWO

1 WA-Br 8:396 (Luther to the Visitors in Thuringia, 25 March 1539); WA 53:255–6 (*Exempel einen rechten christlichen Bischof zu weihen*, 1542).

2 See below, pp. 40 (n. 21), 100.

3 The works which have had the most direct influence on the interpretation presented here are Karl Holl, 'Luther und das landesherrliche Kirchenregiment [1911],' *Gesammelte Aufsätze zur Kirchengeschichte*, vol. 1 (Tübingen, 1948), pp. 326–80; and Hans-Walter Krumwiede, *Zur Entstehung des landesherrlichen Kirchenregiments in Kursachsen und Braunschweig-Wolfenbüttel* (Göttingen, 1967). See also Heinrich Bornkamm, 'Bindung und Freiheit in der Ordnung der Kirche,' and 'Das Ringen der Motive in den Anfängen der Reformatorischen Kirchenverfassung,' in *Das Jahrhundert der Reformation, Gestalten und Kräfte* (Göttingen, 1961), pp. 185–219.

4 On this see Karl Holl, 'Die Entstehung von Luthers Kirchenbegriff,' *Gesammelte Aufsätze* 1:288–325.

5 WA 12:214, 218–19 (*Formula Missae et Communionis*, 1523); ibid., 18:418–19 (*Eyne Christliche vormanung*, 1525); ibid., 19:72–3 (*Deudsche Messe*, 1526).

6 Ibid., 11:261–71 (part II of *Von welltlicher Uberkeytt*, 1523); Holl, pp. 320, 338–9.

7 WA 12:178–92 (*De instituendis ministris Ecclesiae*, 1523); ibid., 6:408 (*An den Christlichen Adel*, 1520); ibid., 11:411–13 (*Das ein christliche Versamlung*, 1523).

8 Ibid., 11:262, 266 (*Von welltlicher Uberkeytt*); LW 45:105. See Holl, p. 330, n. 1, for an array of quotations from other works.

9 WA 32:440 (*Wochenpredigten über Matth. 5–7*, 1523): 'Ein Furst kan wol ein Christen sein, aber als ein Christ mus er nicht regieren: und nach dem er regiret, heisst er nicht ein Christ sondern ein Furst. Die person ist wol ein Christ, aber das ampt odder Furstenthumb geht sein Christentum nicht an ...'

10 Ibid., 11:252 (*Von wellt. Uberkeytt*); LW 45:93.

11 WA 11:249–52; LW 45:89–92.

12 WA 6:404–69.

13 Ibid., p. 404; LW 44:123.

14 WA 6:415–69.

15 See Holl, pp. 327–9; and Karl Müller, *Kirche, Gemeinde und Obrigkeit nach Luther* (Tübingen, 1910), pp. 17–23.

16 WA 6:406, 413; 44:137.

17 WA 6:413–14; LW 44:137.

18 WA 6:415. Also ibid., p. 258 (*Von den guten werkenn*, 1520): 'Sondern das were das best, unnd auch das einige uberbeleibend mittel, szo Kunig, Fursten, adel, Stet und gemein selb anfiengen, der sach ein einbruch mechten, auff das die Bischoff und geistlichen (die sich itzt furchten) ursach hetten zufolgen.'

19 Ibid., pp. 446, 450.

20 *Das eyn Christliche versamlung odder gemeyne recht und macht habe, all lere tzu urteylen, und lerer tzu beruffen, eyn und abtzusetzen ...* (1523), ibid., 11:408–16.

21 Ibid., p. 411; LW 39:308–9.

22 WA 11:413–15; cf. ibid., 12:172, 191 (*De instituendis ministris*); LW 39:311–12.

23 WA 12:206, 214 (*Formula Missae et Communionis*, 1523).

24 WA 10/3:9 (Invocavit Sermons, March 1522); ibid. 8:679 (*Eine treue Vermahnung* etc., 1522).

25 Ibid. 8:679–80; ibid. 18:23, 36 (*Vom Greuel der Stillmesse*, 1525).

26 WA-Br 4:28 (Luther to Elector John, 9 February 1526).

27 WA-Br 3:616 (Luther to Spalatin, 11 November 1525); ibid. 4:29 (Luther to Elector John, 9 February 1526).

28 Ibid. 2:515 (Luther to Spalatin, 5 May 1522), 521 (Luther to Elector Frederick, 8 May 1522).

29 See, for example, ibid., pp. 519–21 (Luther to Elector Frederick, 8 May 1522).

30 In the *Formula Missae* of 1523 Luther emphasizes that pastors may imitate it if it pleases them (WA 12:219–20), and otherwise leaves many matters to the discretion of the pastor (ibid., pp. 209, 210, 211, 214).

31 Ibid., pp. 11–13 (*Ordnung eines gemeinen Kasten*, 1523).

32 WA-Br 3:582 (Luther to Nikolaus Hausmann, 27 September 1525); ibid., p. 595 (Luther to Elector John, 31 October 1525); ibid. 4:133 (Luther to Elector John, 22 November 1526); ibid., p. 135 (Luther to Elector John, 23 November 1526).

33 WA 18:417–18 (*Eyne Christliche vormanung*, 1525); ibid. 19:72 (*Deudsche Messe*, 1526); Holl, pp. 362–3.

34 WA-Br 4:133–4 (Luther to Elector John, 22 November 1526); cf. ibid. 3:628 (Luther to Elector John, 30 November 1525). In the letter of 30 November 1525 Luther clearly states that this compulsion will be applied only to those communities 'wo

man fünde, dass die Leute wollten evangelische Prediger haben.' In the letter of 22 November 1526 no such restriction is stated, but Holl, pp. 364–5, argues strenuously that it is assumed.

35 See n. 26 above.

36 WA 18:417–21 (*Eyne Christliche vormanung von eusserlichem Gottis Dienste vnde eyntracht, an die in Liefflannd*, 1525); LW 53:47. See also WA 19:72–3 (Luther's preface to the *Deudsche Messe*, 1526); and WA-Br 4:157–8 (Luther to Philip of Hessen, 7 January 1527).

37 WA-Br 3:582 (Luther to Nikolaus Hausmann, 27 September 1525): 'Scio reformatione parochiarum opus esse et instituendis uniformibus ceremoniis, iamque hoc saxum volvo, et principem sollicitabo.' See also ibid., p. 583 (Luther to Spalatin, 28 September 1525).

38 Luther first broached the subject of a visitation in his letter of 31 October 1525 to Elector John; ibid., p. 595.

39 Ibid. 4:133–34; WA 26:197–8.

40 WA 26:195–201 (Luther's preface), 202–40 (the *Unterricht*).

41 Ibid., pp. 195–7; LW 40:271.

42 WA 26:200; LW 40:272.

43 See Holl, p. 369; and Krumwiede, pp. 91–109.

44 WA 206:200–1; LW 40:273. See also WA 31/1:207–13 (*Der 82. Psalm ausgelegt*, 1530); ibid. 30/3:520 (*Von den Schleichern und Winkelpredigern*, 1532).

45 See below, pp. 28–34.

46 Sehling 1/1, 142ff.

47 Pp. 372–3.

48 Krumwiede, pp. 107–9, says no; Irmgard Höss, ARG 61 (1970): 144–7 (review of Krumwiede), says yes.

49 Krumwiede, pp. 120–45.

50 See the letter to Daniel Greiser, 22 October 1543 (WA-Br 10:436), in which Luther objects sharply to Duke Maurice of Saxony's new excommunication ordinance, according to which secular officials are to control the imposition and enforcement of the ban. See also the letters to Gabriel Zwilling, 30 September 1535 (ibid. 7:280–1); to Sebastian Steude, 24 August 1541 (ibid. 9:501–2); and to the mayor and city council in Creuzberg, 27 January 1543 (ibid. 10:255–8).

51 See Holl, p. 379, n. 1.

52 In his revised preface for the third edition of the *Unterricht der Visitatoren* (pub. 1545 for use in the bishopric of Naumburg), Luther still spoke of the elector's appointment of visitors as something done 'out of Christian love.' However, the crucial phrases about the elector's not being obligated as a temporal sovereign to appoint visitors or to teach and rule in spiritual affairs (cf. p. 26 above) were deleted in favour of a passage emphasizing that 'hohe ummeidliche Not' has forced

princes, lords, and cities to undertake the 'starke Reformation' of the church which the pope had refused to provide. WA 26:197-8.

53 The notion originated with Hartmann and Jäger. See Martin Brecht, *Die frühe Theologie des Johannes Brenz* (Tübingen, 1966), p. 292.

54 Brecht, pp. 287-92, has argued persuasively that Brenz's earliest, undated, *Obrigkeitsschriften* pre-date the Peasants' Revolt.

55 The literature on this subject is enormous. The following are the basis of the summary offered here: Johannes Wülk and Hans Funk, *Die Kirchenpolitik der Grafen von Württemberg bis zur Erhebung Württembergs zum Herzogtum (1495)* (Stuttgart, 1912); Viktor Ernst, *Eberhard im Bart* (Stuttgart, 1933; rpt. Darmstadt, 1970) pp. 86-95; Alfred Schultze, *Stadtgemeinde und Reformation* (Tübingen, 1918); Bernd Moeller, *Reichsstadt und Reformation*, Schriften des Vereins für Reformationsgeschichte, no. 180 (Gütersloh, 1962); Richard Lossen, *Staat und Kirche in der Pfalz im Ausgang des Mittelalters* (Münster, 1907); Karl Rieker, *Die rechtliche Stellung der evangelischen Kirche Deutschlands* (Leipzig, 1893), pp. 32-9; Willy Andreas, *Deutschland vor der Reformation* (Stuttgart, 1959), chaps. 4 and 6.

56 E.W. Kohls, 'Zur Bedeutung und Geschichte des Begriffes "gemein nutz",' *Die Schule bei Martin Bucer* (Heidelberg, 1963), pp. 121-9; Wilhelm Maurer, *Das Verhältnis des Staates zur Kirche nach humanistischer Anschauung, vornehmlich bei Erasmus* (Giessen, 1930).

57 For the parallel cases of Zwingli and Bucer, see Moeller, *Reichsstadt und Reformation*, pp. 34-55; Robert C. Walton, *Zwingli's Theocracy* (Toronto, 1967), chaps. 1 and 2. See also James M. Kittelson, *Wolfgang Capito: From Humanist to Reformer* (Leiden, 1975), esp. chaps. 5 and 7; and J. Wayne Baker, *Heinrich Bullinger and the Covenant: The Other Reformed Tradition* (Athens, Ohio, 1980), esp. chaps 3-6. For a stimulating general assessment of the contribution of humanists-turned-reformer to the Reformation, see James M. Kittelson, 'Humanism and the Reformation in Germany,' *Central European History* 9 (1976):303-22.

58 Herolt, pp. 108-10, 117-18, 189-90. See chapter one, pp. 4-5.

59 Viktor Ernst, 'Die Entstehung des württembergischen Kirchenguts,' *Württembergische Jahrbücher für Statistik und Landeskunde*, 1911, pp. 377-424: 383-5.

60 Sattler 3:102-22, 132-8; Ernst, 'Kirchengut,' pp. 386, 414; Christian Friedrich von Schnurrer, *Erläuterungen der Württembergischen Kirchen- Reformations- und Gelehrten-Geschichte* (Tübingen, 1798), pp. 120-5.

61 Schnurrer, pp. 126-8; Sattler 3:218-19. After the Interim, Duke Christopher justified his transformation of the monasteries into schools in part on the basis of his rights as *Schirmvogt*: Sattler 4:88-9.

62 Martin Brecht, 'Brenz als Zeitgenosse: Die Reformationsepoche im Spiegel seiner Schriftauslegungen,' BWKG 70 (1970): 5-39, p. 23 (citing the Homilies on Luke of 1531-2/1536). Note also the comments from the Isaiah Commentary of 1544-8, cited on the same page.

CHAPTER THREE

1 Another inhibiting factor in many cases was fear of the emperor and the Catholic estates. Brenz's reaction to this problem will be dealt with in chapter six.

2 'Ablainung: Wie das Euangelium Weltliche Oberkeit nit zu boden stoss Sonder bestetig sie etc.' (ca. end of 1524), *Frühschriften* 1:32–43; 'Sermon: Wars Cristenlichs wesens ein kurtzer bericht und anweysung. Mit antzaig wie Cristenliche Oberkait regirn und handeln soll' (ca. 1524/5), ibid., pp. 43–55; 'Underrichtung der zwispaltigen artickel cristenlichs glaubens' (ca. 1524/5), ibid., pp. 55–111; 'Rhattschlag und Guttbedunckhen herrn Johann Brentii über der Bauren gestelte ... Zwölff Articul ...,' (June 1525), ibid., pp. 132–74.

3 Richter 1:40–9 (the 'Hall Reformation' of 1527); Pressel, pp. 40–2: 'Ursach, warumb ein Christenlicher fürst in seiner dition und landtschafft Christlich gotsdienst anzurichten verschaffen soll' (1 June 1529).

4 *Frühschriften* 1:52–3. The paternal nature of magisterial authority is a constantly recurring theme in Brenz's writings. See, for example: *Opera* 7:321 (Homilies on Acts, 1533); ibid. 6:282 (Homilies on John, 1543–6); ibid. 1:234 (Commentary on Genesis, 1553). See also the Election Day Sermon of 1543, fol. 241a–b (full reference in n. 95 below). Moreover, this paternalistic view of the state is the assumption, spoken or unspoken, of all Brenz's utterances on the exercise of political authority.

5 *Frühschriften* 1:42, 50, 59–60, 135, 144, 171; Pressel, p. 40.

6 *Frühschriften* 1:59–61; Pressel, pp. 40–1.

7 *Frühschriften* 1:140–3. See also ibid., pp. 122–31 (*Von gehorsam der underthon gegen irer oberkait*, 1525).

8 Ibid., p. 144; see also ibid., pp. 35–40.

9 Richter 1:40.

10 Ibid., p. 49.

11 Ibid., p. 40. Brenz cites the *Historia Ecclesiastica Tripartita*, attributed to Cassiodorus, IV.13 and 18, which records incidents of armed violence between Arians and Athanasians in the mid-fourth century.

12 Richter 1:41–2; see also Pressel, p. 41. Brenz did not, however, consider the Christian magistrate bound by the Old-Testament practice of putting false prophets to death. Details in chapter six.

13 Richter 1:41; see also Pressel, pp. 40–2, 88–90.

14 Pressel, p. 42.

15 'Das die underthonen zu Ufferziehung der Jugent guter predinger notdurfftig ...' Stadtarchiv Schwäbisch Hall 4/53, fols. 121a–124b.

16 Pressel, p. 42.

17 See chapter two, pp. 20–3.

18 *Frühschriften* 1:69.

19 Ibid., p. 144.

20 Richter 1:40.

21 *Opera* 5:343 (Commentary on Matthew 1554). In this same work (ibid., p. 344) Brenz speaks of the ancient church as 'deformed' (*de pravo coetu ecclesiae*) because the public magistrates were not members.

22 Pressel, p. 167.

23 See chapter two, p. 21

24 *Frühschriften* 1:137–8.

25 Ibid., pp. 139, 48–50.

26 Ibid., pp. 140–1.

27 Ibid., pp. 140, 141–2.

28 Ibid., p. 144 (cf. pp. 37, 39–40 above).

29 See pp. 44–7 below.

30 *Frühschriften* 1:143: 'Das ist aber alles darumb erzelt ... das man wusse, wie diejhenig, so ytzundt wider ir oberkait auffrurig sein, nicht cristen seyen, sonder aigennutzig heyden ...'

31 Ibid., pp. 96–7. Cf. Luther's views in chapter two, p. 19.

32 See chapter two, p. 20.

33 Stadtarchiv Schwäbisch Hall 4/54, fols. 157b–158a. The following year (1527) Brenz had to repeat the same ideas at far greater length when the city council's *Feiertagsordnung* was denounced by some as a betrayal of the Reformation and a relapse into popery. See 'Aliud prooemium ad repetendum statutum de diebus festivis nuper pronunciatum, sed a quibusdam male feriatis hominibus non tam male intellectum quam pessime interpretatum,' Bayerisches Staatsarchiv Nürnberg 111/11, fols. 175b–177a.

34 See n. 3 above.

35 See below, n. 95.

36 The circumstances are more fully described in chapter six.

37 The question here is whether secular government may take any action at all against the adherents of false doctrine. The question of what specific action ought to be taken will be discussed in chapter six.

38 'Ob ein obrigkeit über das gewissen handle, wann sie mit gewalt die verfüerischen leerer verweiset,' *Frühschriften* 2:501–5.

39 *Opera Omnia* (Antwerp, 1706) 1:398ff. ('Compendium Theologiae, De esse, natura et qualitate conscientiae').

40 'Ob ein weltlich oberkait recht habe, in des glaubens sachen mit dem schwert zu handeln,' *Frühschriften* 2:517–28; also in ARG 60 (1969): 67–75. English translation by J.M. Estes in *Mennonite Quarterly Review* 49 (1975): 28–37. On the anonymous author, see ibid., p. 24.

41 'Antwort auff die vertzeichnus, so auff disse frag (Ob ein weltliche oberkait recht habe, in des glaubens sachen mit dem schwert zu handeln) gestelt ist,' *Frühschriften* 2:528-41.

42 Ibid., p. 528.

43 Ibid., pp. 528-9.

44 Ibid., pp. 531-2, 533-4.

45 Ibid., pp. 539, 541.

46 Ibid., p. 540: 'Dan das stuck ist in die hand der oberkait gesetzt, sie sey recht oder falsch glaubig, das sie in irm gebiet mag new geselschaft, zunfft und rottirung gedulden oder wern auff ir gut ansehen, und ist zu keinem auss not getrungen. So nu ein oberkait ein falschen glauben hat und wil die versamlung der rechtglaubigen in irm gebiet nit gestatten, thut sie wol an im selbs unrecht ... Aber nach der volg irs falschen glaubens thut sie nit unweysslich und unbillich.'

47 Ibid., pp. 521-2.

48 Ibid., pp. 532-4.

49 Ibid., pp. 525-6.

50 Archduke Ferdinand of Austria was elected King of Bohemia in 1526.

51 *Frühschriften* 2:534.

52 Ibid., p. 535. The *Historia Tripartita* is the source of Brenz's historical information.

53 *Frühschriften* 2:483: 'Darzu so mögen die unglaubigen und ketzer eben alss wol vor der welt als byderleut leben als die rechtglaubigen.'

54 Ibid., p. 523.

55 Ibid., p. 538.

56 Ibid., p. 541 (the final sentence of Brenz's 'Antwort'): 'So ist auch der weltlichen oberkait zustendig, das sie aller offentlichen unordnung und verwerung furkome, und *wurt auf ir gewussen nicht gedrungen*, das sie ein new sect, sinagog und offenlich versamlung zu nachtail der rechten cristen einkommen lass, sonder *mag* mit gutem gewussen demselben nachtailigen furnemen der newen sect wern und sie geburlicher, beschaidenlicher, untiranischer weys abstellen etc.' Emphasis added.

57 Hans-Dieter Schmid, *Täufertum und Obrigkeit in Nürnberg*, Schriftenreihe des Stadtarchivs Nürnberg 10 (1972), pp. 291-4. For a brief summary of the problem and a review of the literature, see the introduction to my translation of the anonymous memorandum.

58 'Ob die weltlich christenlich oberkait gewalt hab falsch lerer oder irrig secten zu wern und in gaistlichen sachen der kirchen breuch zu ordnen?' Stadtarchiv Schwäbisch Hall 4/55, fols. 56a-74b. Hereafter cited as 'Osiander.'

59 'Ob ein weltliche oberkait in geistlichen sachen moge ordnen, falsche ler wern und gotloss misbreuch abstellen?' Ibid., fols. 45a-55b. Hereafter cited as 'Linck.' Linck was preacher at the Church of the Holy Spirit in Nuremberg.

60 The Nurembergers' definition of the relationship between secular and spiritual authority comes straight from Luther, with Osiander (fols. 56a–b) quoting almost verbatim from *On Secular Authority* (cf. WA 11:261–71). In this and in other respects in the Nuremberg counter-memoranda are splendid examples of Luther's ideas being used by his followers for un-Luther-like ends.

61 Osiander, fols. 61b–64a; Linck, fols. 45a–b, 48b–49a.

62 Osiander, fol. 57b.

63 Cf. chapter two, pp. 20, 27–8.

64 Osiander, fols. 57b–58a.

65 Ibid., fols. 58a–b.

66 Ibid., fol. 72b; Linck, fol. 49b.

67 Osiander, fols. 57a, 63a, 70a–b.

68 Ibid., fols. 64a–b.

69 Ibid., fols. 67a–68a.

70 Ibid., fols. 68a–69a, 72a, 73b–74b; Linck, fols. 49b–50b.

71 Osiander, fols. 57a, 59a–b, 61b, 73b–74a.

72 Linck, fol. 50a.

73 Ibid., fol. 50b.

74 Ibid., fol. 49b.

75 See above, pp. 45–6.

76 See above, pp. 44–5.

77 See above, p. 36.

78 Details in chapter five.

79 Richter 1:195–7; Sehling 11:171–4.

80 See above, p. 9.

81 See above, p. 43.

82 Pressel, pp. 156–9.

83 Reyscher 8:114 (preamble to the Württemberg Confession, 1551): 'Dann wiewol wir wol wissen, dass zwischen dem Weltlichen vnd Geistlichen Regiment sein vnderschid ist, Jedoch, dieweil der Psalm [2:10–12] vns gantz ernstlich ermanet, vn[d] sagt[:] Lasst euch weisen jr Künig, vnnd lasst euch züchtigen jr Richter auff Erden, dienet dem HERRN mit forcht, und frewet euch mit zittern[,] So haben wir die Götlich Stimm nit verachtet, sonder all vnser fürnemen, vnnd fleiss, vnsers bessten vermügens, der rechten waren Kirchen des Sons Gottes zuhelffen, anrichten sollen.'

84 Martin Brecht, *Die frühe Theologie des Johannes Brenz* (Tübingen, 1966), pp. 241–7.

85 The works are: 1 / *De potestate et Primatu Papae* (1537), CR 3:271–86, which was adopted as an addendum to the Articles of Schmalkalden. On 23 February 1537

Brenz wrote to Johann Bugenhagen (ibid., col. 288) authorizing the latter to sign the
articles and the *De potestate* on his behalf. 2 / *De officio principum, quod mandatum Dei praecipiat eis tollere abusus Ecclesiasticos* (1539). From 1540 on this work
was inserted into all editions of the *Philosophiae Moralis Epitomes*, ibid. 16:85–105.
On 8 January 1540 Melanchthon wrote to Brenz (ibid. 3:924): 'De *officio Principum*
scripsi propter Iuliacensem Cancellarium, cum quo eadem ad verbum disputavi.' 3 /
De officio Principum, quod mandatum Dei praecipiat eis tollere abusus Ecclesiae
(1539, pub. 1541), ibid. 11:432–8. 4 / The section 'De Magistratibus Civilibus et
Dignitate Rerum Politicarum' in the 1535 and 1543 eds. of the *Loci theologici*, ibid.
21:542–54, 984–1015.

86 Ibid. 3:281. See also ibid. 11:434; 16:89–90, 97; 21:1013.
87 See the section 'De officio principum secularium in ecclesia ...' in the Apology of the
Württemberg Confession (1555), *Opera* 8:175–99, esp. pp. 175–9. Here Brenz
defends the right of lay Christians, but especially the princes as foremost members
of the church, to judge, by virtue of the priesthood of all believers, between true and
false doctrine. That it is the prince's duty to promote true preaching, and to banish
false preachers and impious doctrines from the churches in his territory, is simply
asserted (p. 177); no attempt is made to prove it. Hence this work is not the
general theological justification of the state church that its title leads one to expect.
88 See below, p. 55.
89 CR 16:86–7, 94.
90 Ibid. 3:434–5; 16:91–2; 21:553–4, 991–4.
91 Ibid. 3:434; 16:87–8, 91, 95–6; 21:1011–12.
92 Ibid. 3:434; 16:86, 93; 21:553.
93 Esp. Gen. 9:6; Ps. 2:10–12; Is. 49:23.
94 Esp. Rom. 13:3–4; 1 Tim. 2:2; 1 Pet. 2:14.
95 1 / 'De electione Senatus Halensis sermo habitus dominica quinta post trinitatis
Anno 1541,' Landesbibliothek Stuttgart, Cod. theol. et phil. 278 (Homiliae Evangeliorum, quae usitato more in diebus dominis proponuntur), fols. 128b–131b;
2 / 'Homilia habita anno 1543 de Electione Senatus Hallensis,' ibid., fols.
241a–244a; 3 / 'De electione Senatus Homilia, habita anno 1545,' in *Pericopae
Evangeliorum, Quae Vsitato More in praecipuis Festis legi solent, expositae per
Ioan. Brent.* (Frankfurt, 1564), pp. 287–93; 4 / 'Altera Homilia de electione & officio Magistratus, habita 1546,' ibid., pp. 294–300. Hereafter each sermon will be
cited by the date only.
96 1541, fol. 129a; 1543, fol. 241b; 1545, pp. 288–9; 1546, p. 296. Cf. pp. 21, 41 above.
97 *Opera* 1:111–12 (Commentary on Genesis, 1553–7). See also 1541, fols. 129a–b;
1545, pp. 290–3; *Opera* 4:626 (Commentary on Isaiah, 1544–8); ibid. 1:861 (Commentary on Leviticus, 1538 or 39).

98 1541, fols. 129a–b; 1546, p. 297. See also *Opera* 6:354 (Homilies on John, 1543–6).
99 1543, fols. 242a–b.
100 1546, p. 299; 1541, fols. 130a–131a; 1543, fols. 242b–243b.
101 1546, p. 299; 1541, fols. 131a–b; 1543, fols. 243b–244a.
102 See the preamble to the Church Order of 1559, cited on p. 58 below.
103 1546, pp. 297–8.
104 1541, fol. 131a.
105 1541, fols. 129a, 130a, 131b; 1543, fols. 242a, 243b–244a.
106 Hans-Martin Maurer, 'Herzog Christoph als Landesherr,' BWKG 68/9 (1968/9): 112–38, pp. 122, 128–30. See pp. 79–80, 94, 102–3 below.
107 Reyscher 8:114.
108 Ibid., p. 167. See also *Opera* 1:919, 932 (Commentary on Numbers, 1560).
109 Reyscher 8:111. See also *Opera* 6:601 (Homilies on John, 1543–6).

CHAPTER FOUR

1 Karl Müller, 'Die Anfänge der Konsistorialverfassung im lutherischen Deutschland,' *Historische Zeitschrift* 102 (1909): 1–30.
2 Ibid., pp. 3–13.
3 Ibid., pp. 13–14. Marriage came under the jurisdiction of special *Ehegerichte*, not of the *Kirchenrat*.
4 Gerhard Schäfer, *Landeskirchliches Archiv Stuttgart: Übersicht über die Bestände und Inventar der Allgemeinen Kirchenakten* (Stuttgart, 1972), p. 14.
5 Hauptstaatsarchiv Stuttgart A63, B. 10: Christopher's instructions to Brenz (drafted by Brenz himself), July 1553; and Brenz's report to Christopher, 'Acta zu Newenburg in der Pfaltz, in mense Augusto Anno 53.'
6 Pressel, pp. 447–50: 'Bedenken, die Reformation und Visitation der Kirchen und hohen Schulen in der Pfalz betreffend.'
7 The editors of Sehling 14 (Kurpfalz) completely overlooked the influence of Württemberg. For a summary of that influence, see Martin Brecht's review of the Sehling volume in *Zeitschrift für Württembergische Landesgeschichte* 28 (1969): 465–8. For a discussion of the origins and development of the *Kirchenrat* in the Palatinate, see Volker Press, *Calvinismus und Territorialstaat: Regierung und Zentralbehörden der Kurpfalz, 1559–1619* (Stuttgart, 1970), pp. 114–29; 218–20, 238–53, 284–7. Press, like the Sehling editors, ignored the Württemberg archives and thus has nothing to say about the influence of Brenz or the Württemberg model.
8 Müller, pp. 18–23; Hans-Martin Maurer and Kuno Ulshöfer, *Johannes Brenz und die Reformation in Württemberg* (Stuttgart and Aalen, n.d.), pp. 197–200.
9 See above, pp. 33–4.

10 Friedrich Wintterlin, *Geschichte der Behördenorganisation in Württemberg* (Stuttgart, 1904), pp. 24–6.

11 Hans-Martin Maurer, 'Herzog Christoph als Landesherr,' BWKG 68/9 (1968–9): 112–38, pp. 115–20.

12 Müller, pp. 14–17.

13 See Martin Brecht, 'Die Ordnung der württembergischen Kirche im Zeitalter der Reformation,' *Kirchenordnung und Kirchenzucht in Württemberg vom 16. bis zum 18. Jahrhundert* (Stuttgart, 1967), pp. 9–52; and James M. Estes, 'Johannes Brenz and the Institutionalization of the Reformation in Württemberg,' *Central European History* 6 (1973): 44–59.

14 *Frühschriften* 1:144–9.

15 Ibid., pp. 144–6.

16 Ibid., p. 149.

17 ARG 11 (1914): 285–6 ('Gutachten wegen Verwertung des Kirchenguts,' 1526); Köhler, pp. 390–1 (Brenz to the city council of Schwäbisch Hall, 28 January 1531).

18 The problem of ecclesiastical discipline will be dealt with more fully in the following chapter. Here only as much of that story will be told as is necessary to maintain the continuity of the story of Brenz's early efforts in the area of ecclesiastical administration.

19 Richter 1:46.

20 Ibid., pp. 45–6.

21 Ibid., p. 46: 'Vnd ob etwas anders in der kirchen ausserthalb der gemeinen ordnung zu thon were solt es vorhin an die bestimpten von der Oberkait gelangen von den selbigen ainer gantzen Oberkait furgebracht werden. Welche so es nutzlich fur die kirchen wurd angesehen approbirt oder so es fur untuglich geacht verwurffe Darmit nit einer Itliche sonderliche person Irs gefallens in der kirchen ordnung zu stolzieren vnd leben gestat wurd.'

22 'Ordnung des Sends,' 28 January 1531, in Köhler, pp. 391–6.

23 Albert Michael Koeniger, 'Brenz und der Send,' in *Beiträge zur Geschichte der Renaissance und Reformation* (Munich and Freising, 1917), pp. 208–24: 220–1.

24 'Ein abredt der theologen zu Onoltzbach ...,' dated 'umb Valentinii im 31. jar.' Stadtarchiv Schwäbisch Hall 4/54, fols. 151b–152b.

25 'Gutachten der Nürnberger Theologen über die Sendordnung von Johannes Brenz,' May 1531, in Gerhard Müller and Gottfried Seebass, eds., *Andreas Osiander d. Ä. Gesamtausgabe*, vol. 4: *Schriften und Briefe, Mai 1530 bis Ende 1532* (Gütersloh, 1981), pp. 236–9.

26 'Gutachten der Ansbacher Theologen über den 'Neuen Begriff',' December 1531, in *Osiander Gesamtausgabe* 4:382–8.

27 Ibid., pp. 384–5: 'Nachdem aber dennoch der ban oder excommunication zur erhalltung christlicher communion und kirchenpolicey nötig ist ... so sihet uns für nutz

und nötig an, das zuvor in einer yetlichen rifier ettlich auss den fürnemsten kyr-
chendiener, auch sonst auss dem kyrchenvolck ettlich frum, redlich, verstendig
christen erwelet, die heiss man gleich, wie man wöll, visitatores, superattendentes,
presbyteros ecclesiae, judices rerum ecclesiasticarum oder sonst, wie man will,
deren ampt sollt sein, in den sträfflichen lastern, so des bans wirdig seyen, zu
urteilen, item die kyrchenordnung handzuhaben, item in eesachen zu erckennen
und anderst, so zu der kyrchenpolicey gehört, zu administriern; dan wo das nit
geschicht, so achten wir, der offenlich ban mög nit angericht werden, und bsorgen,
die gestellte kyrchenordnung werde mehr ein unordnung sein, dweill mortuae leges
sine vivis legibus nymmer kein bstandt haben.'

28 This is indicated by the reference to rural chapters in the concluding paragraph of
the memorandum; ibid., p. 388: '[W]ir befinden, das ... diese kyrchenordnung kein
ordnung bleiben kan oder mag, on angerichte kyrchenpolicey under den personen
der kyrchen, nemlich das ettlich zu visitatores oder superattendentes oder judices
rerum ecclesiasticarum oder capitula stättlich verordnet wurden ...' The district of a
chapter was a deanery (decanat).

29 A senatus presbyterorum was established in Nuremberg on 20 May 1533. The
relevant Ratsbeschluss is printed in Mitteilungen des Vereins für Geschichte der
Stadt Nürnberg 34 (1937): 128–9. Apparently no superintendents were appointed
at this time: the Ratsbeschluss instructs the rural pastors to take their problems
directly to the theologians in Nuremberg. I have no information concerning similar
measures in Brandenburg-Ansbach.

30 'Ordnung der Visitation,' Pressel, pp. 166–70.

31 See above, p. 9.

32 Pressel, pp. 167–8.

33 Ibid., pp. 168–70.

34 Ibid., p. 170.

35 Ibid., p. 156 (Brenz to Joachim Camerarius, 17 September 1535): 'Ego permissu
principis demum repetam post autumnum, fortassis revocandus ad visitationem
ecclesiarum.'

36 Brecht, Kirchenordnung und Kirchenzucht, pp. 24–6.

37 Reyscher 8:48.

38 Ibid., p. 49.

39 Ibid., p. 59.

40 Julius Rauscher, ed., Württembergische Visitationsakten, 1 (Stuttgart, 1932): xxviii.

41 Brecht, Kirchenordnung und Kirchenzucht, p. 26.

42 Ibid.

43 Reyscher 8:66–9. On the question of the date, see Brecht, Kirchenordnung und
Kirchenzucht, p. 27, n. 72.

44 Reyscher 8:67. On the latter question, decisions were to be rendered by the 'Rent-
kammerräte sampt andern darzu geordneten.'

45 Ibid., pp. 69–80.

46 Ibid., pp. 71–5. Reyscher's footnotes give the 1544 text.

47 Ibid., pp. 75–7.

48 Ibid., pp. 77–9.

49 See chapter one, p. 7.

50 Pub. by Georg Lenckner in *Württembergisch Franken* 49 (Neue Folge 29, 1965): 16.

51 In the preface to the Church Order of 1543 Brenz wrote: 'Dann, auch das wie bey diser rohen, frechen, und undanckbaren welt, durch versaumnus der Schulen und kirchen zubesorgen, die *Ministeria* der kirchen nit allerdings, mit so geleerten personen, wie die notdurft wol erfordert, und man gleichgern wollte, versehen werden möchte ...' From the original edition (see Köhler, no. 122), which has no pagination in the preface.

52 For information about the revived Hall chapter we are dependent upon the second-hand accounts in Julius Hartmann and Karl Jäger, *Johann Brenz*, 2 vols. (Hamburg, 1840) 2:78–80; and Julius Gmelin, *Hällische Geschichte* (Schwäbisch Hall, 1899), pp. 757–8. The sources they used have apparently been lost. There are, however, a few scraps of information in the Church Order of 1543 and in Herolt's chronicle.

53 The Church Order of 1543 (see n. 51 above), p. xcvi, refers to 'annual synods.'

54 Herolt, p. 119. Hartmann/Jäger 2:80, and Gmelin, p. 757, assert that Brenz was made superintendent.

55 Hartmann/Jäger say one, Gmelin says two.

56 Reyscher 8:74. The records of one such meeting, held in Sindelfingen in 1544, have been preserved. See G. Bossert, 'Acta in Synodo Sindelfingensi,' BWKG 10 (1908): 1–31.

57 Reyscher 8:79.

58 Ibid., pp. 79–80.

59 Ibid., pp. 80–92.

60 Ibid., pp. 92–3 ('Befehl an die Amtleute, das Interim verkündigen zu lassen,' 20 July 1548).

61 See chapter one, p. 15.

62 A fragment of the original ordinance survives in the Hauptstaatsarchiv Stuttgart A63, B. 10. See Brecht, *Kirchenordnung und Kirchenzucht*, pp. 33–4, for a summary and analysis.

63 Viktor Ernst, 'Die Entstehung des württembergischen Kirchenguts,' *Württembergische Jahrbücher für Statistik und Landeskunde*, 1911, pp. 377–424; pp. 399–400.

64 Ibid., pp. 386–92.

65 Reyscher 8:100–5.

66 The original ordinance, once thought lost, is in the Landeskirchliches Archiv, Stuttgart. See Brecht, *Kirchenordnung und Kirchenzucht*, pp. 35–6.

67 Ernst, 'Kirchengut,' pp. 400–4.
68 The greatest loss occurred when Spanish troops ransacked the Stuttgart archives during the Thirty Years War. See Wilhelm Lempp, *Der Württembergische Synodus, 1553–1924* (Stuttgart, 1959), p. 53.
69 See nn. 62–7 above.
70 Reyscher 8:273.
71 Ibid., pp. 100, 102–3.
72 Ibid., p. 273.
73 Ibid., p. 275.
74 Ibid., pp. 100–2, 275–82.
75 Ibid., pp. 101, 238–9, 270–3, 275, 280.
76 See above, p. 62.
77 Maurer/Ulshöfer, p. 152.
78 Reyscher 8:238–9.
79 Ibid., pp. 271–2. Cf. above, p. 62.
80 Ernst, 'Kirchengut,' pp. 406–8.
81 See below, pp. 102–3.
82 Reyscher 8:102–3, 274–5.
83 Ibid., pp. 222–34. An 'Instruktion' (now lost) on the appointment of new clergymen was in force in July 1553, when Brenz recommended its adoption in Pfalz-Neuburg. See Haupstaatsarchiv Stuttgart A63, B. 10.
84 See above, p. 69.
85 Reyscher 8:223–8, 234.
86 Ibid., pp. 222–3.
87 Ibid., p. 228.
88 Ibid., pp. 245–56.
89 Ibid., pp. 245–6.
90 Julius Rauscher, *Württembergische Reformationsgeschichte* (Stuttgart, 1934), p. 193.
91 Eugen Schneider, *Württembergische Reformationsgeschichte* (Stuttgart, 1887), p. 114.
92 Reyscher 8:246–50.
93 Ibid., pp. 250–1.
94 Ibid., pp. 251–2.
95 Ibid., pp. 252, 266, 269–70.
96 Ibid., p. 103.
97 The full title was 'gemeiner Conuentus des Consistorij bey vnser Cantzley der Superintendentz halben,' ibid., p. 269.
98 In the 'Ordnung des Sends' of 1531: Köhler, p. 392, n. 1. In 1526 Brenz had made the same point in his Commentary on Ephesians. See Walther Köhler, ed.,

Johannes Brenz' Kommentar zum Briefe des Apostels Paulus an die Epheser (Heidelbrg, 1935), p. 57.

99 Lempp, *Synodus*, p. 19.
100 See above, p. 65.
101 Reyscher 8:256–60. The original ordinance of 1553 survives in the Landeskirchliches Archiv, Stuttgart. See Brecht, *Kirchenordnung und Kirchenzucht*, pp. 37–8.
102 Reyscher 8:260–5.
103 The territorial visitation will be discussed in chapter five.
104 Maurer, pp. 122–4.
105 Reyscher 8:256, 259–60.
106 Ibid., pp. 257–9.
107 Ibid., pp. 248–9.
108 Ibid., pp. 256–7.
109 Maurer, pp. 124–5.
110 Ibid., p. 124, n. 29.
111 Reyscher 8:256, n. 29.
112 Maurer, p. 125.
113 Reyscher 8:259.
114 See above, pp. 54–7.

CHAPTER FIVE

1 For general developments in Upper Germany and Switzerland, see Walther Köhler, *Zürcher Ehegericht und Genfer Konsistorium*, 2 vols. (Leipzig, 1932/42).
2 F. Donald Logan, *Excommunication and the Secular Arm in Medieval England* (Toronto, 1968), pp. 14–16.
3 *Frühschriften* 1:100–2: 'Underrichtung der zwispaltigen artickel cristenlichs glaubens.' Cf. WA 6:64.
4 See n. 11 below.
5 Walther Köhler, ed., *Johannes Brenz' Kommentar zum Briefe des Apostels Paulus an die Epheser* (Heidelberg, 1935).
6 *Frühschriften* 2:45–53 (from a series of sermons preached during Lent 1527).
7 Ibid., p. 52.
8 Commentary on Ephesians, p. 57.
9 *Frühschriften* 2:49, 52–3; Commentary on Ephesians, p. 57.
10 Albert Michael Koeniger, 'Brenz und der Send,' in *Beiträge zur Geschichte der Renaissance und Reformation* (Munich and Freising, 1917), pp. 208–24: 208–16. See also *Realencyclopädie für protestantische Theologie und Kirche*, s.v. 'Send, Sendgericht,' by Albert Hauck.
11 Richter 1:45–6: 'Von der Kirchen Straff vom Ban und Synodo.'

12 See chapter four, n. 21.

13 Richter 1:46.

14 Bayerisches Staatsarchiv Nürnberg, 111/11, fols. 171a–173b. On the date, see Martin Brecht, 'Anfänge reformatorischer Kirchenordnung und Sittenzucht bei Johannes Brenz,' *Zeitschrift der Savigny-Stiftung für Rechtsgeschichte*, Kanonistische Abteilung, 86 (1969): 322–47, p. 326, n. 20. See ibid., pp. 336–8, for a summary of the mandate.

15 Bayerisches Staatsarchiv Nürnberg, 111/11, fols. 174a–175b.

16 Ibid., fol. 171a.

17 Ibid., fols. 171a–172b. The mandate also contains (fols. 172b–173a) regulations governing the uniform observance of holidays and the marriage of minors, matters of no interest here.

18 Ibid., fols. 173a–b. The mandate calls the inspectors simply 'die verordneten.' Brenz called them 'accasuatores publici": ibid., fol. 175a.

19 Ibid., fol. 175a: 'Cognominantur enim vernacula lingua beinlin, kleckstein, verretter etc.'

20 Ibid., fol. 173b.

21 Ibid., fols. 178b–179a: Brenz's sermon inaugurating the 'Ordnung etlicher kirchenbreuch' (Order of Public Worship) of 1527.

22 Ibid., fols. 174a–b.

23 Köhler, pp. 391–6.

24 Ibid., pp. 390–1 (Brenz to the city council, 28 January 1531). Why the council asked Brenz for this ordinance is not indicated, but see p. 90.

25 Koeniger, 'Brenz und der Send,' pp. 218–21, demonstrates this in some detail.

26 Julius Hartmann and Karl Jäger, *Johann Brenz*, 2 vols. (Hamburg, 1840), 1:332.

27 At any rate, this is the conclusion one draws from the absence of a single scrap of evidence for its existence. How could such a court have functioned in an area in which the clergy were still largely outside the control of the city council?

28 Hartmann/Jäger 1:396. The 'ordnung des sends' is mentioned in a memorandum of the Ansbach theologians dating from mid-February 1531: Stadtarchiv Schwäbisch Hall 4/54, fol. 151b.

29 See the *iudicium* of the Ansbach theologians (May 1531) in Gerhard Müller and Gottfried Seebass, eds., *Andreas Osiander d. Ä. Gesamtausgabe*, vol. 4: *Schriften und Briefe, Mai 1530 bis Ende 1532* (Gütersloh, 1981), p. 256.

30 H. Westermayer, *Die Brandenburgisch-Nürnbergische Kirchenvisitation und Kirchenordnung, 1528–1533* (Erlangen, 1894), pp. 85–7; Adolf Engelhardt, *Die Reformation in Nürnberg*, vol. 2, in *Mitteilungen des Vereins für Geschichte der Stadt Nürnberg* 34 (1937): 114–16.

31 'Gutachten der Nürnberger Theologen über die Sendordnung von Johannes Brenz,' May 1531, in *Osiander Gesamtausgabe* 4:236–9, esp. pp. 237–8.

32 Pressel, pp. 117–18: 'Verzeichnus auff die Nürnbergisch pesserung in der gstellten ordnung der Kyrchenbreuch,' 15 May 1531. (Date according to Westermayer, p. 84.)

33 The reference is to article 4 of the recess of the conference at which the Schmalkaldic League was founded (31 December 1530). See Ekkehart Fabian, ed., *Die Schmalkaldischen Bundesabschiede, 1530–1532* (Tübingen, 1958), pp. 13–14; and St L. 16:1769–70.

34 Engelhardt, p. 117.

35 'Gutachten der Ansbacher Theologen über den 'Neuen Begriff',' in *Osiander Gesamtausgabe* 4:382–8.

36 Ibid., pp. 383–4.

37 Ibid., pp. 384–5. See chapter four, n. 27.

38 Richter 1:202–3, and Sehling 11:185–6 (Brandenburg-Nuremberg, 1533); Reyscher 8:46–8 (Württemberg, 1536); Richter 2:15–16 (Schwäbisch Hall, 1543).

39 Pressel, pp. 110–11.

40 Martin Brecht, *Kirchenordnung und Kirchenzucht in Württemberg vom 16. bis zum 18. Jahrhundert* (Stuttgart, 1967), pp. 19–21.

41 Pressel, pp. 169–70.

42 See pp. 54–5.

43 Landesbibliothek Stuttgart, Cod. theol. et phil. 278, fol. 243b (Election Sermon of 1543).

44 *Pericopae Evangeliorum ... expositae per Ioan. Brent.* (Frankfurt, 1564), p. 299 (Election Sermon of 1546).

45 H. Lietzmann, H. Bornkamm, et al., eds., *Die Bekenntnisschriften der evangelisch-lutherischen Kirche*, 2nd ed. (Göttingen, 1952), pp. 456–7.

46 WA-TR 4:278–80.

47 WA-Br 10:436–7.

48 Reyscher 12:193–239.

49 Ibid., pp. 196–205.

50 Pressel, p. 386.

51 Reyscher 8:192–3.

52 The synod was established in May 1553, and Brenz's description of the meeting in question (see n. 50 above) was written ca. 10 September 1554.

53 Pressel, p. 386.

54 Ibid., pp. 252–4. See also Brecht, *Kirchenordnung und Kirchenzucht*, p. 41. n. 109.

55 Reyscher 8:265–9.

56 Pressel, p. 387: '... causa rite et legitime cognita ac perspecta ex permissu et concessione Illustriss. vestrae Celsitudinis excommunicetur.'

57 Most of the sources for the Lyser-Andreä affair (i.e., those not printed elsewhere) are found in Otto Matthes, '10 Brief aus den Jahren 1523–1590 aus dem Besitz Johann Valentin Andreäs, Teil 2: Ein Kirchenzuchtplan Jakob Andreäs,' BWKG 62 (1962): 124–253, esp. pp. 124–98.

58 'Epistola Casp. Liseri ad Ducem Wirtemb. Christophorum de reproducenda Censura Ecclesiastica s. Excommunicatione contra improbos' (6 September 1554): Sattler 4:71–5, p. 72.

59 Brecht, *Kirchenordnung und Kirchenzucht*, p. 40.

60 Sattler 4:73. Viret's plan was in his *De origine, continuatione, usu, auctoritate atque praestantia ministri verbi Dei, et sacramentorum* ... (Geneva, 1554).

61 Sattler 4:73, 75.

62 Matthes, p. 125 (Andreä to Duke Christopher, 2 November 1554).

63 Ibid., pp. 125, 174–5, 176.

64 Sattler 4:76 (Christopher's notation at the end of Lyser's letter).

65 Lyser had also expressed himself in favour of the election of pastors by the congregations: CR 43:51 (Lyser to Calvin, 27 February 1554).

66 'Brentii Consilium in causa Censurae Ecclesiasticae ad Lyseri epistolam' (ca. 10 September 1554): Pressel, pp. 385–8.

67 Sattler 4:72.

68 On this point cf. *Opera* 5:345 (Commentary on Matthew, 1554): 'Etsi autem multi sumunt Coenam Domini indigne, et impoenitenter, tamen quotquot eam, iuxta publicam Ecclesiae sue ordinationem sumunt, non sunt ab aliis temere et suo ipsorum iudicio condemnandi. Si videris hominem nuper ebrium Coenam Domini sumere ... cogites tecum: ... Vidisti quidem peccatum illius, sed non vidisti suspiria eius: heri deliquit, hodie poenituit ... [N]ullus qui profitetur poenitentiam reiieciendus est a Coena Domini ...' See also Reyscher 8:253.

69 Pressel, p. 387: '... non possum nec debeo Illustrissimae Vestra Celsitudini consulere, ut permittat Pastori Nürtingensi novum Consistorium et novos pontificios Canones in sua Ecclesia instituere ...'

70 Matthes, p. 174: 'Deutscher Bescheid des Herzogs Christoph vom 11. September 1554 an Caspar Lyser.'

71 Ibid., pp. 124–7.

72 See the 'Deutsches Protokoll vom 24. November 1554' in Matthes, pp. 178–9 (text), and 179–83 (commentary). The remonstrance is found in the Hauptstaatsarchiv Stuttgart A63, Bü. 15, fols. 94a–107b (draft in Brenz's hand), and fols. 55a–57b (fair copy).

73 *Opera* 5:343–6. Date from Brecht, 'Anfänge,' p. 344.

74 For a different view, see Brecht, 'Anfänge,' p. 346. For my objections to that view, see *Church History* 41 (1972): 477, n. 53.

75 Richter 2:194–6.

76 Hauptstaatsarchiv Stuttgart A63, Bü. 10 (fols. unnumbered): 'Bedenken der verordneten Räte über die 23 Artikel des Herzogs.' See Brecht, *Kirchenordnung und Kirchenzucht*, p. 45, n. 127.

77 Text in Matthes, pp. 193–6.

78 Text of Christopher's comments in Matthes, pp. 230–1.

79 Hans-Martin Maurer, 'Herzog Christoph als Landesherr,' BWKG 68/9 (1968/9): 112–38, pp. 120–8.

80 The ordinance of 13 February 1557 is summarized in Brecht, *Kirchenordnung und Kirchenzucht*, pp. 47–9.

81 Reyscher 8:260–5.

82 Maurer, p. 125, n. 32.

83 See above, p. 79.

84 Maurer, pp. 125–32.

85 Hauptstaatsarchiv Stuttgart A63, Bü. 15, fols. 112a–116b: 'Unterthenig bericht der Theologorum, das bedencken De publica excommunicatione belangendt,' 1565 (in Brenz's hand).

86 Ibid., fols. 110a–b: memorandum of the Oberräte, with the concluding notation, 'Beleibt auch bey disem bedenckhen.'

CHAPTER SIX

1 For a useful general introduction, see Cynthia Grant Schoenberger, 'The Development of the Lutheran Theory of Resistance: 1523–1530,' *The Sixteenth Century Journal* 8 (1977): 61–76.

2 Richter 1:42–3.

3 St L. 15:2204.

4 Ibid., pp. 2205–6, 2254; 16:187–8.

5 Ibid., 15:2253–4.

6 'Ob die bundsvereinigung vermog, das die geystlich nit allein in irer weltlichen, sonder auch in irer geystlichen jurisdiction von den bundsstenden beschirmpt sollen werden,' pub. by Walther Köhler in ARG, 10 (1912–13): 176–82.

7 René Hauswirth, *Landgraf Philipp von Hessen und Zwingli, 1526–1531*, Schriften zur Kirchen- und Rechtsgeschichte, Nr. 35 (Tübingen and Basel, 1968), pp. 34–5, 100–1.

8 Hans von Schubert, *Bekenntnisbildung und Religionspolitik, 1529/30 (1524–1534)* (Gotha, 1910), pp. 185–7.

9 Luther to Elector John, 6 March 1530. Text in Heinz Scheible, ed., *Das Widerstandsrecht als Problem der deutschen Protestanten, 1523–1546*, Texte zur Kirchen- und Theologiegeschichte, Heft 10 (Gütersloh, 1969), pp. 60–3; and in WA-Br 5:258–61. See also WA 19:632–45 (*Ob Kriegsleute auch in seligem Stande sein können*, 1526).

10 Scheible, *Widerstandsrecht*, pp. 29–39.

11 v. Schubert, pp. 193–5; Harold J. Grimm, *Lazarus Spengler: A Lay Leader of the Reformation* (Columbus, 1978), pp. 142–3.

12 Scheible, *Widerstandsrecht*, pp. 40–2; Pressel, pp. 44–6.

13 v. Schubert, pp. 195–8.

14 Scheible, *Widerstandsrecht*, pp. 43–7; v. Schubert, pp. 199–202.

15 v. Schubert, pp. 204–9.

16 'Ablainung der Einred auff das gestellt bedencken, Ob k. Mt. in sachen des Evange-liums mög mit gutem gwissen widerstandt gescheen etc.' Pressel, pp. 47–63, where the date is incorrectly given as November 1529. Abridged version, with corrections of Pressel's misreadings, pub. by Walther Köhler in ARG 11 (1914): 287–90.

17 ertzschenck, ertzmarshalk, ertzkamerer, ertzdruchsess.

18 'Ob der abschied des ytzigen Augspurgischen reichstags wider daz Evangelium gefiele und kayse. Mt. wolt mit gwalt oder krieg demselbigen volg thon, was eim Cristenlichen fursten hierin mit guttem gwissen zu thon gebür,' pub. by Walther Köhler in ARG 24 (1927): 300–1.

19 WA-Br 5:653–5.

20 For an account of the conference, see Ekkehart Fabian, *Die Entstehung des Schmal-kaldischen Bundes und seiner Verfassung, 1524/29–1531/35*, Schriften zur Kirchen- und Rechtsgeschichte, Nr. 1, 2nd ed. (Tübingen, 1962), pp. 118–24.

21 Scheible, *Widerstandsrecht*, pp. 63–6.

22 Ibid., p. 67. But (pp. 67–8) the theologians then went on to recommend extremely far-reaching concessions (i.e., no resistance to the enforcement of the Augsburg Recess of 1530) in order to avoid bloodshed and win time. The jurists (p. 68) found this recommendation 'unhelpful.'

23 Ekkehart Fabian, ed., *Die Schmalkaldischen Bundesabschiede, 1530–1532* (Tübin-gen, 1958), p. 12.

24 Karl Schornbaum, *Zur Politik des Markgrafen Georg von Brandenburg vom Beginne seiner selbständigen Regierung bis zum Nürnberger Anstand, 1528–1532* (Munich, 1906), pp. 164, 484. The margrave's invitation to Brenz (15 January 1531) and Brenz's reply (18 January) are in Pressel, pp. 104–5.

25 Scheible, *Widerstandsrecht*, pp. 83–8.

26 Ibid., pp. 83–6.

27 The authors quote Accursius's gloss on D. I.1.3.

28 Published by Walther Köhler in ARG 13 (1916): 233–6.

29 Scheible, *Widerstandsrecht*, pp. 86–7. This passage contains loud echoes of the conclusion to Luther's *Ermahnung zum Frieden* of 1525: WA 18:332–4.

30 Scheible, *Widerstandsrecht*, pp. 87–8.

31 Schornbaum, pp. 165–6, 174–81, 199–230.

32 Martin Brecht, *Die frühe Theologie des Johannes Brenz*, Beiträge zur historischen Theologie, Nr. 36 (Tübingen, 1966), pp. 272–3.

33 Ibid., pp. 296–7. The same interpretation of Daniel 7 is found in Luther's *Heerpre-digt wider den Türken* (1529), WA 30/2:166; and in his preface to the book of Daniel (1530), WA *Deutsche Bibel* 11/2:12.

34 The following comments are based primarily on Hans Baron, 'Religion and Politics in the German Imperial Cities during the Reformation,' Part I, *English Historical Review* 52 (1937): 405–27.

35 Kuno Ulshöfer, 'Die evangelische Politik der Reichsstadt Hall vom Augsburger Reichstag 1530 bis zum Eintritt der Stadt in den Schmalkaldischen Bund,' *Württembergisch Franken* 55 (Neue Folge 45, 1971): 67–83, pp. 67–9.

36 See above, n. 9.

37 See above, n. 33.

38 Schornbaum, pp. 166–73.

39 For a more detailed account, see Ulshöfer, pp. 70–81.

40 Texts pub. by George Lenckner in *Württembergisch Franken* 49 (Neue Folge 39, 1965):7–10 (1536), 10–12 (1537).

41 The text of the treaty (Fabian, *Entstehung*, pp. 349–53, esp. p. 352) does indeed rule out any aggressive action against the emperor, but, by placing no limits on the right of armed resistance to aggression, it tacitly sanctions resistance to aggression from the emperor.

42 Text in St L. 16:1821–6. Hall was listed among the estates covered by the terms of the peace (col. 1822). Brenz overlooked the fact that the peace had not been confirmed by the imperial diet and was therefore not binding on the Catholic estates, who were not a party to it.

43 Ulshöfer, p. 81.

44 See above, pp. 7–8.

45 Text in BWKG 32 (1928):20.

46 Text in ibid., pp. 20–4; here esp. pp. 21–2.

47 Ibid., pp. 23–4.

48 Hans-Martin Maurer and Kuno Ulshöfer, *Johannes Brenz und die Reformation in Württemberg* (Stuttgart and Aalen, n.d.), p. 140. For a fuller account of Christopher's problems and policies in the years 1550–2, see Viktor Ernst, ed., *Briefwechsel des Herzogs Christoph von Wirtemberg*, 4 vols. (Stuttgart, 1899–1907), 1:ix–xli (Ernst's introduction).

49 The standard work on the subject of Brenz and the Anabaptists is Gottfried Seebass, *'An sint persequendi haeretici?* Die Stellung des Johannes Brenz zur Verfolgung und Bestrafung der Täufer,' BWKG 70 (1970):40–99. See Seebass's footnotes for the older literature, which is now mostly out of date. I have adopted many of Seebass's judgments and conclusions as my own.

50 *Quellen zur Geschichte der Wiedertäufer*, Vol. 1:*Herzogtum Württemberg*, ed. Gustav Bossert (Leipzig, 1930), pp. 1*–2*.

51 *Deutsche Reichstagsakten, Jüngere Reihe*, vol. 7/2, ed. Johannes Kühn (Stuttgart, 1935; rpt. Göttingen, 1963), p. 1016.

52 Bossert, *Quellen*, p. 2*, lines 4ff.

53 Seebass, pp. 42-3. See also Hans-Dieter Schmid, *Täufertum und Obrigkeit in Nürnberg*, Schriftenreihe des Stadtarchivs Nürnberg, Nr. 10 (Nuremberg, 1972), pp. 182-95.

54 WA-Br 4:498-9 (Luther to Linck, 14 July 1528). See Seebass, p. 44, n. 14.

55 Seebass, pp. 44-5; Schmid, pp. 199-200.

56 'Ob ein weltliche oberkeyt, mit gotlichem und billichem rechten möge die widerteuffer durch fewr oder schwert vom leben zu dem tod richten lassen,' *Frühschriften* 2:480-98.

57 English version by Roland Bainton (New York, 1935; rpt. 1965). Brenz's memorandum is found on pp. 154-69. In the following pages, the translation of direct citations to the Brenz memorandum is my own, based on the German text, though I have not hesitated to adopt a felicitous phrase here and there from Bainton's version.

58 Bainton, pp. 128-9.

59 *Frühschriften* 2:481-5; Bainton, pp. 155-8. The reference to the hangman as learned doctor comes almost verbatim from Luther's *An den christlichen Adel* (1520): WA 6:455. Cf. also ibid., 1:624 (Conclusio LXXX of the *Resolutiones* of 1518); and ibid., 11:261-71 (part II of *Von welltlicher Uberkeytt*, 1523).

60 *Frühschriften* 2:485-7; Bainton, pp. 158-60.

61 *Frühschriften* 2:487-8; Bainton, p. 160.

62 *Frühschriften* 2:488-9; Bainton, p. 161.

63 *Frühschriften* 2:489-90; Bainton, p. 162.

64 *Frühschriften* 2:490-2; Bainton, pp. 162-4.

65 *Frühschriften* 2:492-3; Bainton, pp. 164-5. The text of the decree which Brenz used reads: 'Si quis rebaptizare quempiam de ministris catholicae sectae fuerit detectus, una cum eo, qui piaculare crimen commisit, si tamen capax criminis sit per aetatem, cui persuasum sit, ultimo supplicio percellatur.' Modern critical editions of the decree (*Codex Just.*, I.6.2) read: 'Si quis rebaptizasse, ex quo lex lata est, quempiam de *mysteriis* catholicae sectae' etc.

66 *Frühschriften* 2:493-4; Bainton, pp. 165-6.

67 *Frühschriften* 2:494-6; Bainton, pp. 166-7. The sections of the imperial law referred to are: *Codex Theod.* XVI.6.1 and 2, and *Codex Just.* I.6.1 (rebaptizing bishops); *Codex Theod.* XVI.8.7 and *Codex Just.* I.7.1 (apostates); and *Codex Just.* I.7.3 (greater heretics).

68 *Frühschriften* 2:496-7; Bainton, pp. 168-9. Brenz's chief source of information about 'bloodthirsty bishops' was the *Historia Tripartita* XI.3 and XII.4.

69 *Frühschriften* 2:497-8; Bainton, p. 169.

70 CR 2:18 (Melanchthon to Myconius, February 1530).

71 Georg Lenckner, 'Täufer im Gebiet der Reichsstadt Schwäbisch Hall,' *Württembergisch Franken* 48 (Neue Folge 38, 1964):16-28.

72 Seebass, pp. 48–9.

73 Ibid., p. 50; Schmid, pp. 189–91.

74 Seebass, p. 50; Schmid, pp. 196, 198–9.

75 *Reichstagsakten* 7/1:240, 243–4.

76 WA 26:145–6 (*Von der Wiedertaufe an zwei Pfarherrn*, January 1528); WA-Br 4:498–9 (Luther to W. Linck, 14 July 1528).

77 Seebass, pp. 50–1.

78 *Frühschriften* 2:476–80.

79 Seebass, pp. 51–2.

80 Bossert, *Quellen*, pp. 3*–5*. The endorsement was really pro forma: few Protestant estates actually enforced the decrees.

81 CR 2:17–18 (Melanchthon to Myconius, February 1530); ibid., pp. 549–50 (Melanchthon to Myconius, 31 October 1531); ibid., 4:737–40 ('Bedenken der Theologen zu Wittenberg: ob man die Wiedertäufer mit dem Schwert strafen möge,' ca. January 1531); and WA 31/1:207–13 (*Der 82. Psalm ausgelegt*, 1530). On the date of the Wittenberg 'Bedenken' (incorrectly put at 1541 in CR), see Seebass, pp. 77–8, n. 141.

82 CR 2:549–50.

83 *Chronica, Zeitbuch vnnd Geschichtbibel* (Darmstadt, 1969: facsimile of 1536 ed. pub. in Ulm), fols. ccv (verso) – ccviij (recto) in the third *Chronica*.

84 For some examples, see Joseph Lecler, S.J., *Toleration and the Reformation*, trans. T.L. Westow, 2 vols. (New York and London, 1960), 1:361–2, 379; 2:261, 278, 450. See also Bainton, pp. 107–11. In *The Bloudy Tenent* (1644), Roger Williams makes brief reference to Brenz in a list of the opinions of those opposed to religious persecution. See *The Complete Writings of Roger Williams*, Vol. 3 (New York, 1963), pp. 35, 200–1. I have not been able to determine which of Brenz's works Williams cites (evidently not the memorandum of 1528).

85 Seebass, pp. 53–5, 58–60; Schmid, pp. 48–9; *Frühschriften* 2:498–9.

86 'Ob ein obrigkeit über das gewissen handle, wann sie mit gewalt die verfüerischen leerer verweiset,' *Frühschriften* 2:501–5.

87 The letter (26 March 1530) in which Spengler asks Brenz to write a memorandum is in *Frühschriften* 2:512–16. On the anonymous memorandum, see n. 40, chapter three.

88 *Frühschriften* 2:528–41. See n. 41, chapter three.

89 See above, pp. 44–7.

90 *Frühschriften* 2:501, 504–5.

91 See above, p. 44.

92 See above, p. 125.

93 *Frühschriften* 2:532, line 19.

94 See above, pp. 45–6.

95 *Frühschriften* 2:529–31.

96 See above, p. 9.

97 Seebass, pp. 70–1.

98 Ibid., p. 71.

99 *Frühschriften* 2:573–5.

100 Seebass, p. 73, assumed this. Since then an autograph by Brenz has been found. See *Frühschriften* 2:547–8.

101 Seebass, pp. 71–2.

102 Ibid., pp. 73–4.

103 Ibid., pp. 76–7. Margrave George's letter and Brenz's reply are in Pressel, pp. 104–5.

104 'Vom underschidt der widertauffer,' *Frühschriften* 2:575–6.

105 Epistula 185.VII.25.

106 Seebass, p. 75.

107 See WA 31/1:208–9 (*Der 82. Psalm ausgelegt*, 1530).

108 Seebass, pp. 77–9.

109 Ibid., pp. 80–1. The text of the mandate is in *Württembergisch Franken* 48:25–6 (see n. 71 above).

110 Claus-Peter Clasen, *Die Wiedertäufer im Herzogtum Württemberg und in benach-barten Herrschaften* (Stuttgart, 1965), p. 29.

111 Seebass, p. 82; Clasen, *Wiedertäufer*, pp. 34–5. The 'Ordnung der widertaufer' of 1536 is in Bossert, *Quellen*, pp. 57–60.

112 See above, p. 12.

113 Seebass, pp. 82–4. The memoranda of the jurists and the theologians are in Bossert, *Quellen*, pp. 50, 53–7.

114 Reyscher 8:103.

115 Ibid., pp. 247, 254, 262–3.

116 Followers of Caspar Schwenckfeld von Ossig (1489–1561), mystic and lay theolo-gian, whose unorthodox doctrines (e.g., the deification of the humanity of Christ) and rejection of all ecclesiastical authority made him anathema to the established Protestant churches.

117 Bossert, *Quellen*, pp. 128–30; Seebass, pp. 84–5.

118 Bossert, *Quellen*, pp. 136–7.

119 Ibid., pp. 133–6.

120 Ibid., pp. 137–41.

121 Seebass, p. 86. As Seebass notes, Count Wolfgang did not expunge the references to the imperial law. On the other hand, he did not execute any Anabaptists either: Claus-Peter Clasen, *Anabaptism: A Social History, 1525–1618* (Ithaca and London, 1972), p. 383.

122 Bossert, *Quellen*, pp. 187–95. Here Bossert incorrectly gives the date as 1559. He corrects himself on pp. 1020 and 1021 (Nr. 103 in the *Nachtrag*).

123 Ernst, *Briefwechsel* (see above, n. 48) 4:415 (Duke Christopher to Count Palatine Wolfgang, 9 September 1557). The imperial recess is in Bossert, *Quellen*, pp. 7*–9* (see esp. section 92 on p. 9*).

124 Seebass, pp. 87–8.

125 *Prozess wie es soll gehalten werden mit den Wiedertäuffern* (Worms, 1557); printed in Bossert, *Quellen*, pp. 161–8.

126 Ibid., pp. 165, fn. b, and 166, fn. c.

127 Clasen, *Anabaptism*, pp. 382–3.

128 Bainton, p. 58.

129 Seebass, pp. 89–90.

130 Bossert, *Quellen*, pp. 168–71.

131 Reyscher 8:241–5.

132 Bossert, *Quellen*, pp. 1022–47. Bossert gives '1558 nach Juli 25' as the date, which cannot be correct because of the references in the text (p. 1022) to the published Church Order of 1559.

133 Ibid., pp. 1025–34. Cf. p. 137 above.

134 Ibid., p. 1030.

135 Seebass, pp. 91–2; Clasen, *Wiedertäufer*, pp. 43–4.

136 Thus the comments of Wilhelm Bidembach on the treatment of *Vorsteher* (Bossert, *Quellen*, p. 280; cited in Seebass, p. 92): 'Vitam nulli auferendam, got geb, was er für articul defendier, quia queritur correctio, que non est in occidendo. sei crudele, licet in Mose wer ainer versteinigt worden; que severitas in evangelio ufgehebt; nusquam reperitur, das die apostel noch Christus zu töten befolhen, man findet auch nit in ecclesiastica historia, das heretici getodt worden seien. Constantinus hat die Arianer auch nit töten lassen, noch Marcianus die Euticheten töten lassen. Unde leges codicis, que occidunt, meinen andere greuliche hereticos, die offentlich gelestert oder zu irem glauben zwang und gwalt gebraucht. Do man sie aber bi uns nun lediglich verweisen sollte, non placet, quia grave aliis et contra reichsconstitutionem. Auch nit mit ruten ushowen lassen, quia offendiculum et scandalum, als gescheh es umb des glaubens willen.'

137 See above, p. 60.

138 Sehling 13:112–13; 14:230.

139 The text is preserved only in the revised form used in the Electorate; ibid., 14:236–9. See ibid., pp. 29–30, and Seebass, pp. 93–4.

140 Seebass, p. 95.

141 Clasen, *Anabaptism*, p. 421.

142 See above, p. 136.

AFTERWORD

1 See, for example, the comments cited in Immanuel Mann, 'Zur Predigttätigkeit von Johannes Brenz in Hall: Untersuchungen zu den Predigten von Johannes Brenz über das erste Buch Samuel,' BWKG 45 (1941):8–49, p. 31; and Martin Brecht, 'Brenz als Zeitgenosse: Die Reformationsepoche im Spiegel seiner Schriftauslegungen,' ibid., 70 (1970):5–39, p. 21.
2 Mann, 'Predigttätigkeit,' pp. 32–4; Brecht, 'Brenz als Zeitgenosse,' pp. 24–5.
3 For numerous examples, see, in addition to the *Ratswahlpredigten* discussed in chapter three, *Frühschriften* 1:174–201; 2:297–339.

Bibliography

I. UNPUBLISHED PRIMARY SOURCES

Bayerisches Staatsarchiv Nürnberg
  Repertorium 111 / Ansbacher Religionsakten
Hauptstaatsarchiv Stuttgart
  Repertorium A63 / Religions- und Kirchensachen
Stadtarchiv Schwäbisch Hall
  Signatur 4/53–5 / Brentiana Sammlung
Württembergische Landesbibliothek Stuttgart
  Cod. theol. et phil. 278 / Homiliae Evangeliorum quae usitato more in diebus dominis
  proponuntur.

II. PUBLISHED PRIMARY SOURCES

Brenz, Johannes *Frühschriften*. Edited by Martin Brecht et al. 2 vols. Tübingen,
  1970/74
– *Pericopae Evangeliorum, Quae Vsitato More in praecipuis Festis legi solent, expositae
  per Ioan. Brent*. Frankfurt, 1564
– *Operum Reverendi et Clarissimi Theologi, D. Ioannis Brentii, Praepositi Stutgardiani
  Tomus Primus [Secundus, etc.]*. 8 vols. Tübingen, 1576–90
Buder, G. 'Zwei unbekannte Bedenken von Johannes Brenz an Herzog Ulrich und Her-
  zog Christoph über das Interim.' *Blätter für Württembergische Kirchengeschichte* 32
  (1929): 10–37
Calvin, John *Calvini Opera Quae Supersunt Omnia*. Edited by C.G. Bretschneider et al.
  Corpus Reformatorum, vols. 29–87: Braunschweig, 1863–1900
Castellio, Sebastian *Concerning Heretics, Whether they are to be persecuted ...* Trans-
  lated and edited by Roland H. Bainton. New York, 1935; reprint 1965

Deutsche Reichstagsakten, Jüngere Reihe. Vol. 7. Edited by Johannes Kühn. Stuttgart, 1935; reprint Göttingen, 1963

Ernst, Viktor, ed. *Briefwechsel des Herzogs Christoph von Wirtemberg.* 4 vols. Stuttgart, 1899–1907

Estes, James M. ' "Whether Secular Government Has the Right to Wield the Sword in Matters of Faith." An Anonymous Defense of Religious Toleration From Sixteenth-Century Nürnberg.' *Mennonite Quarterly Review* 49 (1975):22–37

Fabian, Ekkehart, ed. *Die Schmalkaldischen Bundesabschiede, 1530–1532.* Tübingen, 1958

Franck, Sebastian *Chronica, Zeitbuch vnnd Geschichtbibel.* Ulm, 1536; facsimile reprint Darmstadt, 1969

Köhler, Walther *Bibliographia Brentiana.* Berlin, 1904; reprint Nieuwkoop, 1963

– 'Brentiana und andere Reformatoria.' *Archiv für Reformationsgeschichte* 9 (1911/12):79–84; 10 (1912/13): 166–97; 11 (1914):241–90; 13 (1916):228–39; 14 (1917): 143–52; 24 (1927):295–301; 26 (1929):250–64

–, ed. *Johannes Brenz' Kommentar zum Briefe des Apostels Paulus an die Epheser.* Heidelberg, 1935

Lenckner, Georg 'Autographa Brentiana.' *Württembergisch Franken* 49 (Neue Folge 39, 1965):3 – 18

Lietzmann, H. and Bornkamm, H., eds. *Die Bekenntnischriften der evangelisch-lutherischen Kirche.* 2nd ed. Göttingen, 1952

Luther, Martin *D. Martin Luthers Werke, Kritische Gesamtausgabe.* 58 vols. in 73. Weimar, 1883–

– *D. Martin Luthers Werke: Briefwechsel.* 15 vols. Weimar, 1930–78

– *D. Martin Luthers Werke: Tischreden.* 6 vols. Weimar, 1912–21

– *Dr. Martin Luthers Sämmtliche Schriften.* Edited by Johann Georg Walch et al. 23 vols. in 25. St Louis, 1881–1910

– *Luther's Works.* Edited by Jaroslav Pelikan, Helmut T. Lehmann, et al. 52 vols. to date. St Louis and Philadelphia, 1955–

Matthes, Otto '10 Briefe aus den Jahren 1523–1590 aus dem Besitz Johann Valentin Andreäs, Teil 2: Ein Kirchenzuchtplan Jakob Andreäs.' *Blätter für Württembergische Kirchengeschichte* 62 (1962):124–253

Melanchthon, Philip *Philippi Melanchthonis Opera Quae Supersunt Omnia.* Edited by C.G. Bretschneider et al. *Corpus Reformatorum,* vols. 1–28: Halle, 1834–60

Müller, Gerhard and Seebaß, Gottfried, eds. *Andreas Osiander d. Ä. Gesamtausgabe.* Vol. 4: *Schriften und Briefe, Mai 1530 bis Ende 1532.* Gütersloh, 1981

Ordnung der Kirchen inn eins Erbarn Raths zu Schwäbischen Hall Oberkeit und gepiet gelegen. Schwäbisch Hall, 1543

Pressel, Theodor, ed. *Anecdota Brentiana: Ungedruckte Briefe und Bedenken von Johannes Brenz.* Tübingen, 1868

Quellen zur Geschichte der Wiedertäufer. Vol. 1: *Herzogtum Württemberg.* Edited by Gustav Bossert. Leipzig, 1930

Rauscher, Julius, ed. *Württembergische Visitationsakten.* Vol. 1. Stuttgart, 1932

Reyscher, August Ludwig, ed. *Vollständige, historisch und kritisch bearbeitete sammlung der württembergischen geseze.* 19 vols. in 28. Stuttgart and Tübingen, 1828–51

Richter, Aemilius Ludwig, ed. *Die evangelischen Kirchenordnungen des sechszehnten Jahrhunderts.* 2 vols. Weimar, 1846; reprint Nieuwkoop, 1967

Sattler, Christian Friedrich *Geschichte des Herzogthums Würtenberg unter der Regierung der Herzogen.* Vols. 3 and 4. Tübingen, 1771

Scheible, Heinz, ed. *Das Widerstandsrecht als Problem der deutschen Protestanten, 1523–1546.* Texte zur Kirchen- und Theologiegeschichte, no. 10. Gütersloh, 1969

Schiess, Traugott, ed. *Briefwechsel der Brüder Ambrosius und Thomas Blaurer.* 3 vols. Freiburg, 1908–12

Sehling, Emil, et al., eds. *Die evangelischen Kirchenordnungen des XVI. Jahrhunderts.* Vols. 1–5: Leipzig, 1902–13. Vols. 6 et seq.: Tübingen, 1955–

Von Gottes gnaden vnser Christoffs Herzogen zu Württemberg vnd zu Teckh, Grauen zu Mümpelgart, etc. summarischer vnd einfältiger Begriff, wie es mit der Lehre vnd Ceremonien in den Kirchen vnsers Fürstenthumbs, auch derselben Kirchen anhangenden Sachen und Verrichtungen, bissher geübt vnnd gebraucht, auch fürohin mit verleihung Göttlicher gnaden gehalten vnd volzogen werden solle. Tübingen, 1559; facsimile reprint Stuttgart, 1968

Württembergische Kommission für Landesgeschichte *Württembergische Geschichtsquellen.* Vol. 1: *Geschichtsquellen der Stadt Hall,* vol. 1. Edited by Christian Kolb. Stuttgart, 1894

III. SECONDARY ACCOUNTS

Andreas, Willy *Deutschland vor der Reformation.* Stuttgart, 1959

Baker, J. Wayne *Heinrich Bullinger and the Covenant: The Other Reformed Tradition.* Athens, Ohio, 1980

Baron, Hans 'Religion and Politics in the German Imperial Cities during the Reformation.' Part I. *English Historical Review* 52 (1937):405–27

Bornkamm, Heinrich *Das Jahrhundert der Reformation, Gestalten und Kräfte.* Göttingen, 1961

Bossert, Gustav *Das Interim in Württemberg.* Schriften des Vereins für Reformationsgeschichte, no. 12. Halle, 1895

Brecht, Martin 'Anfänge reformatorischer Kirchenordnung und Sittenzucht bei Johannes Brenz.' *Zeitschrift der Savigny Stiftung für Rechtsgeschichte,* Kanonistische Abteilung, 55 (1969):322–47

– 'Brenz als Zeitgenosse: Die Reformationsepoche im Spiegel seiner Schriftauslegungen.' *Blätter für Württembergische Kirchengeschichte* 70 (1970):5–39

- 'Die Chronologie von Brenzens Schriftauslegungen und Predigten.' *Blätter für Württembergische Kirchengeschichte* 64 (1964):55-74
- *Die frühe Theologie des Johannes Brenz.* Tübingen, 1966
- *Johannes Brenz: Neugestalter von Kirche, Staat und Gesellschaft.* Stuttgart, 1971
- *Kirchenordnung und Kirchenzucht in Württemberg vom 16. bis zum 18. Jahrhundert.* Stuttgart, 1967.

Clasen, Claus-Peter *Anabaptism: A Social History, 1525-1618.* Ithaca and London, 1972
- *Die Wiedertäufer im Herzogtum Württemberg und in benachbarten Herrschaften.* Stuttgart, 1965

Engelhardt, Adolf *Die Reformation in Nürnberg,* vol 2. In *Mitteilungen des Vereins für Geschichte der Stadt Nürnberg* 34 (1937)

Ernst, Viktor 'Die Entstehung des württembergischen Kirchenguts.' In *Württembergische Jahrbücher für Statistik und Landeskunde.* 1911. Pp. 377-424
- *Eberhart im Bart.* Stuttgart, 1933; reprint Darmstadt, 1970

Estes, James M. 'Church Order and the Christian Magistrate According to Johannes Brenz.' *Archiv für Reformationsgeschichte* 59 (1968):5-23
- 'Johannes Brenz and the Institutionalization of the Reformation in Württemberg.' *Central European History* 6 (1973):44-59
- 'Johannes Brenz and the Problem of Ecclesiastical Discipline.' *Church History* 41 (1972):464-79
- 'The Two Kingdoms and the State Church According to Johannes Brenz and an Anonymous Colleague.' *Archiv für Reformationsgeschichte* 61 (1970):35-49

Fabian, Ekkehart *Die Entstehung des Schmalkaldischen Bundes und seiner Verfassung, 1524/29-1531/35.* Schriften zur Kirchen- und Rechtsgeschichte, no. 1. 2nd ed. Tübingen, 1962

Gmelin, Julius *Hällische Geschichte.* Schwäbisch Hall, 1899

Grimm, Harold J. *Lazarus Spengler: A Lay Leader of the Reformation.* Columbus, 1978

Hartmann, Julius and Jäger, Karl *Johann Brenz: nach gedruckten und ungedruckten Quellen.* 2 vols. Hamburg, 1840

Hauswirth, René *Landgraf Philipp von Hessen und Zwingli, 1526-1531.* Schriften zur Kirchen- und Rechtsgeschichte, no. 35. Tübingen and Basel, 1968

Holl, Karl *Gesammelte Aufsätze zur Kirchengeschichte.* Vol. 1. Tübingen, 1948

Kantzenbach, Friedrich Wilhelm 'Der junge Brenz bis zu seiner Berufung nach Hall im Jahre 1522.' *Zeitschrift für bayerische Kirchengeschichte* 32 (1963):53-73
- 'Johannes Brenz und die Reformation in Franken.' *Zeitschrift für bayerische Kirchengeschichte* 31 (1962): 149-68
- 'Theologie und Gemeinde bei Johannes Brenz, dem Prediger von Hall: Sein erstes Wirken für die kirchliche Neuordnung der Reichsstadt von 1522 bis ca. 1526.' *Blätter für Württembergische Kirchengeschichte* 65 (1965): 3-38

Kittelson, James M. 'Humanism and the Reformation in Germany.' *Central European History* 9 (1976):303–22
- *Wolfgang Capito: From Humanist to Reformer.* Leiden, 1975
Köhler, Walther *Zürcher Ehegericht und Genfer Konsistorium.* 2 vols. Leipzig, 1932/42
Koeniger, Albert Michael 'Brenz und der Send.' In *Beiträge zur Geschichte der Renaissance und Reformation.* Munich and Freising, 1917
Kohls, E.W. *Die Schule bei Martin Bucer.* Heidelberg, 1963
Krumwiede, Hans-Walter *Zur Entstehung des landesherrlichen Kirchenregiments in Kursachsen und Braunschweig-Wolfenbüttel.* Göttingen, 1967
Kugler, Bernard *Christoph, Herzog zu Wirtemberg.* 2 vols. Stuttgart, 1868/72
Lecler, Joseph, S.J. *Toleration and the Reformation.* 2 vols. New York and London, 1960
Lempp, Wilhelm *Der Württembergische Synodus, 1553–1924.* Stuttgart, 1959
Lenckner, Georg 'Täufer im Gebiet der Reichsstadt Schwäbisch Hall.' *Württembergisch Franken* 48 (Neue Folge 38, 1964): 16–28
Logan, F. Donald *Excommunication and the Secular Arm in Medieval England.* Toronto, 1968
Lossen, Richard *Staat und Kirche in der Pfalz im Ausgang des Mittelalters.* Münster, 1907
Mann, Immanuel 'Zur Predigttätigkeit von Johannes Brenz in Hall: Untersuchungen zu den Predigten von Johannes Brenz über das erste Buch Samuel.' *Blätter für Württembergische Kirchengeschichte* 45 (1941):8–49
Maurer, Hans-Martin 'Herzog Christoph als Landesherr.' *Blätter für Württembergische Kirchengeschichte* 68/9 (1968/9):112–38
- and Ulshöfer, Kuno *Johannes Brenz und die Reformation in Württemberg.* Stuttgart and Aalen, n.d.
Maurer, Wilhelm *Das Verhältnis des Staates zur Kirche nach humanistischer Anschauung, vornehmlich bei Erasmus.* Giessen, 1930
Moeller, Bernd *Reichsstadt und Reformation.* Schriften des Vereins für Reformationsgeschichte, no. 180. Gütersloh, 1962
Müller, Karl 'Die Anfänge der Konsistorialverfassung im lutherischen Deutschland.' *Historische Zeitschrift* 102 (1909):1–30
- *Kirche, Gemeinde und Obrigkeit nach Luther.* Tübingen, 1910
Press, Volker *Calvinismus und Territorialstaat: Regierung und Zentralbehörden der Kurpfalz, 1559–1619.* Stuttgart, 1970
Rauscher, Julius *Württembergische Reformationsgeschichte.* Stuttgart, 1934
Rieker, Karl *Die rechtliche Stellung der evangelischen Kirche Deutschlands.* Leipzig, 1893
Schäfer, Gerhard *Landeskirchliches Archiv Stuttgart: Übersicht über die Bestände und Inventar der Allgemeinen Kirchenakten.* Stuttgart, 1972

Schmid, Hans-Dieter *Täufertum und Obrigkeit in Nürnberg*. Schriftenreihe des Stadtarchivs Nürnberg, no. 10. Nuremberg, 1972

Schneider, Eugen *Württembergische Reformationsgeschichte*. Stuttgart, 1887

Schnurrer, Christian Friedrich von *Erläuterungen der Württembergischen Kirchen-Reformations- und Gelehrten-Geschichte*. Tübingen, 1798

Schoenberger, Cynthia Grant 'The Development of the Lutheran Theory of Resistance:1523–1530.' *The Sixteenth Century Journal* 8 (1977):61–76

Schnornbaum, Karl *Zur Politik des Markgrafen Georg von Brandenburg vom Beginne seiner selbständigen Regierung bis zum Nürnberger Anstand, 1528–1532*. Munich, 1906

Schubert, Hans von *Bekenntnisbildung und Religionspolitik, 1529/30 (1524–1534)*. Gotha, 1910

Schultze, Alfred *Stadtgemeinde und Reformation*. Tübingen, 1918

Seebass, Gottfried 'An sint persequendi haeretici? Die Stellung des Johannes Brenz zur Verfolgung und Bestrafung der Täufer.' *Blätter für Württembergische Kirchengeschichte* 70 (1970):40–299

Strauss, Gerald *Luther's House of Learning: Indoctrination of the Young in the German Reformation*. Baltimore and London, 1978

Ulshöfer, Kuno 'Die evangelische Politik der Reichsstadt Hall vom Augsburger Reichstag 1530 bis zum Eintritt der Stadt in den Schmalkaldischen Bund.' *Württembergisch Franken* 55 (Neue Folge 45, 1971):67–83

Walton, Robert C. *Zwingli's Theocracy*. Toronto, 1967

Westermayer, H. *Die Brandenburgisch-Nürnbergische Kirchenvisitation und Kirchenordnung, 1528–1533*. Erlangen, 1894

Wintterlin, Friedrich *Geschichte der Behördenorganisation in Württemberg*. Stuttgart, 1904

Wülk, Johannes and Funk, Hans *Die Kirchenpolitik der Grafen von Württemberg bis zur Erhebung Württembergs zum Herzogtum (1495)*. Stuttgart, 1912

Wunder, Gerd 'Der Haller Rat und Johannes Brenz 1522–1530.' *Württembergisch Franken* 55 (Neue Folge 45, 1971):56–66

Ziemssen, Ludwig 'Das württembergische Partikularschulwesen 1534–1559.' In Württembergische Kommission für Landesgeschichte, *Geschichte des humanistischen Schulwesens in Württemberg* 1:468–599. Stuttgart, 1912

Index